Clergy Malpractice in America

LANDMARK LAW CASES

&

AMERICAN SOCIETY

Peter Charles Hoffer
N. E. H. Hull
Series Editors

MARK A. WEITZ

Clergy Malpractice in America

Nally v. Grace Community Church of the Valley

UNIVERSITY PRESS OF KANSAS

© 2001 by the University Press of Kansas

All rights reserved

Published by the University Press of Kansas (Lawrence, Kansas 66049), which was
organized by the Kansas Board of Regents and is operated and funded by Emporia
State University, Fort Hays State University, Kansas State University, Pittsburg State
University, the University of Kansas, and Wichita State University

Library of Congress Cataloging-in-Publication Data

Weitz, Mark A., 1957–

Clergy malpractice in America : Nally v. Grace Community Church of the Valley /
Mark A. Weitz.

p. cm.—(Landmark law cases & American society)

Includes bibliographical references and index.

ISBN 0-7006-1125-8 (cloth : alk. paper) — ISBN 0-7006-1126-6 (pbk. : alk. paper)

1. Nally, Walter—Trials, litigation, etc.   2. Grace Community Church of the
Valley (Sun City, Calif.)—Trials, litigation, etc.   3. Freedom of religion—United
States.   4. Clergy—Malpractice—United States.   5. Suicide—Religious aspects—
Christianity.   I. Title.   II. Series.

KF228.N27 W45 2001

342.73'0852—dc 21   2001026126

British Library Cataloguing in Publication Data is available.

Printed in the United States of America

10   9   8   7   6   5   4   3   2   1

CONTENTS

{ v }

In this fascinating and deeply moving study of a grieving family's lawsuit against a charismatic evangelical church, Mark Weitz, a lawyer and historian, explores one of the fastest growing and most novel areas of con-tort law: clergy malpractice. Constitutional torts combine constitutional issues, here the First Amendment's protection of freedom of worship from government interference, with a tort (civil wrong) suit against ministers for malpractice. Can the parents of a young suicide convince the courts that lay ministers in a church should be liable when the advice they give to the victim may have contributed to his decision to end his life? Must ministers or counselors inform parents or trained doctors when they know that a parishioner in their care is contemplating suicide?

Nally v. Grace Community Church became the focus of national attention when the California appeals courts reversed a lower court's dismissal of the suit. Churches all over the country were concerned that the Nally family's contentions changed the nature of church-state and clergy-lay relations. Weitz handles both the complex legal questions and the wider religious and political implications of the case in evenhanded and yet compassionate fashion. Over the decade and a half that he studied the case, Weitz gained the trust of participants on both sides, and adds their accounts, revealing the hidden story of personal feelings and motivation to the public record of legal thrust and counterthrust. The story that follows is a lucid account of a complex area of emerging law and a remarkable tale of ordinary people looking to the law for justice and vindication.

At the same time, Weitz's sharply delineated depictions of the rise of the fundamentalist movement and the changing demographic and historical context of the Los Angeles region in the 1960s and 1970s fit the suit into its own time and place. In his hands, the case becomes a window through which we can see how a cultural of material progress based on educational and professional achievement came into conflict with a culture based on the search for salvation in spiritual exclusivity—a conflict that the courts struggled to resolve.

Introduction

William Prosser, the authority on American tort law, once observed that more than any other branch of the law, the law of torts is a battleground for social theory. In the half century following World War II this connection between law and culture found its way to a new place on the battlefield: religion. By the 1980s America had become a land where many people no longer believed in miracles, at least not the religious kind, and a nation that once welcomed God into all aspects of community life had grown unsure as to exactly where religion fit in American culture. As the country moved out of the depression and World War II and into the 1950s and the cold war, it became more than a modern, industrialized nation. America continued a process that actually began in the late 1800s and early 1900s, the secularization of society and culture. Increasingly, Americans looked for answers to life's most troubling problems and pitfalls in places other than church and God. The ramifications of this trend were to have unimaginable consequences in 1980.

Oliver Wendall Holmes defined a landmark case as one that "exercises a kind of hydraulic pressure which makes what previously was clear seem doubtful, and before which even well settled principles of law will bend." *Nally v. Grace Community Church* is such a case. Prior to its filing in 1980, the notion of suing a priest, clergyman, or a church would have been almost sacrilegious for the vast majority of Americans throughout our 200-year history. If such a thing were even suggested to most Americans in prior generations they would have replied that "No one sues God, or any of God's servants, for goodness' sake. America was founded by people fleeing religious persecution. We are One Nation, Under God."

This reaction would not have been out of place. The First Amendment implicitly, if not expressly, states that one could not sue a church. The courts are the judicial organs of the state and the state is prohibited from doing anything that would excessively entangle it in the business of a church. Although the government can show deference to religious organizations, such treatment must be evenly applied so as not to elevate the beliefs of one faith over those of another. The tax-exempt status enjoyed by religious bodies is an example of the limited state action permitted under the Constitution. In the face of such religious, cultural, and legal traditions one would have to ask, "What were the Nallys thinking?" By the time the case had run its course, suing a minister or a church no longer seemed so outrageous. The idea that the First Amendment protected a church when it had hurt or injured someone seemed a little less tenable. The case moved through four weeks of trial, two trips to the state court of appeals, and a final rendezvous with the California Supreme Court, and more than one well-settled legal principle bent in the face of the storm raised by the suit. The longer the case progressed, the more places along the wall that guards the citadel of religious freedom in America came under assault by others willing to follow the example set by the Nallys.

Prior to *Nally*, religion had experienced only limited governmental interference and had its rights under the First Amendment either solidified or at worst limited by being more clearly defined. Virtually every instance dealt with an occasion where the matter in question involved applying secular regulations to a function or aspect of a religious body that was itself secular. Unemployment taxation, education, and medical care for minor children were the most glaring examples of government intrusion into religious affairs. *Nally* raised an issue of government interference into an area that seemed on its face to be a purely religious function. When the California Supreme Court finally laid the case to rest in November 1988, Holmes's words would continue to echo, because what had once been clear was no longer so.

Almost from the inception of organized religion, priests, ministers, rabbis, vicars, and all other religious leaders irrespective of title have counseled their flock. The technical term is pastoral counseling. Broadly speaking, it refers to the counseling done by ministers in the course of their religious duties. For those who hold themselves out as ministers, priests, or pastors, there is no greater role than that of counselor and it is inextricably intertwined with God's work. For most of American history this counseling role posed no problem for society. However, as the medical field became more professionalized in the early twentieth century and the need for counseling services grew rapidly, the church's counseling role came to coexist alongside a growing body of "professionally" trained counselors, people who looked to medical explanations for the answers to mental health. Without ever being addressed, the natural question that begged for an answer was: What, if anything, could a religious counselor not do in an area that became emersed in professional, medical, and secular standards?

The question became even more acute after 1960 when the need for counseling services began to surpass the ability of the professional community to service everyone. As the demand for social and psychological counseling outstripped the profession's ability to supply assistance, professionals came to look increasingly more to nonprofessional counselors to handle problems that were considered the exclusive bailiwick of professional psychiatrists and psychologists. Nonprofessionals encompassed virtually everyone in the mental health field who lacked a license. To become a licensed psychiatrist or psychologist required a doctorate and accreditation by a state medical licensing agency. By the 1960s, colleges and universities simply could not produce enough Ph.D.'s and M.D.'s to meet the demand for professional counselors.

It is impossible to determine if the incidence of mental illness increased. All that is certain is that the frequency with which people sought help began to increase at an alarming rate. Americans began to rely heavily on counseling services at work, through volunteer organizations, YMCAs, schools, shelters, welfare agencies, and a spectrum of community-based institutions. These facilities rarely had accredited professionals among their staff. In time, even hospitals would see the majority of their mental health staff filled by nonprofessionals, even though a professional was on hand to supervise their activities.

Competition for clientele no longer posed a problem: there were plenty of sick to go around. Although a growing fear of potential liability began to surface, the larger issue among the professional community was the concern for the overall quality of American mental health care. What could a nonprofessional competently handle? Who would set those standards? What type of cases are clearly beyond a nonprofessional's ability to handle? All of these issues, although troubling to professionals, were easily answered by individuals who had been counseling their whole lives in a calling that was as old as man and religion. For the clergy this problem was no problem at all, at least not on the surface. Not until Kenneth Nally locked himself inside a small closet at a friend's house sometime between March 30 and April 1, 1979, and ended his life with a shotgun blast to the head.

Kenneth had been a member of Grace Community Church and for at least the previous year had been actively receiving counseling from the church's pastoral counseling service. A bright, intense, and outgoing young man, Ken grappled with many of the same beasts that young people in the late 1970s faced. Fear of failure, the pressure of finding and maintaining personal relationships, career choices, and coping with the pressures and hassles of modern life posed problems for many young people. College had separated Ken Nally from home for the first time and the loss of companionship with his parents and brother created a void in his life. Personal relationships with women posed their own form of pressure. On top of all of this, in 1974 Ken converted from the religion of his youth, Catholicism, to a fundamentalist Protestant faith. It was there he sought out church counselors for problems that ultimately proved too difficult for Ken to handle.

Grace Community Church believed and continues to believe in the literal interpretation of the Bible and that its teachings were beyond question by man. An aspect of this belief was that the only religiously proper way to counsel matters of the heart or mind was through direct reference to biblical scripture. Grace rejected the utility of secular psychiatry and psychology unless the professional practitioner shared Grace's biblical beliefs. When Kenneth Nally took his own life the congregation mourned, but its doctrine told the membership that God had called an errant soul home and that despite the suicide, Kenneth was with God.

In another time and under different circumstances the story would have ended there. But this was America in 1980. Religion continued to spark controversy as the Moral Majority blasted its message out over the airwaves to anyone who would listen. Unlike the late 1800s and early 1900s, when religious institutions were in conflict with one another and secular society over the effects of modernization in America, in the 1980s secular America began to see religion as a threat to basic constitutional freedoms. Religion not only wanted to condemn conduct it deemed inappropriate, but seemed willing to use political and private avenues to dictate proper cultural standards. What Americans read, what they watched on television, what their children were being taught in school became the focus of religious efforts to bring about moral conformity.

On a personal level Kenneth Nally's conversion had caused a good degree of trauma within his family. He seemed to embrace his religious beliefs with the same intensity that characterized his other endeavors. His new beliefs left him feeling his family, all Catholic, were doomed to eternal damnation unless they joined him in his new community. The family resisted and Kenneth's father, Walter, saw his son's conversion attempts as a threat to the family's Irish-Catholic beliefs. The conflict that ensued between father and son only made matters worse. As institutions often do, Kenneth's new church had come between him and his family and had erected an almost unscalable wall between son and father.

When Kenneth committed suicide in 1979 his family, Walter Nally in particular, were left with many more questions than answers. As Walter Nally probed deeper into the years, months, and days prior to Kenneth's death, he developed a picture of his son's state of mind and came to believe that the church and its pastoral counselors had been responsible for his son's untimely and tragic death. By March 1980, Nally was convinced that the church and its pastors, John MacArthur in particular, had killed his son. On March 31, 1980, almost one year from the date of Kenneth Nally's death, Walter and Maria Nally filed suit in the Superior

Court of the state of California for the county of Los Angeles against Grace Community Church of the Valley and four of its pastoral counselors, asserting the novel theory of clergy malpractice for the negligent and careless manner in which it and they had counseled their son, conduct they alleged resulted in his death.

This, then, is the story of a landmark case in the area of religious freedom. Within it are many stories: A family's quest to understand the death of one of its members and a father's need to understand the death of his son; a church's journey into previously uncharted waters, a journey that would test the strength of its convictions and call into question the protections it had enjoyed for most of its existence. It is the story of a minister who had taken a small congregation in the late 1960s and built it into a teeming community of almost 20,000 strong, a community and a man that stood to lose much if this case were to be lost. It is also the story of America, a nation that looked at God and religion differently than it did fifty years before; a nation with different concepts of blame and legal responsibility. America was about to find out what price it was willing to pay for religious freedom and perhaps define the extent to which it would allow religion to act, before such actions were no longer protected as belief but became subject to society's judgment as conduct. This case is also the story of a judicial system and its judges, men faced with questions that no one had ever confronted in precisely this way. Three lawyers whose paths had never before crossed would become locked in a struggle that for each was perhaps the most important case he had ever tried. Although *Nally* arose from tragic circumstances that led a young man to kill himself, the real story is about people who struggled to give meaning to Kenneth Nally's inability or unwillingness to continue. Its roots go back long before April 1, 1979, and will have ramifications far beyond the present. For some, the case ended in November 1988; for others, it will never end. It is a story that for our purposes began with a knock on the Nallys' door one morning in April 1979.

CHAPTER I

Is It Permanent?

"Dad! There's someone at the door to see you." Eighteen-year-old Walter Nally Jr. was uncertain what the uniformed police officer standing on his front step wanted, but something in his gut told him it was not good. As his father came out of the kitchen and into the foyer where the police officer waited, the elder Nally's instincts took over. The son of an Irish cop in Chicopee, Massachusetts, Walter Nally Sr. knew this was not a social call and without the officer uttering a word, Nally asked, "Is it permanent!?"

Forty-eight hours before, Walter had watched in tears as his son Kenneth slowly drove away from the family home, distraught over his life, his right arm rendered lifeless by a suicide attempt just three weeks before, driven by an internal conflict that seemed beyond the ability of anyone else to relieve. Kenneth's overdose of prescription drugs three weeks before had not been his first effort to take his own life, but it was the first such attempt his family was aware of. As Kenneth disappeared that morning, Walter could only hope for the best, although after almost two days of searching with no luck, he feared the worst.

"Yes, Mr. Nally, I am afraid it is," replied the officer, who then went on to explain the discovery of a body at the home of Ernie Hauser, a body that they believed to be Kenneth's. Regrettably, the deceased would have to be identified by a family member because the shotgun Kenneth used to commit suicide had rendered his facial features unrecognizable. Walter Jr. fell into hysteria almost immediately. Maria had not been home and on her return from the grocery store Walter broke the news to her. After doing the best he could to calm his son and wife, both nearly hysterical at the news that their worst fears had come to pass, Walter Nally pulled himself together for what promised to be a lonely trip to the coroner's office to identify his boy. Kenneth was twenty-four years old when he took his own life and the Nallys confronted the sorrow unique to parents in the death of a child.

Walter Nally Sr. was a third-generation Irish American whose roots went back to his great-grandfather, Edward Patrick Nally, who immigrated to the United States in 1846. Walter grew up fast in a tight-knit, Irish-Catholic community under the watchful eye of his father. In 1951 he left home and joined the navy, a decision that would not only take him far from his small community and his past, but would lead to his future. When he was stationed in Japan, Walter Nally met his wife, Maria, in the most unlikely of circumstances: receiving a blood transfusion in Yakusuka Naval Hospital. The pretty nurses were usually reserved for officers. Not this time. Someone had slipped up and the pretty young Japanese girl attending him left the young staff sargent from Massachusetts thunderstruck.

Before Nally could leave for the coroner's office, people began calling and coming to the house. He was amazed at how quickly word had spread of Ken's death. Bobby Azzaritto, a childhood friend of Ken's and a member of Grace Church, was the first to appear. He was followed soon by more members of Grace Church: some Walter Nally knew, others he did not. Among the mourners and well-wishers were Lynn Cory and Duane Rea. At the time, Walter Nally knew them only as Ken's friends and fellow members of the church to which he had devoted so much of his last years. In time, Mr. Nally would come to believe these two were actually responsible for the death of his son. As people poured into the Nally home, Walter kept thinking in the back of his mind that Maria must not know how Kenneth took his own life. How he was going to prevent this he was unsure, but he knew he had to try.

Maria Nally was no stranger to hardship and sorrow. Born the daughter of a devout Buddhist family, her father survived a gunshot wound to the head in Indo-China during the 1930s, only to return to Japan to die in a flood, leaving his family to endure the rigors of war alone. Maria grew up in Kobe and knew the ravages of modern warfare firsthand. Bombing and the human carnage left in its wake were constant reminders of a world that had seemingly gone mad. Although she survived the war and married her handsome young American sailor, the hardship was far from over.

America in the 1950s was anything but accepting of difference. An Asian-American couple in the wake of World War II had to deal with a country that not only drew comfort in "sameness" but felt an acute sense of insecurity with anything Asian. Even the naval priest in Japan cautioned the couple against a "mixed marriage." Walter Nally's parents were split initially: His mother was critical, fearing the marriage would fail, whereas his father simply said that anyone Walter loved would be a fine wife. Cultural differences within the family nevertheless existed. Walter's father scared Maria when she first met him, but in time, the big Irish cop with a strong personality and his new daughter-in-law became close.

As his house quickly filled up with people he did not know, the elder Nally grew increasingly uncomfortable. Walter felt the same inability to connect with these people that he had experienced with Kenneth in the last years of his life. Somehow the "Grace" people, even though well intentioned, carrying their Bibles and trying to convert souls, seemed out of place in the immediate wake of his son's death. Besides, Nally needed to get to the coroner's office and identify Ken's body. It was a trip he would not have to make.

After explaining to Duane Rea that the coroner's office was waiting, Nally got his first insight into the extent to which Grace Community Church was connected to some of the secular institutions in the San Fernando Valley. With well over 20,000 members, the church touched many aspects of the surrounding community. Its membership and leadership reached into the highest levels of law enforcement. Pastor Rea placed a call to Robert Vernon, a church elder and the deputy chief of the Los Angeles Police Department. Within a matter of minutes the coroner's office had been contacted, and the decision had been made that an on-site inspection of the body was unnecessary and that identification would be accomplished through Ken's dental records. From that moment, Walter Nally understood that this church had "clout," political power that he had seen work back in Massachusetts as a boy. When someone or something important wanted or needed anything, it just happened.

As Rea quickly resolved what had promised to be a terribly difficult trip to the coroner's office, Nally could only think how strange it was to live one's life in a community and yet never know that certain people and institutions even existed. So it had been with him and Grace Community Church.

The Nallys came to California in 1965, a move precipitated by a health condition Kenneth developed. Named in honor of Maria's father, "Kenneth" was as close as the Nallys could get to "Kenshin," and with his birth Walter Nally's mother accepted Maria completely. But as fate would have it, the Nallys would soon leave Massachusetts. As a child Kenneth suffered from asthma and his parents began to look for a place with a climate more conducive to Ken's needs. The development of the asthmatic condition coincided with a job opportunity as the vice president of a southern California company. With real estate still cheap, the Nallys settled into a comfortable home in the hills of the San Fernando Valley in a quiet little community called Tujunga.

In California the family became the typical post–World War II baby boom family. Kenneth and his younger brother, Walter Jr., born in 1960, attended Catholic schools and ran around safe neighborhoods doing the things kids do. Kenneth endured all the growing pains of an adolescent and some that were unique to a boy of mixed ancestry. The first time someone called him a "dirty Jap," Ken was both shocked and hurt. Although racial prejudice did not end in California, a few quick boxing lessons from his dad helped alleviate the source of the comments. In time Kenneth overcame both childhood bullies and his asthmatic condition, and grew into a strong young man, athletically talented, with a love for baseball. In high school he excelled both academically and athletically, demonstrating an intensity that characterized anything he tried. All of this growth and development, both as a family and Kenneth individually, occurred in almost complete ignorance of another family and another community that also traced its beginning to the early and middle 1950s. Grace Community Church of the Valley grew up just down the freeway in Sun City.

———

Grace Community Church of the Valley began inauspiciously in July 1956. A group of twenty-five Baptist families had become disenchanted with the lack of Sunday school classes at the Village Church in Burbank. In an effort to rectify the problem and direct more attention to the development of their children, this small nucleus formed a new church, unconnected to any specific denomination and open to anyone that wanted to attend. At first the congregation met in a converted house in Van Nuys, but the membership grew so quickly that a hole had to be cut in the walls so the entire congregation could see its preacher, Dr. Don Householder. Within a year the church purchased land and built a permanent structure. Still basically Baptist, Grace Church experienced a rapid growth. Six hundred people attended the first services in the new facilities on June 30, 1957.

By 1959 Sunday school attendance alone had risen to 558. The church bulletins reflected Grace's goal to become the center of the community. The emblem on the bulletin depicted a hub, drawing people to Sunday services from as far as an hour's drive away. The congregation began the practice of a "prayer chain," where personal hardships or needs were shared with the congregation, which prayed as a body for a good outcome. One example was Dr. Householder asking the congregation to pray for the injured son of a fellow minister who was hurt in an automobile accident. By 1963 the church had begun to reach beyond its community and far abroad, sending missions to places like Okinawa, Formosa, Hong Kong, Ecuador, and Colombia.

In 1965, Dr. Householder died of a heart attack while preparing a sermon at his desk. His successor, Dr. Richard Elvee, brought national credibility to the growing church, having succeeded Billy Graham as president of Northwestern College in Minneapolis before leaving to join Grace Church. Elvee's tenure proved short. On September 5, 1968, he too died of a heart attack in church. The church elders began a search for Dr. Elvee's replacement and in January 1969 they offered the job to a young preacher with apparent but as yet unproven promise, who could trace his "linage of the cloth" back over the last five generations of his family. Grace's third minister would be John A. MacArthur, the son of a minister, the same boy injured in an auto accident whom the congregation had prayed for almost ten years before.

———

John MacArthur was in Scotland when he received word that Kenneth Nally was dead. Just a week before, Kenneth had stayed at MacArthur's home. The minister and his wife, Patricia, had offered their home in an effort to help the troubled young boy. When the MacArthurs left for Scotland, Kenneth went home. Years later MacArthur would say that when he heard the news, "he was saddened, but not shocked." Still, such a tragic loss could not help but cause MacArthur to reflect on his own life and what had brought him to this point.

Born in Los Angeles, California, on June 19, 1939, John MacArthur was the son of a Texas minister, Dr. John MacArthur Sr. The elder MacArthur preached and traveled throughout the Midwest, had his own nationally broadcast radio show, wrote a few books, and became one of America's first televison evangelists in the 1960s. Young John MacArthur, who his father called "Johnny," was always close to his father and says he always knew he was destined for the ministry. Called to Christ at age seven after he had lied about taking part in vandalizing a local school, John MacArthur remembered that he and his best friend, Eddie, talked about how they would be ministers with their own churches. When MacArthur was a senior in high school, Eddie's car slid off the road and he was killed in the accident. Several years later MacArthur barely survived a similar accident. As the news of Kenneth's death sank in, he recalled having told Kenneth about his own brush with death and how it taught him the fragility of life. MacArthur knew then that one never knows how long they have. As so often happens, teacher and student had now switched roles and Kenneth demonstrated with finality what MacArthur already knew.

John MacArthur graduated from Los Angeles Pacific College

in 1961, majoring in religion and minoring in history and Greek. Three years later he graduated magna cum laude from Talbot Theological Seminary in La Miranda, California. The same year he was ordained by the Independent Fundamental Churches of America of Westchester, Illinois. With his credentials in hand, MacArthur took a position as an assistant professor at Los Angeles Baptist College in 1965 and the following year he became a faculty representative at Talbot Theological Seminary. MacArthur felt destined to be called to Grace Church. He shunned the notion that church was only a once-a-week gathering of people dressed in their best. MacArthur wanted much more, and in 1969, with only four years of experience, he stepped up to the biggest challenge of his life and assumed the leadership of a growing congregation in the heart of what had become an exciting and decadent place to live.

———

Los Angeles in the 1960s and 1970s offered both the best and worst of American urban living. Metropolitan Los Angeles comprised Los Angeles, Orange, Riverside, Ventura, and San Bernardino Counties. By 1970 the region had a population of over 7 million, with Los Angeles County accounting for 71 percent of that total, including both the Nally family and Grace Church.

By the mid-1960s L.A. had already begun to develop some of the problems that would become synonymous with its name. Air pollution, traffic congestion, water shortages, the disappearance of natural landscape, and the decline of the ecosystem all plagued Los Angeles. Despite these environmental concerns, some people saw the city as "Incredible Los Angeles," the first truly American city, a place that had shaken off the model of old European-style cities like New York and Chicago and become a place where opportunity abounded. Hollywood and Disneyland were not merely places and institutions, they represented infinite possibility.

For all of its opportunities, Los Angeles had an undesirable side. Human growth brought with it human vice and by 1965 when the Nallys arrived, Los Angeles had a growing crime problem, including a steady escalation in the use and sale of illegal drugs. Although cocaine had yet to become the drug of choice, marijuana, heroin, and illegal pharmaceutical drugs had already become problems. In 1964 over one-half of California's 346,000 cases of juvenile delinquency, robbery, rape, homicide, and auto theft occurred in Los Angeles County. The same year Los Angeles had the dubious honor of being the bank robbery capital of the United States, with 121.

Los Angeles also suffered from other problems of growth. Increased size brought a loss of community, the sense of belonging that binds people together. Although its proponents argued that Los Angeles had "community," they also had to admit that it was not always obvious or easy to find.

"Sixty Suburbs in Search of a City" described Los Angeles in the 1960s. A fragmented metropolis that social scientist Melvin Webber referred to as the "non-place urban realm," a collection of people without roots. A society of artificial community constructed by people fleeing small towns and eastern urban areas, who built their community around groups of far-flung social contacts and activities totally unconnected to any local neighborhood. One Los Angeles city planner summarized the development of the city's growth as "chaos." The physical shape of Los Angeles made it less conducive to developing community and culture. The increasing size of Los Angeles denied the inhabitants any sense of stable attachment.

Still, there was community. The Los Angeles metropolitan area had 180 identified cities and towns within its five-county area in 1970. More important, community seemed to be more than just a series of destinations to be reached from one's residential stronghold. In a 1970 survey, almost 70 percent of Mexican Americans, 65 percent of blacks, and 61 percent of whites made the statement, " I feel a part of my neighborhood."

Even among people who did not conceive of community in neighborhood terms, there was a sense of belonging and attachment. The picture of Los Angeles as people whose lives centered around far-flung activities and social connections may have been true. But as historian John Findlay observed, the city's residents maintained a sense of community through "mental maps," a selective familiarity with other people and places that screened out certain parts of the city, but actually created a sense of identity and community with the areas they frequently traveled to or used. Although not "traditional" community, it did provide a sense of belonging.

Whether one saw Los Angeles community as nontraditional or nonexistent, some of the people that did feel a sense of community often did so in response to shared hardship. The population growth that resulted brought an increase in both the black and Hispanic populations. By 1970, 830,000 blacks accounted for 10.8 percent of the metropolitan population and the Mexican-American population stood at 1.7 million. Both groups struggled to find their piece of the dream.

Unemployment, poor-paying jobs, and housing discrimination posed problems for both Hispanics and blacks. Some described the Mexican-American population as almost invisible, yet in the Anglo portion of Los Angeles they could be seen wherever low-paying laborers were present. The 1970 census revealed that the average median income among blacks in Los Angeles was $7,500, for Mexican Americans it was $8,900, and for white families it was $11,400. The racial distinctions were even greater in the area of education. Ninety-six percent of black students attended predominantly black schools with dropout rates between 25 and 50 percent of the enrollment. By comparison, white school dropout rates were as low as 1 percent in some schools and never exceeded 34 percent. Hopelessness is never easy to bear, but the pain is much *culture* more acute in an age and area of abundance. The Watts riots of 1965 served as a reminder that Los Angeles had a growing population that did not reap the benefits of life in America's "first city."

Lost in the affluence and despair was that Los Angeles had become home to people who identified themselves less by their wealth or their ethnicity, and more by their beliefs. Sexual freedom, gay liberation, and a host of New Age religious groups all found a home in Los Angeles. Although some saw this emerging culture as an aspect of individual freedom, others would see it as the destruction of family values. William Irwin Thompson suggested society in southern California was on the "edge of history."

Los Angeles residents could change their house, job, wife, and religion at will. Thompson saw a lack of stability and tradition, a society with too much freedom that survived only by clinging to the fantasies offered by Disneyland.

Despite his qualifications, there were some among his flock that thought John MacArthur was not ready to lead in 1969. They questioned his Greek language skills, thought he might be too young. Some members took offense at MacArthur's beliefs that women's biblical station relegated them to staying at home, a position he eventually rescinded in the face of criticism after considering firing several women who were employed by Grace. Still, John MacArthur's appointment met with general approval. Most people expected great things from the young preacher, and MacArthur did not disappoint them.

In 1969 John MacArthur set about building Grace Church. The grounds of the church still had a dozen chicken coops on the premises where the homeless slept. He had both the homeless and the coops removed to make room for expanded youth services, and brought buses in to transport the children to Sunday school. MacArthur arranged for the church to buy property that adjoined its existing structure, thus expanding its physical facilities and its potential for membership. By 1973 Grace provided both financial assistance and pastoral help to surrounding smaller churches, in effect seeding the community with self-replicas.

Perhaps the most important aspect of Grace's services was its pastoral counseling program. Three individuals brought in by MacArthur became the heart of the program. Lynn Cory reflected the "new blood" that John had brought into Grace to invigorate its youth programs. Cory, a native Californian, was a few years older than Ken Nally when the two met in 1973. Although he had a college education and had been in the military, Cory had no particular training as a counselor outside training that he received from Grace Church. He held no medical degrees or certifications in mental health counseling.

Cory's main asset was his flamboyant personality, which made it possible for him to relate to Grace's younger membership. Cory and his wife Joan, "Jo" to her friends, liked rock music and the louder form of gospel tunes than the music traditionally associated with the fundamentalist faiths. Cory took charge of the "College-Age Group," an important ministry at Grace that consisted of about 400 college-age members of Grace, further divided into cells, or smaller, more manageable groups. Ken and Cory quickly found common interests in sports. Many people at Grace saw Cory as John MacArthur's pupil, and when Ken and Cory began socializing more closely, MacArthur sometimes accompanied them to football and basketball games. Ken grew to trust Cory and when the pressure got too much to bear, Ken turned to Cory first and Cory directed Ken to Duane Rea.

Duane Rea was not only a believer, he was tied to John MacArthur through marriage. Rea had married MacArthur's sister-in-law, and Rea and his wife joined Grace shortly after MacArthur became the pastor. Rea was both a pastor and one of thirty-eight people, pastoral and lay, that comprised Grace's biblical counseling center. Biblical counseling literally meant using the Bible as the tool for resolving both spiritual and mental health problems. Grace Church taught that at the root of all problems lay sin. Conditions such as addiction, depression, and anxiety were manifestations of unresolved sin. If one could gain control of sinful conduct, the underlying problem would disappear. The Bible held the answers to how one should act, and by following its teachings one could alter his or her conduct and resolve problems. Like MacArthur, Rea was a staunch advocate of biblical counseling but had no medical or professional counseling training. As a former mechanic and fireman, Rea acquired most of his counseling knowledge through reading on his own. It would be Rea who would spend the most time with Kenneth as the young man struggled to resolve the many problems that plagued him after he started college.

Like all of Grace's counselors, Rea had no formal training as a counselor. He had been counseling people since his early twenties and freely acknowledged that some of these people had severe emotional and mental problems, but he lacked any formal education. Nevertheless, he and MacArthur believed he had the "gift," an innate ability through God's intervention to counsel troubled people. Not only did Duane Rea believe he possessed this ability, but he openly acknowledged that there were others at Grace with the God-given talent to counsel, particularly Richard Thomson.

Rich Thomson had come to Grace in 1976 and had taken charge of its growing pastoral counseling program. Thomson himself represented somewhat of a reclamation project. Thomson met MacArthur in seminary: his first year was MacArthur's last. At Talbot, Thomson began to experience severe depression and was told by members of Talbot to seek out John MacArthur. MacArthur remembered Thomson and began trying to help him, assistance that took both spiritual and financial forms. As Thomson came out of his depression and got back on his feet he finished his seminary training and remained in close contact with MacArthur. He became a member of Grace Church and in 1978 accepted the position as director of the Grace counseling program, where he served until 1980. Although Thomson would not have as much direct contact with Ken Nally as Rea, his role as the director and trainer of those that did would push him to the forefront of the controversy.

––––––

As the Nally home continued to fill with Grace Church members, Maria Nally sat on her bed trying to come to grips with a reality too horrible to admit. She had known Ken was troubled. In many ways her relationship with Ken had grown stronger as her eldest boy struggled to reconcile his internal conflicts. Maria Nally could identify with Kenneth's struggle to reconcile his new faith with his family better than anyone else. She had done the same thing decades before when she converted from the religion of her family, Buddhism, to Catholicism. Her father was not only a Buddhist, but she had uncles who were priests. More than anyone, Maria Nally understood what it meant to follow one's own conscience. Her mother had wept when Maria told her that she wanted to be baptized a Catholic. In an effort to save her family the grief that her conversion had caused years before, Maria Nally tried to go the extra mile for Kenneth. Walter Nally had been willing to go to church with Kenneth on occasion, a trip that he found boring after about the first hour, but Maria Nally had gone several steps beyond. At Ken's insistence she not only went to church without telling her husband, but attended one of the postsermon sessions at Grace set up to bring in new members.

Maria Nally recalled Ken telling her to walk through a door, which she did, finding herself in a large room with tables, behind which sat a neatly dressed man or woman with a name tag that said "Hello. Welcome to Grace Church. My name is . . ." Maria Nally sat down at a table and said "hello" to a woman named Nancy. Nancy had asked, "Are you Christian?" Maria remembered responding, "Yes, I am Catholic." She also remembered being shocked when her polite hostess then quickly told her that she was not a Christian, that as a Catholic she had not been born again, and that until she was born again, she was destined to go to hell.

Maria did not understand. "What do you mean, born again?" she asked. "You must join Grace Church, accept Jesus Christ as your savior, and then you will be saved," responded Nancy. None of this made sense to Maria. The notion that one could gain salvation without living a good life seemed impossible. She left without committing to join Grace. Ken was waiting anxiously when she emerged and wanted to know what happened. She honestly was not sure, nor did she commit to going back to church with Ken the following Sunday.

However, Maria Nally did share another experience with Kenneth that Walter Nally did not. Like her son, she had firsthand knowledge of Grace's counseling services. Although Walter Nally knew many of the people now mingling in their home because of Ken's interaction with them, Maria had personal knowledge of at least one of Grace's pastors, Duane Rea.

In 1976, at Kenneth's insistence, Maria sought out Rea to help resolve problems she and Walter Nally were having. Mr. Nally had been the victim of a corporate buyout that saw the removal of all of the upper management of the company he had worked for since coming to California. Between December 5, 1976, and May 1977, Maria met with Duane Rea three times. Maria confided in Rea about problems at home, most of which stemmed from her husband's inability to find work. Rea counseled her to throw her husband out of the house. Quoting from scripture, Rea said, "That if he shall not work, neither shall he eat." If Walter Nally was not employed, Maria should not allow him to remain at home. Much of Ken's new religion was a mystery to Maria, but she knew that there was no way she was going to throw her husband out of the house. When she finally told Rea how she felt, Rea lamented that "Your son and I had hoped you would see the truth and perhaps could later marry a Christian man from the church. Ken and I will pray for you."

Although this was the last time Maria Nally made an effort to meet Kenneth more than halfway, it had not been the only effort, and was not the most extreme. In 1974, Maria followed Kenneth's suggestion that they enroll Walter Jr. into Village Christian School. Wally was having problems at Our Lady of Lourdes, the Catholic school Kenneth had attended. Unlike Kenneth, his grades were far from exemplary. The school was part of Village Christian Church, one of the churches taking leadership from Grace. MacArthur's four children attended the school and Ken badly wanted Wally to go. For Ken it was a way to bring Wally into the Grace community. For Maria Nally it was a way to keep her family intact in the face of the strain it was under. Walter Sr. was under so much pressure that he did not even realize Wally was not going to Catholic school until it was time to write checks one month, and an invoice from Village Christian School came up for payment. The elder Nally could only shake his head and conceded this one. One more thing he knew nothing about.

As time went on Walter and Maria Nally would find that there were many things they did not know, things about Kenneth they thought they should have known, information they believed could have saved Kenneth's life. Kenneth's suicide was not his first attempt. His overdose of medication three weeks earlier was also not his first try. Ken had displayed suicidal tendencies since at least 1973 and had tried to commit suicide on several other occasions, once with pills and another time by jumping off a building, attempts Grace and its counselors came to understand but did not share with Ken's family. This fact lay at the heart of Walter and

Maria's lawsuit and their belief that the church and its pastors had a duty to disclose this information to them.

———

Kenneth Nally's depression seemed to follow closely on the heels of his leaving home for college. Although Cal State Irvine was only an hour and a half from home, still, he was farther from his family than he had ever been. Irvine lasted only one year. Ken's grades were good, but he hated the school. Part of the problem may have been the demise of Ken's relationship with his high school girlfriend. By Christmas, Ken was ready to leave. In the spring of 1973 Ken transferred to UCLA. At UCLA Ken met people who would lead him to Grace Community Church. As part of his sojourn into self-discovery, Ken had grappled with the issue of God and religion. A note in Ken's Bible revealed that he had "been saved" on April 20, 1973.

Years later Walter Nally would reflect on what had transpired and recall that Ken had gradually stopped going to church with the family. Special occasions like Christmas or Easter were the only times Ken went to Catholic mass. Ken had come to believe that his depression might be connected to his religious beliefs. With friends at UCLA he began to try different churches. Ken had heard about Grace Community and with Steve Black, a friend who lived in the same dorm, he began to frequent Sunday services. One evening at UCLA, with Steve Black as a witness, Ken embraced his new faith.

Following his conversion to Grace Church Ken's life began to improve, at least in the short term. Conversion to his new faith came with the same intensity Ken displayed in everything else he did. But the more intensely he embraced his new religion the worse things seemed to get at school, and UCLA offered little relief for the problems that plagued Ken. At times his grades fell off, he grappled with bouts of depression, and even attempted suicide, attempts his family knew nothing about. Although the demise of his relationship with his girlfriend clearly contributed to his depression, part of Ken's problem seemed to lay in his inability to reconcile his new faith with the secular education he was receiving at UCLA. [5]

Grace Church taught that the Bible was factually and historically correct, but college biology clearly did not mesh with a belief that the world was created in the year 4004 B.C. Part of Ken's motivation for coming to UCLA was to become a doctor. Chemistry and the hard sciences lay between him and his goal. The inability to reconcile his biblical beliefs with his secular studies not only severely hurt his grade point average, but ultimately ended his aspirations to go to med school. He failed a science exam at UCLA when he explained that Earth was only 6,000 years old and God had placed old bones and artifacts in the ground to test mankind's faith. Ken wandered from major to major, uncertain which road to take, but sure that the key to his future lay within the pages of the Bible.

The harder Ken Nally studied the Bible the more he came to believe that unless he could convert his family, they were destined to suffer eternal damnation. Already troubled by the problems commonly encountered by young people in college, Ken now added to the mix a deep evangelical mission to convert his family, a goal that was destined to fail, as each member of his family rejected his entreaties with varying degrees of intensity. Ken's attempts to convert his family slowly eroded the features they had held in common.

Always somewhat tumultuous, like many relationships between fathers and their eldest sons, it seemed to Walter Nally that everything with Ken now had as its ultimate goal the conversion of the family. Baseball, golf, and vacations provided no relief. Although Kenneth had succeeded in getting his younger brother into Village Christian School, Wally began to have trouble with the teachers at Village School. About that time Walter Sr. began to have trouble paying for the school. When Walter took Wally out of Village, Kenneth saw it as one more form of resistance by his father to Ken's attempts to "save" his family. The harder Ken tried to convert his family the more they resisted, and he began to spend more time at Grace Church and less time visiting home. He explained that to live at home was to "live with sinners," an idea that infuriated his father and confused his mother.

The situation at UCLA worsened. Ken was passing, but barely.

He finally sought relief at a campus counseling center called Shepard House. This session in March 1975 revealed that Ken had entertained thoughts of suicide. As he moved into his last year he began to fight with the issue of what he would do for a career. He had finally majored in ecology, which at the time held very little prospect of a future. With nowhere else to turn, Kenneth became convinced that he wanted to be in seminary, and after graduating from UCLA he took steps to get into Talbot. For a year Ken attended seminary classes in a program at Grace called LOGOS. During this period he began to believe he might want to pursue the law and be a Christian lawyer. He was influenced by Sam Ericsson, an attorney and church member who would later become a central figure in the controversy that unfolded. During the same period Ken began to exhibit severe emotional problems. At one point he told his father that he was seeing a Christian psychologist in Van Nuys. Although Walter knew little of what was discussed between his son and the doctor, he was told only that Ken was feeling "calmer."

About the time that Ken came to grips with his career decisions, he also became involved with a girl, Katie Thayer. Katie went to Grace, was a devoted follower of John MacArthur's teachings, and from all indications Katie and Ken became close. However, this relationship proved to be as unstable as most of Ken's relationships, and by 1978 the couple was having problems. More important, Ken's circle of friends and confidants had grown considerably smaller and his willingness to share his feelings with those he did trust lessened as he turned more inward.

In 1978, years of conflict both internally and externally with his family had begun to take their toll. Ken sought help with Grace Church's counseling program. He approached Lynn Cory initially and Cory sent him to Duane Rea. Rea and Ken had talked informally for years, but in 1978 they formed what Rea would characterize later as a formal counseling relationship. During the course of this relationship Ken revealed much of what had transpired during his adult life. He shared his suicidal thoughts with Rea, told him of his failed attempts while at UCLA, and expressed a general sense of depression and frustration with life. It became apparent to Rea that at the core of Ken's problems lay his relationship with both his father and his girlfriend. For Rea the issue was simple: Sin lay at the heart of Ken's problems. The inability to forgive his father and make peace with him and his sinful feelings toward Katie, particularly his desire for intimacy outside of matrimony, were the problems that troubled Ken.

Their formal counseling relationship continued for about four months, but the informal one lasted over a year. Still, Ken did not seem to improve. Reconciling with his father proved easier to discuss than to accomplish, and his feelings for Katie Thayer proved no easier to reconcile. Ultimately, Rea, with Thomson's approval, broke off the formal counseling relationship with Ken. When asked why, Rea responded, "Ken wasn't doing his homework."

The Nallys argued later that at the moment Kenneth confided in Rea about his suicidal tendencies the problem had become deeper that Rea could handle. At the same time that Rea was getting in over his head, Kenneth was putting more importance in his relationship with the pastor. For the Nallys this was the point that Rea should have stepped away and referred Kenneth to a professional. In their eyes it was Rea's own arrogance, belief in the Bible, or his single-minded but unjustified belief in God that caused the tragedy.

In December 1978 Ken's relationship with Katie Thayer fell apart. In a letter to Ken she indicated that they had no future together. Despondent, Ken went to her and begged her not to give up. He convinced her to come to counseling with Lynn Cory. Despite Cory's best efforts, the break in the relationship seemed irreparable. During these sessions with Cory and in other meetings with Grace pastors in early 1979, Ken sought the answer to a troubling theological question. Would a person who committed suicide forfeit eternal salvation? Rich Thomson's response was unequivocal, and it was this belief and Thomson's expression of it that would drag the church into eight years of litigation. Thomson told Ken, "If you have received the Lord, if you are Born-Again, then you are saved." Thomson told his students in counseling classes that "The Bible tells us in Corinthians and other places that suicide for the believer is the Lord saying, 'Okay, come on home. Can't use you anymore on Earth, if you are not going to deal with those things in your life, come on home.' "

In Thomson's defense, he did not invent this doctrinal position of the effect of suicide on the salvation of a true believer. Many Protestant denominations and leaders, including John MacArthur, believed that once one was saved in Christ he or she did not lose that grace by killing themselves. Years later, on the witness stand, Thomson, Rea, and MacArthur all emphatically denied that they ever advocated that Ken commit suicide. Suicide is wrong. However, once the message is delivered the sender often has little control over how it is interpreted by the recipient. Such was the case with Ken Nally.

Ken's depression seemed to worsen. In repeated efforts to reconcile with Katie he told her that if he killed himself he would be with the Lord and that all of his sufferings would at least be over. Katie knew Ken well enough to know that he really believed that suicide might offer a way out of his misery without jeopardizing his salvation.

By February 1979, Ken's mother had seen enough to know that things were not right. She questioned him as to what was wrong. All Ken could say was, "I can't cope." Even apparently good news brought no relief. Ken had been accepted into law school at the place of his choice, Southwestern Law. On February 18 Maria arranged for Ken to see a psychiatrist, a Dr. Milestone, and during that session the psychiatrist gave Ken a prescription of Elavil, a tricyclic antidepressant. The drug did not seem to help. Perhaps part of the problem was that while all of this was transpiring, Ken was taking a course at Talbot Theological College on how to minister to the sick and dying. The class took the students to hospitals and mortuaries and gave extensive seminars on coping with death. The last entry in Ken's appointment diary for 1979 was a reminder to be at the seminar on the theological aspects of death and dying.

On March 12, 1979, Ken took a major step toward the fulfillment of his theological understanding of suicide. Sometime in the early morning after learning his close friend Mike McKillop had died at a Veterans' Administration hospital, he took an overdose of the

Elavil Dr. Milestone had prescribed. His parents found him unconscious on the bed in his room later that morning. Rushed to Verdugo Hills Hospital, Ken recovered. Walter and Maria Nally were completely taken by surprise and faced a tough decision. With Ken in the hospital and under supervision, what were they going to do with him? Was he so great a risk to himself that he needed to be committed to a psychiatric facility, even if against his will?

Ken was still not saying much to his parents. But while he was in the hospital at Verdugo Hills, members of Grace Church routinely visited his room. On one occasion Pastor MacArthur and Ken were alone when Ken told him that he "was sorry he had failed. When I get out I'll do it again. I won't fail next time." Whether MacArthur passed this off as a postsuicide depression, a statement that stemmed from the embarrassment Ken brought on himself for trying in the first place, or whether MacArthur felt like Ken's statements were given in the confidence of a pastor-penitent relationship, the pastor said nothing to anyone about Ken's promise to try again, at least not until after Ken was dead. Later that night Duane Rea visited Ken. While the two were alone Ken told Rea what he had told MacArthur: "If I'm given the opportunity, I'll do it again."

As Ken recovered the Nallys grappled with what to do next. Part of the difficulty in making an informed decision was that Walter and Maria Nally knew very little about the last six years of Ken's life. Walter Nally did not even know that Ken had been to Dr. Milestone in February. The Nallys knew nothing of any suicide attempts until the one in March 1979. They knew nothing about his suicidal predisposition manifested in statements to friends and counselors at Grace Church. They knew nothing about his promise to try again when he got out. All they knew for sure was what the attending physician at Verdugo Hills Hospital, Dr. Christine Evelyn, told them: that Ken had tried to kill himself with Elavil and that he seemed to be recovering.

The Nallys hesitated to involuntarily commit Ken. Maria flatly said, "Kenny is not crazy and I won't put him in a nuthouse." Walter Nally felt the same way, but both understood the severity of the situation. Their unwillingness to commit Ken would later become a key issue in the trial as Grace Church alleged and offered evidence that it was the family's own negligence that caused Ken's death. But, as the Nallys later testified, despite Ken's statements to Grace pastors and some of his close friends, statements that neither Maria nor Walter were privy to at the time, Ken continued to deny he was suicidal when questioned by Dr. Evelyn.

Evelyn believed Ken was recovering well physically and explained that the paralysis he felt in his right arm was only temporary. Often referred to as "Saturday Night Palsy," the condition was common among alcoholic patients who fall asleep in their chairs, cutting off the blood flow to the arm. Such a loss of blood apparently occurred when Ken overdosed. Evelyn explained that she could not and would not release Ken until he had seen a resident psychiatrist at Verdugo Hills, a Dr. Hall. Evelyn found Ken's depression hard to understand, given his physical good looks and apparent intelligence. It was not that "beautiful people" could not suffer from depression, it just seemed to her and others that Ken had so much to be positive about. Regardless of his physical and mental attributes Evelyn made an appointment with the staff psychiatrist for Ken. Despite an initial reluctance, Ken finally gave in when Evelyn explained he would not be allowed to leave the hospital until he had seen Dr. Hall.

Dr. Hall spent about an hour with Ken. He had the chart and medical records from Verdugo Hills, but little else. Hall later commented that Ken displayed an emotional maturity level of someone ". . . fifteen or sixteen. Unwilling to carry the conversation, not volunteering information, he gave vague answers . . . but did reveal that religion was very important to him and that the counseling he received from the religious leaders was something he relied very heavily on." Attempts to get Ken to be more specific about the type of counseling he received at Grace proved futile. "Biblical counseling" was as explicit as Ken was willing to be. However, what did concern Hall was Ken's statement that "My counselors have advised me not to go to a psychiatrist. In fact I did want to check with them before coming to see you, to see if it was all right, but I was unable to."

After an hour Hall invited Walter Nally to join him and Ken in his office so the three of them could discuss Ken's condition. Hall explained various aspects of depression. Walter Nally questioned whether this could be some kind of chemical imbalance in Ken's blood. When treatment was discussed, one thing was clear: Ken adamantly opposed any kind of hospitalization. Hall suggested they treat Ken on an outpatient basis and he made an appointment for March 23, 1979. Ken agreed and Hall said, "I think we can discharge you tomorrow."

The next day Ken left the hospital. His father picked him up and drove him home. Ken agreed to stay for lunch, but insisted that he be taken to the church to speak with Lynn Cory. When he got home his mother was waiting. Mother and son embraced and wept. After lunch, Walter Nally drove Ken to the church and waited there for him. Ken spent time alone with Lynn Cory and when the two emerged, Cory told Walter that "Kenneth had agreed to go over to Pastor MacArthur's house for a few days." The elder Nally was crushed and he told Ken how disappointed both he and Maria were that he was not coming home. As happens often when children grow up and leave, other people and institutions come between children and their parents. So it had happened with Kenneth and his family.

A few days became a week and when MacArthur and his family left for a trip to Scotland that had been planned for some time, Kenneth returned home. The time Ken spent at home was occupied with reading the Bible and listening to tapes of John MacArthur's sermons and teachings. "What could he be listening to on those tapes?" thought Walter. Maria could not understand why he would not watch television. Ken explained that "a born-again Christian does not watch T.V." By Saturday morning, March 30, Ken was extremely agitated. He hoped he and Katie might resolve their problems but she had not called him. To make matters worse, Ken's arm did not come around as he had hoped and believed it would. The playful ribbing of his brother did not help. "It seems to be getting smaller," Wally joked.

Ken dressed and went to his car. His father followed him, pleading to know why Ken was so distraught. As Ken backed out of the driveway Walter Nally kept pace with the slow-moving vehicle, all the while begging to know why Ken was so upset. Ken finally blurted out, "It's my arm, see how it is?" "What about it?" Walter asked, still walking to keep pace with Ken's car. "They told me it was because of my sin. They told me it was God's punishment, Dad!" Walter Nally could not believe his own ears. "Tell me which one of those bastards said it!" Ken was already gone mentally. He turned to face the road and increased his speed. His father struggled to hold on to the door handle. Unable to keep pace with Ken as he picked up speed, Walter Nally stumbled and fell in the street. As he watched Ken pull away, part of him knew that was the last time he would see his son. Nally did not know then and does not know today for certain where Kenneth spent his last days. All he knows for sure is that sometime between the morning Ken pulled out, March 30, and the knock at the door on April 1, he took his own life.

CHAPTER 2

Some Answers, More Questions

Finally, around 3:30 in the afternoon the Nally house emptied, leaving the family alone with its grief. Walter Nally's first concern was to protect Maria from the reality of how Kenneth had taken his life. Duane Rea had been adamant that Grace Community Church would handle the funeral arrangements. Nally was too weary to argue, but could only watch in amazement that afternoon as Rea took control of the phone, making what seemed like endless phone calls. As the day came to a close Nally took Rea aside and asked him, "For the sake of my family, would you promise me one thing? That you won't be telling other people how my son died." Rea assured him, "I will tell nobody."

So many questions, so few answers. What began as grief would soon turn into anger. Walter Nally had a lot of catching up to do, and as he began to probe into his son's life over the past several years he would reach the conclusion that Kenneth's death was the fault of this church and its counselors. Although it took months before he could reach that conclusion, it took a considerably shorter time for Nally to become angry with Grace and its ministers. The anger would feed an already growing need to understand Kenneth's life in the years prior to his death.

As Walter and Maria Nally packed to spend a few days at Walter's cousin's, Ken's car arrived. The police had found it several blocks from Ernie Hauser's home. Duane Rea drove it home and left it in the driveway. Walter Nally went outside to inspect it and first noticed that it was cleaner than he could ever remember. The inside was cleaned out, including all the Grace Church cassette tapes that Ken was always listening to. The one remaining tape that was left was in the cassette deck, "The History of Grace."

The funeral occurred several days later and between Ken's death and the end of the funeral Duane Rea made a series of mistakes that would lead Walter Nally to pursue Rea, Cory, Thomson, MacArthur, and the church for over eight years. Prior to the funeral Nally drove down to Grace Church to finalize the arrangements. In the course of conversations with Rea, the pastor told Walter, "Kenneth wasn't the only one. This isn't the first time that this has happened at our church. There have been other suicides, young men and women who have killed themselves." Rea's words did not fully sink in at the time. Nally remained concerned that others would find out how Ken had died. Rea assured him they would not.

As the conversation wandered Walter Nally learned more about Rea, this former mechanic and fireman who had counseled Kenneth. The obvious question to Nally was, "Are you trained as a counselor? Do you have a degree as a psychiatrist?" Rea seemed amused by the question and explained that he counseled straight from the Bible. Psychiatrists and psychologists taught beliefs that were inconsistent with Grace's teachings. Some, including Rea, believed that secular mental health professionals were satanic. Walter wondered if John MacArthur understood what kind of pastor he had working for him. Later, Wally explained to his dad that Rea was MacArthur's brother-in-law, and that MacArthur knew all about Rea.

The day of the funeral was bright and clear. The Nallys went to Catholic mass and then made their way to Grace Church for the funeral. The place was packed. First Lynn Cory spoke, followed by several of Ken's friends, who gave eulogies. Duane Rea then got up. "It is not my purpose to eulogize Ken," he said. "Ken disobeyed God in the final act of his life. He took what did not belong to him." Despite Walter Nally's emphatic pleas that no one know that Kenneth had killed himself, Rea made it clear to even the most ignorant observer that Ken had committed suicide. He did not stop there. Rea then offered to read from a card found at the scene of Ken's death, a card the Nallys knew nothing about. Rea could not find the card so he resorted to a passage from scripture. Walter Nally could not stop thinking there might have been a note, some explanation of why Ken killed himself. As the service broke up and people made their way by car to the grave site no one wanted to discuss Ken with the Nallys. Walter recalled feeling that something was wrong here. Rea's sermon was unsettling, not only to the Nallys, but to many of the Grace Church community.

Following the graveside service the Nallys went back to Walter's cousin's home. The sermon had been a disaster so far as Walter Nally was concerned, compounded by learning in the few days preceding the service that Duane Rea was not even a qualified counselor. In the aftermath of the funeral Rea made one more mistake. He went to see Walter Nally and brought with him a paper. Rea explained that it was a written testimonial Ken had given to the board of elders at Grace Community Church as a prerequisite to admission into the LOGOS program that preceded Talbot Theological Seminary. Rea told Mr. Nally that the testimonial revealed that Ken had tried to kill himself prior to 1979, and remarked that "that is why I was not surprised when he finally succeeded."

Nally could not believe what he read. Ken's testimonial recounted prior suicide attempts dating back to 1973. Rea admitted the church knew all about these attempts and Ken's testimonial seemed to prove that the upper echelons of Grace Church also knew. Rea went on to explain that Ken's death was the result of unresolved sin, that he, Lynn Cory, and Rich Thomson had tried to counsel Ken but that Ken could never do what was required to overcome his problems. As the conversation continued Rea made it clear that the beliefs he advocated, those that had been apparent in Ken's conduct toward his family, emanated directly from the teachings of John MacArthur.

Walter and Maria Nally stayed at his cousin Edward's for almost two months. For most of the time Walter Nally wrestled with the new information that Rea had given him. Attempts to reach John MacArthur had proven futile. Apparently MacArthur had tried unsuccessfully to reach the Nallys by phone, and on May 3, 1979, he wrote Walter and Maria a one-page letter that began, "My heart is heavy as I write this letter." He explained how he had heard of Ken's death while in Scotland and how hard he and his wife Patricia had tried to give Ken something positive to hold on to in the week prior to the suicide. MacArthur conceded that "In a real sense,

I failed to do what I so desperately needed to do—give him hope." But MacArthur also believed the fault lay with Ken entirely. "None of us could force him to override his will—so the act was his alone and no one else carried any guilt, at all, before God."

The letter appears to have been a sincere effort on MacArthur's part to offer comfort and closure on Ken's death. It did neither. Walter Nally did not think that "the act was Ken's alone." Regardless of whether anyone else felt a sense of guilt, Nally believed that there was enough fault to go around, a belief that grew as he began to dig deeper into his son's life. In Ken's desk he found biblical verses on index cards and a *Los Angeles Times* newspaper clipping about a Gigi Allison. The young girl had killed herself by jumping off a bridge at Santa Rosa. She was a member of Grace Church and her family was Catholic. Rea's words now began to make sense: Ken had not been the only one, there were others.

As Walter Nally began to investigate he discovered members of Grace Church who had committed suicide, disappeared without a trace, or otherwise exhibited extreme antisocial behavior. Three people, including Ken, had committed suicide since 1978. Walter Nally tracked deaths and disappearances at Grace for the ten-year period from 1978 to 1988 and ultimately found twenty-five instances. Half were unidentified or their names were withheld from publication. A total of eleven were suicides. Although indicative of a troubling trend, the suicide numbers from 1978 to 1980 did not seem out of line with the suicide rate within the surrounding community.

Between 1955 and 1980 the suicide rate among young people from ages fifteen to twenty-four rose dramatically in America and remained high. The National Center for Health Statistics indicated that the suicide rate doubled for young women, going from 2 to 4.3 per 100,000 people, and more than tripled for men, going from 6.3 to 20.2 per 100,000. By 1980 the United States ranked among the nations with the highest rate of young male suicides, surpassing both Japan and Sweden, two countries with historically high suicide rates. The absolute numbers for suicides among men fifteen to twenty-four in America went from a few hundred per year to over 5,000 per year. By 1984 suicides among young men represented 20 percent of the 23,000 suicides in the United States each year.

The mental health profession was at a loss to explain the rise in suicides among young American men. Change in the quality of family life and an increase in the intensity of competitive pressures to succeed, including pressure to perform at college and professional school, were seen as the primary cause of the rising suicide rate. Research at Harvard, Yale, and the University of California at Berkeley revealed some interesting but inconclusive data.

Most college-age male suicides were doing better than average in their studies, but had performed poorly during the most recent grading period. The majority did not seek psychiatric help, but those who had did not discuss suicide and were not seen as suicidal. Most male victims did, however, give some kind of warning sign to teachers or friends and even the parents of these suicide victims recognized some level of dissatisfaction with their academic performance.

Ken Nally had clearly experienced the frustration with his scholastic life that seemed indicative of the problems that plagued many of the young men who committed suicide at or near the time Ken killed himself. Physical environment may or may not have contributed to Ken's death. Burbank and the immediate vicinity experienced a high incidence of suicide in 1978. Burbank police sergeant Don Brown estimated that in 1978 Burbank averaged four attempts and one successful suicide per month. What alarmed Brown was not only the frequency, but the age of the victims. Of the twenty-one suicides in Burbank during 1978, twelve were under the age of twenty, and five were under age twenty-five. In addition to academic pressures common to the age group, young people had to cope with the stresses of urban living, growing up too fast, and the apparent loss of community and a sense of belonging.

Some of the cases of suicide and strange behavior that Walter Nally uncovered involved individuals who were members of the church. Others, however, had only attended services. Were these people the product of Grace Church's teachings and ministry, or were they already severely misguided or ill, and just happened to lose hope or self-control while looking for answers at Grace? It was almost impossible to prove any connection between Grace Church and the incidences of suicide or deviant behavior. Still, Walter Nally did not see this as a societal issue, but rather an apparent epidemic of suicides and violent behavior at Grace. "What were these people teaching?" he asked himself.

Among his son's personal effects Walter Nally found a letter dated March 9, 1979, two days before Ken's failed attempt to commit suicide in the Nally home. The short letter was from Lynn Cory and it made reference to a tape Ken had apparently been listening to as well as another tape he should consider. Cory recommended the tape as a means to get a pulse on one's motivations. "They are subtle, you know. Our hearts are deceitful and desperately wicked and a tape like this is good to keep it in check."

Most of Ken's tapes had disappeared following his death, but Walter Nally discovered that he could buy them at the Grace bookstore. He bought some tapes and as he listened to them he became deeply disturbed. He began to believe that Ken's death might have been prevented, that what had actually caused Ken's suicide was the manner in which Grace Church and its pastors had counseled Ken. More important, at a time when Walter and Maria Nally had to make a crucial decision as to how to treat Ken, Grace's pastors withheld information that would have greatly influenced the Nallys' decision.

What Walter Nally heard on the Grace tapes reinforced his belief that the church was a cult. He could recall going to see Father Lawrence, his Catholic priest, shortly after Ken's death. Father Lawrence had been shocked to learn that the Grace counselors had treated Ken's depression as solely the result of sin. He had explained that "Although Christian counseling had its place in helping people, a priest or minister must realize that there are some problems that must be left to the medical profession to treat. Catholic priests know a lot about sin and its results ourselves and we know enough to be able to say that a lot of so-called sinning is only the result of sickness."

Nally reached a point where he could no longer reconcile Grace's counseling practices with what had happened. Although it is easy to see how Walter Nally or anyone of the Catholic faith might have drawn that conclusion, Grace was not a cult, but an example of an American fundamentalist Protestant church.

———

Religious fundamentalism had existed long before Walter Nally and Grace Church crossed paths. Fundamentalism grew out of challenge to Protestant evangelical theology that arose during the tumultuous sixty-year stretch in America from 1870 to 1930. During this era three developments began to undermine Protestantism in America: evolution, the scientific study of religion, and the changing face of American culture brought on by growth, immigration, and industrialization.

Presented for the first time in 1859, Charles Darwin's theory of evolution posed a two-part problem. First, it drew into question the traditional notion stated in Genesis that God created "the beast of the earth after his kind." The Bible is clear: God made man, then God made animals. Evolution says man evolved from lower species. From this notion of slow development came the idea that evolution could now explain man's presence on earth and could do so without the necessity of God. Herbert Spencer, a contemporary of Darwin's, went a step further and suggested that since life constantly evolved from the simplistic to the complex, Christianity itself might no longer be necessary. A primitive belief in God might have helped early man cope with life, but man no longer needed God.

Closely related to evolution, scientific inquiry posed the second challenge confronting Protestant theology. The education system in Germany in the late nineteenth century stressed scientific inquiry and freedom for research. In the process it took education away from church control and placed it in the hands of secular institutions. Building on Enlightenment thinking in the eighteenth century, scientific criticism of the Bible not only attempted to place Christianity within the context of a wave of primitive religious beliefs systems that deserved no special recognition, but questioned the validity of many of the stories contained within its text. The natural next step was to compare the Bible with other ancient documents and conclude that the Bible was flawed, and ultimately so was the Christian belief in Jesus Christ.

By the early 1900s Protestant theology had split into liberal and conservative components. Liberal Protestantism had in effect reconciled itself with modernism. In the words of Protestant theologian Charles Briggs, "the sacred scriptures do not describe for us all questions of orthodoxy. They do not answer the problems of science, of philosophy and history. They do not cover the whole ground of theology." Liberalism or modernism sought to redefine theology to make it compatible with the ever-changing face and dynamics of American society. The resurrection need no longer be seen as an actual physical event, but could be conceived in purely spiritual terms, not so much as an event but part of an unfinished process. In short, liberal thought showed a willingness to conform religion to America and gave up the attempt to conform America to religion.

Conservative theologians rejected liberalism's accommodation to modern American society. Through the efforts of men like Edgar Youngs Mullins, B. B. Warfield, Robert Speer, and Gresham Machen, conservative Protestantism reaffirmed the aspects of traditional Protestant thought that were under such severe attack. Chief among their reaffirmations were that the Bible was infallible and that Christ was the son of God, made human, and actually rose from the dead to cleanse the sin of mankind.

As important as the individual responses of conservative Protestant theologians was to the fight, perhaps the most important response to liberalism came from a combined Protestant evangelical response. Between 1910 and 1915 the Testimonial Publishing Company, housed on the grounds of the Moody Bible Institute of Chicago, published twelve booklets under the collective title of *The Fundamentals: A Testimony of the Truth*. Bankrolled by Lyman and Milton Stewart, owners of the Los Angeles–based Union Oil company, *The Fundamentals* were sent, free of charge, to pastors, missionaries, preachers, theologians, seminary students, and YMCA secretaries across the globe. The booklets represented the combined efforts of Methodists, Presbyterians, Baptists, Episcopalians, and ministers of unaffiliated Protestant churches who faced head-on the wave of liberalism sweeping America. Within *The Funda-mentalist* lay the essentials for orthodoxy: the complete inerrancy of the Bible, the virgin birth, Christ's atonement and resurrection, and dispensationalism. These five points of fundamentalism became the focus of doctrinal struggles through the 1920s as the fundamentalists, as they became known, defended their orthodoxy against the modernists.

Protestantism went through a sixty-year internal struggle, one that eventually destroyed any semblance of Protestant unity, but American society literally passed it by. As conservatism battled liberal thought, America slipped further away from religion during the twentieth century. The Great Depression caused most Americans to question whether God even existed, and if he did, to ask why he had abandoned so many of them. As a direct result of the depression, government became an increasingly active partner in the everyday life of Americans, a trend that continues today. The battle among Protestants paled in comparison to the postwar battle with communism that saw the United States move to the forefront of the global struggle. At home, education became increasingly more public and less Christian and as the country emerged from World War II, it found itself bathing in a new power and prosperity that brought about the secularization of American culture.

It was no longer a two-sided debate between modernism or conservatism. A third option had appeared, the resolution of problems and conflicts via nonreligious answers and institutions. In part because of their unbending devotion to their conservative principles, fundamentalists completely lost credibility with mainstream America. Most Americans saw them as illiterate country bumpkins. However, although these conservative people retreated from public life, fundamentalism did not disappear. Instead, it built a network of churches, denominations, Bible schools, seminaries, Bible camps, missionary houses, and publishing houses that, although absent from public circles, became the basis of fundamentalism's resurgence during the 1970s.

Grace Community Church exemplified the evolution of fundamentalism and its resurgence, a small group of people seeking to bring their religious institutions more in line with their basic religious needs. For Grace it was Sunday school instruction for children that became the motivating force behind the unaffiliated Protestant church. From its humble beginnings, far from the mainstream of Los Angeles life, Grace Church grew to a thriving congregation of 20,000 by the 1970s.

Grace Church's doctrine is set out in a statement titled "What We Teach," and reflects the key tenants of fundamentalism. Grace teaches that the Bible is "absolutely inerrant in the original documents, infallible, and God breathed. We teach the literal, grammatical-historical interpretation of Scripture which affirms the belief that the opening chapters of Genesis present creation in six literal days." Jesus Christ was virgin born and "accomplished our redemption through the shedding of his blood and sacrificial death on the cross." At Grace, "the truth of the scriptures stands in judgment of men, never do men stand in judgment of it."

Part of this story is a reflection of fundamentalism's history. Born out of the need to defend itself against modern America and the destruction of traditional Protestant theology, fundamentalism took an all-or-nothing view of the world. There was only one correct way and any other way was unacceptable. Although Grace Church was part of the wave that became the resurgence of fundamentalism, it never lost the sense of having to defend its beliefs. Grace Church followed a strict adherence to its own doctrine and taught that although "there may be several applications of any given passage of scripture, there is but one true interpretation." Interpretation at Grace is the interpretation of its leader, John A. MacArthur.

What Walter Nally saw as a "cult" was in reality a fundamentalist religious institution whose present-day practices and beliefs were deeply rooted in the unbending principles of the founders of fundamentalism. One of the most obvious manifestations of this unyielding attitude lay in the way that outsiders were treated. As Kenneth repeatedly told his family, if you are not saved in the way Grace believes one must be saved, you do not have eternal salvation and are "damned as sinners." Therefore, not only did Walter Nally and his family struggle with the schism that existed between the family and Ken, but they also understood that insofar as Grace and its community was concerned, they were infidels, nonbelievers, destined to eternal damnation.

This feeling of being an outsider became an important component of the lawsuit between the Nallys and Grace. In some ways it made the litigation a battle that was very much grounded in theological differences between Catholics and Protestants, liberals and conservatives of all faiths, those who believed the Bible's teachings belonged in a narrow area of life and those who believed the Bible offered all that one needed to answer every problem in life, including issues of mental health.

When John MacArthur assumed leadership at Grace Community Church in 1969, fundamentalism was on the verge of a resurgence that to some degree continues today. During the 1950s and 1960s fundamentalism had begun to reemerge from decades spent in revival tents and small, nondenominational churches throughout America. The movement grew strength by attacking communism as something not only un-American in a secular sense, but as un-Christian. By bootstrapping the older fundamentalist concepts of salvation with the theme of nationalism and patriotism, fundamentalism began the long road back into the public arena during the 1960s. With men like Billy Ray Hargis and Robert Welch, the founder of the John Birch Society, fundamentalism slowly made its way closer to mainstream America.

As a portion of America became disillusioned with change and reform that dominated the 1960s and started into the 1970s, fundamentalism took on a unique character in California. Rather than embrace the secular themes of nationalism and patriotism, the Jesus people, or "Jesus freaks" as they were referred to, exemplified a type of fundamentalism that not only advocated that Jesus Christ offered the only way to salvation, but rejected any notion that the church should be part of mainstream American political culture or the American political establishment. This aspect of fundamentalism found its energy from young people and focused on Jesus as a "revolutionary." They saw themselves as a small island of virtue in a sea of sin and reveled in the notion that society saw them as social outcasts. One publication actually played on this

aspect of the Jesus movement by showing how Christ would have
been depicted in the 1970s:

WANTED: JESUS CHRIST
Alias: The Messiah, Son of God, King of Kings, Lord of Lords,
Prince of Peace, etc.
Notorious leader of underground liberation movement
Wanted for the following charges

—Practicing medicine, wine-making and food distribution
without a license
—Interfering with businessmen in the Temple
—Associating with known criminals, radicals, subversives,
prostitutes and street people
—Claiming to have the authority to make people into God's
children

BEWARE:—This man is extremely dangerous. His insidiously
inflammatory message is particularly dangerous to young people
who haven't been taught to ignore him yet. He changes men
and claims to set them free
WARNING: HE IS STILL AT LARGE!

The Jesus movement did not survive as the primary organ of
fundamentalism in the 1970s and 1980s. However, its message that
America was socially and spiritually corrupt did endure and became a major theme of fundamentalism's most prominent spokes-
men. Men like Jerry Falwell, the leader of the Moral Majority, and
Pat Robertson, founder and director of the 700 Club, pointed
directly to the moral depravity of America. John MacArthur, living and preaching in the heart of Los Angeles County, would also
see this issue as a crucial component to his message. However,
unlike the Jesus freaks, who rejected involvement in American culture and politics, the new fundamentalists placed themselves
directly within secular institutions in an effort to use the system to
bring about change.

Equally important was a focus on youth. Jerry Falwell's princi-
pal vehicle for his brand of fundamentalism became Liberty College. John MacArthur stressed the importance of young people,

and anyone attending a Grace service could see the emphasis on youth. However, the youth that flocked to MacArthur's pulpit were not the social rebels identified with the Jesus movement of the 1970s, but young, middle- and upper-class men and women. Fundamentalism had emerged from the fringes of American society where it had languished since the late 1920s. It now appealed to people in the mainstream of America, present and future leaders of the community. Grace's board of elders included professionals from all walks of life, including Los Angeles assistant police chief Robert Vernon.

When asked why fundamentalism took off in some parts of California and not others, MacArthur replied that many factors were involved, but basically, "God does what he does when he does it." However, an energetic Protestant population was not the product of an overnight transition in Los Angeles. Southern California had strong Protestant roots dating back to the middle 1800s. American Protestants heard the call from New York as early as 1849 when the *Baptist Home Mission Record* exhorted them to

> Go where the waves are breaking
> On California's shore
> Christ's precious gospel taking,
> More rich than golden ore

A strong fundamentalist presence followed in the early decades of the twentieth century. Although traditionally held to be strongest in rural areas of the South and the Midwest, as America moved into the twentieth century fundamentalism experienced significant growth in America's cities, and Los Angeles was no exception.

According to the Religious Bodies Census, between 1916 and 1936 over one-third of Protestant churches claiming to be "definitely fundamentalist," meaning they belonged to the World's Christian Fundamentals Association and their doctrine conformed to the five fundamentals, were located in urban areas. As the fastest growing western urban area of that era, Los Angeles was home to the Stewart brothers and the Bible Institute of Los Angeles (BIOLA), an offshoot of the Moody Bible Institute in Chicago. Aimee Semple McPherson and Robert "Fighting Bob" Schueler launched significant Protestant radio ministries from California in the two decades between the world wars. From Los Angeles, Robert Fuller sent his "Old Fashioned Revival Hour" over the airwaves in 1933, and by 1937 his program was distributed to over 450 radio stations nationwide, making him the first national radio minister.

Los Angeles also had a population that drew heavily from the South and Midwest, areas identified as strongholds of fundamentalism. The "southernization" of Los Angeles occurred in the 1920s and 1930s and saw 250,000 white immigrants from Texas, Oklahoma, Missouri, and Arkansas, followed a decade later by 300,000 "Okies." World War II continued the inmigration of southerners. As Japanese Americans were forced into internment camps, 620,000 more "Okies" joined those who had come in the 1930s. Predominantly Protestant, this new wave came to California to man the military defense plants that had sprung up across southern California.

Some historians explain the relationship between fundamentalism and urbanization as a religious response to growth and the many vices that accompanied it, particularly those associated with industrialization. However, Los Angeles does not fit this description. Fundamentalism in southern California seemed to respond to a sense of alienation that came with urban living. Rather than a rural versus urban confrontation, Los Angeles was actually built by Protestant migrants, many from rural communities, and these people used their faith and the volunteer organizations that were so crucial to their religious life to not only build the great western metropolis, but to cope with what it became.

In the years following World War II Los Angeles continued its role as a center for fundamentalists and evangelicals. Neoevangelicalism emerged, a movement that rejected old-line fundamentalism's anti-intellectual conservatism. The most successful proponents were Robert Fuller, who used his radio ministry to launch the Fuller Theological Seminar in 1947, and Billy Graham, whose eight-week postwar revivalism in 1949 converted several celebrities and caught the attention of *Time* magazine and the *Los Angeles Times*. Both publications heralded Graham as a "rising young evangelist." Paralleling Graham's efforts was an emerging network of youth ministries.

Campus Crusade for Christ began on the campus of the University of California at Los Angeles and spread nationwide.

There is no single reason why fundamentalism caught on in the northern Los Angeles area. Strong roots dating back to the 1920s, a growing population that migrated from areas of traditional Protestant strength that provided a receptive audience to the emerging fundamentalist leadership, and an urban fundamentalist tradition contributed to the growth of institutions like Grace Church. MacArthur concedes that Grace rode the crest of the Jesus movement by taking the old fundamentalist message and personalizing it, taking Christ off the shelf, so to speak. The music at services and the focus on youth all came from a refinement of the Jesus movement. Grace's growth paralleled the growth of new Christian publications and the Living Word Bible took the message of God out of the archaic and allowed the everyday person to understand its teachings. During the 1970s the evangelical message became very aggressive, an aggressiveness that would give rise to the charismatic movement and see churches generate billions of dollars in revenue, something MacArthur himself was familiar with and conceded that "we are both better and worse for it."

Obviously not everyone in California was fundamentalist or even Protestant, for that matter. By 1980, when *Nally* was filed, the 2.2 million California Protestants made up only 9 percent of the state's 23,600,000 population. However, it was an active, energetic minority and Grace Church epitomized the religious traditions that had been developing since the early 1900s, Its followers did not see Los Angeles as an example of cultural and intellectual freedom, but as a place where the vast majority of people had lost their way. The "Hub,' the symbol of Grace Church, reflected more than a desire for community, but a need to spread its message and to reclaim the city from the social and cultural forces that threatened the metropolis that previous Protestant generations had helped to build.

When Kenneth Nally took his life in April 1979, he had been a member of a church that was far from being a cult. Yet to those who did not belong to the Grace community, Grace seemed to exhibit the fervent, uncompromising attitude that most Americans identified with cults. More important to the Nallys, Grace seemed to exert the type of control over their son that they normally associated with cults. This was a nation and a state that only too recently had absorbed the shock of the Jonestown massacre. To Walter Nally, Ken's behavior, his resistance to his own family, and rejection of the religion of his childhood began with his involvement at Grace. The information discovered from talking to Grace pastors, listening to the same tapes Ken had listened to, and reading his son's own words led Walter Nally to the conclusion that Ken's death was a direct result of Grace's influence. It was the influence transmitted by Grace's pastors and counselors that had prevented Ken from getting the help he had so desperately needed, help that Ken would not accept because it came in the form of secular institutions and physicians that Grace rejected as sinful and satanic.

It's Not About Religion

Ed Barker was a thirty-seven-year-old solo practitioner in 1979 when Walter Nally walked into his humble office in downtown Los Angeles. Barker attended college at the University of Pittsburgh, but went West and finished his undergraduate work at UCLA. From there he just kept going, got his law degree from UCLA, and went into solo practice in the middle of one of the largest and fastest growing cities in the world in 1969. Ed specialized in personal injury, not an uncommon specialty for a one-man show. In a city the size of Los Angeles it offered the promise of a lucrative if unsteady practice.

Ed Barker was bright in a purely legal sense. He coauthored portions of the California Tort Code and he knew and understood tort law. He combined what he knew with a genuine love for debate. Years later his wife, Juan, would say that "some people do law for whatever reason, Ed did it because that was what he was supposed to do. He was a great trial lawyer." Finally, Barker had a quality that every lawyer should have, but one that a solo practitioner cannot survive without: He never believed he was outgunned, not during this case, not during any case. He had a partner for a brief period, Bob Long, but having grown up on the insurance defense side of the docket, Long was accustomed to a steady paycheck. Plaintiff's law offered no such security.

At the time Walter Nally first appeared, Ed Barker was looking hard at another case. Like the Nallys', it would be a big case, a time-consuming case, and the type of case a solo practitioner could manage only one at a time. Walter Nally would come in, Barker would send him back for more data. Nally would come back, and Barker would send him back out. Eventually Nally's bulldog tenacity won over Barker and he took the case. He took the case knowing that no one had ever really sued a church for malpractice before. Barker knew that even though California had laws that governed counselors, specifically laws that imposed duties on professionals to prevent the suicides of people in their care, the California legislature had specifically excluded the clergy from licensing requirements, and at best pastoral counselors were deemed nonprofessionals.

By 1980 America was more litigious than it had ever been before. The statistics on the number of lawsuits showed a dramatic increase since World War II, an increase disproportionate to the increase in population. At the turn of the twentieth century the cry had been caveat emptor, buyer beware! Now it was caveat vendor, seller beware! Torts, the legal body of law governing noncontractual liability, had been on the rise throughout the twentieth century. By 1980 American law boasted well-developed notions of strict liability for products, regardless of a showing of fault. Complex comparative negligence statutes that sought to apportion each person's liability within a particular transaction as precisely as possible existed in every state. In short, America had become a land preoccupied with "fault," and no one was exempt.

A litigious society does not explain completely why Walter and Maria Nally had a chance to win their case. Not only were Americans suing one another at a record pace under legal theories that seemed to be continuously developing, but religion as a target had become much more palatable to Americans in the 1980s. Despite a variety of contradictory studies that tended to disagree on whether church attendance was rising or declining, both attendance and a belief that religion was an important part of American life had declined from the 1950s. More important, studies showed that secularization, a trend that had been on the rise since the turn of the twentieth century, had made serious inroads into church attendance and the role of religious institutions. Churches were no longer "the" community institution, but rather one of many institutions that people could and did look to for companionship, guidance, and assistance. Overall church attendance in America was declining from the 1950s but on the rebound from its low point in the 1960s. Where growth in attendance did occur, it could be found in Protestant churches. Regardless of the level of church attendance, America had become an increasingly secular land. This secularization in turn gave rise to a battle that saw the fundamentalist churches on the forefront. However, unlike the struggle among Protestants that characterized the first rise of evangelical fundamentalism, this battle pitted evangelicals directly against secular America.

The rise of fundamentalism in the early twentieth century occurred mainly within the context of a battle "among" Protestants. Although modernism, Darwinism, and scientific inquiry might have threatened man's eternal soul, conservative Protestantism did not seem to threaten modern man, at least not the rights and privileges that secular society felt were central to a Democratic, if not godly, society. However, the rise of fundamentalism that culminated in the late 1970s and early 1980s took on a distinctly different tenor. In increasing numbers Americans felt that evangelical Protestantism, conservative fundamentalism, or whatever one chose to call the zealous religious leaders that flooded the airwaves, was willing to enforce its religious morals at the expense of the constitutional protections guaranteed to all Americans. It was not enough that children should not read certain books, see certain movies, or be exposed to certain curricula, but fundamentalists believed those books, movies, and courses of study should be banned. Fundamentalism in the 1980s was no longer merely behind-the-scenes Bible classes and youth camps. It was a multibillion-dollar machine, equipped with sophisticated media and publication infrastructure that sent its message out to everyone in America, including those in political office. Not only was it vocal, it had become powerful: many Americans were afraid of fundamentalism, or at least its most obvious manifestations.

By 1981 the Moral Majority Inc. claimed established chapters in all fifty states. A study released in the *Dallas Times Herald* in 1981

{ *Clergy Malpractice in America* }

indicated that the Moral Majority's fund-raising efforts successfully doubled the organization's coffers from the previous year.
Jerry Falwell claimed to have 25 million viewers each week for his
Old Time Gospel Hour, a figure he boasted doubled during his
efforts in 1980 to influence Ronald Reagan's choice of a vice-
presidential running mate. Detractors claimed the figure for active
viewers was much smaller, more along the lines of 3 million. The
truth lies somewhere in between. But data from a 1981 nationwide
probability sample of Americans indicated that significant numbers, sometimes a majority of some state populations, identified
with the Religious Right's stance on such issues as abortion, homo-
sexuality, women's rights, and school prayer. In April 1980 the
Washington for Jesus rally drew approximately 200,000 people
from across the country. Protestant fundamentalism had a clear
political agenda and by the 1980s there were signs it was making
inroads into politics.

The Christian Voice, a fundamentalist political action group,
began in California in 1979 and within a year claimed 187,000
members, with clergymen making up 20 percent of its membership. By 1982 its membership had almost doubled to 328,000,
including 40,000 ministers. Using its California base of support
and Hollywood connections, the organization launched televison
campaigns featuring Ephrem Zimbalist Jr. and Buddy Ebsen
promoting prayer in the schools and other moral issues. On the
Christian Voice congressional advisory committee sat men like
James McClure of Idaho, Gordon Humphery of New Hampshire,
William Dannemeyer of California, and Orin Hatch of Utah. In
1979 the organization introduced an unsuccessful bill to proclaim
the United States a "Christian nation." In 1980 it issued the first
of its "moral report cards" on U.S. senators and representatives,
rating each on a list of issues such as school prayer, abortion, and
other planks of the fundamentalist right platform. That same year
the Voice established a "Christians for Reagan" branch with a $1
million budget for recruiting fundamentalist support for Reagan's
presidency.

To see the nature and extent of the conflict one need only look
at the antifundamentalism literature coming out in the late 1970s

and early 1980s. Titles like *Liberty and Justice: Defending a Free Society from the Radical Right's Holy War, Liberty and Justice for Some,* and *Holy Terror: The Fundamentalist War on America's Freedoms in Religion, Politics, and Our Private Lives* are but a few of the myriad books that attested to fears within secular America that fundamentalism posed a threat to values and freedoms guaranteed by the U.S. Constitution. A Harris poll in July 1981 reflected this backlash and showed that by a 2–1 majority, Americans opposed the efforts of Moral Majority preachers to force television networks and advertisers to remove "immoral" programming. A study of the Dallas–Ft. Worth Metroplex in 1981 by Anson Shupe and William A. Stacey showed signs of the same resistance to the Religious Right in a region and among people that should have been its most ardent supporters.

The DFW Metroplex in 1981 had 4 million people, making it as large or larger than either Mississippi or Louisiana. Situated at the north-central corner of Texas in the heart of the Bible Belt, the region served as the headquarters for the Southern Baptist Convention, James Robison's Evangelical Association, and the nation's second largest Southern Baptist congregation. The study found that among middle-class, home-owning voters, twice as many people opposed the Moral Majority as supported the organization. Even among clergymen, support of the moral majority was far from overwhelming. The study concluded that despite its efforts, fundamentalism did not go unopposed, and serious resistance existed to the ongoing attempt of the Religious Right to reshape America.

In some ways the opposition groups spawned by the Moral Majority/Religious Right provide the best evidence of its strength. People for the American Way, formed in 1980 by writer/producer Norman Lear, was a nonprofit, nonpartisan organization dedicated to fighting what it perceived as the Religious Right's encroachment on fundamental liberties such as free speech and free press. Among its board members were Public Library chairman Andrew Haiskell, former congresswoman Barbara Jordan, and former Warner Bros. board chairman Ted Ashley. The organization's national advisory counsel included Protestant, Catholic and Jewish ministers, the president of Notre Dame University, the U.S. representative to UNICEF, present and former national congressmen, and the heads of national business corporations.

Using its wide-based and prominent leadership, People for the American Way tried to educate Americans to the threat posed by politically active fundamentalist religious groups. Part of the educational process focused on identifying the many organizations that comprised the Religious Right. One publication identified thirty separate groups headquartered in all parts of the United States, including three organizations in addition to the Christian Voice that were based in southern California.

Despite a strong fundamentalist effort to influence national elections, success did not come immediately. Exit polls among New York and Indiana voters in November 1980 showed that there was still an effective resistance to the Religious Right's efforts to sway the election. The polls indicated that Democratic candidates marked for evangelical or conservative attack did as well or as poorly as nontarget candidates. However, even the pollsters conceded that the potential for influencing elections remained, in light of what they identified as sophisticated, well-financed technological support, and the "driving sentiments undergirding its [Religious Right's] efforts."

Jerry Falwell, Pat Robertson, and James Robison were among the more well-known "electronic ministers" and were unaffected by the data that reflected a grass-roots resistance to their movement. Men like Paul Weyrich led the zealous "preachers into politics" movement, stating that "This is really the most significant battle of the age-old conflict between good and evil, between the forces of God and forces against God, that we have seen in this country . . . and as such we feel not just a political commitment to change this institution, but a moral, and if you will a religious commitment to battle these forces." This was not the internal struggle within Protestantism that characterized the early twentieth century, this was a contest between secular and evangelical America, a battle waged on all fronts.

The fundamentalists' intensity did not escape mainstream America or its political leaders. Senator Robert Packwood put the fears of many Americans into context in a 1981 article in the *Port-land Oregonian:* "God does not speak to any of us and say, 'You are right and those who disagree with you are wrong.' If any of us thinks God has ordained us to speak for Him, we are wrong. Worse, if we are in positions of power and believe we speak for God, we become dangerous."

The 1980 pollsters' admonitions concerning the Religious Right's capacity to influence the political process came to fruition as the 1980s ended. One of the most revealing indicators of the shift in fundamentalist religion's goals and approach to the political process lay in its willingness to adapt and the success that came from its sustained effort. After almost eight years of trying to influence American politics on a national level, Pat Robertson's Christian Coalition shifted its focus toward state and local contests. In 1988, Christian-backed candidates in California won three of five important congressional contests, six of twelve of its targeted state assembly races, and a significant number of city council and school board elections. Nationally, candidates backed by the Religious Right won 40 percent of the 500 races monitored by People for the American Way.

In Grace Church Ed Barker had a defendant that possessed all of the physical manifestations of a Radical Right religion: physical size, large membership, widespread ministry, a well-known leader, and an unbending belief in its own message that characterized American fundamentalism. These fears only mounted as prominent fundamentalist leaders like Jerry Falwell openly professed the Moral Majority's goal to recover control of a godless country: "The role of government," Falwell believed, was "to minister justice and to protect the rights of its citizens by being a terror to evil-doers within and without the nation." He often said that "The idea that religion and politics don't mix was invented by the devil to keep Christians from running their own country." Not every American included him or herself within the term "their." At least not the same "their" that included Reverend Falwell.

The fear was that religion would go too far and this fear made many Americans highly suspicious of evangelicals like John MacArthur. Barker was counting on this fear and the notion that fundamentalism did not know when to stop. As one Methodist minister said:

> Recently I watched a movie on television in which one brother killed another, married his wife, then the son of the murdered man killed the wrong person thinking it was his uncle; the daughter of the wrong person went mad and his son decided on vengeance after she had committed suicide, and the movie ended with both young men, the mother, and the uncle all dead. But Sir Laurence Olivier played Hamlet so well, I would hesitate to come out against it.

Organizations similar to People for the American Way began to spring up carrying the message that "The attacks on liberty waged by the Radical Right will continue unabated unless citizens mobilize to defend our heritage of freedom." Ed Barker had to take this fight out of the schools, off the floors of state houses, and into the courthouse. But it would be getting into the courthouse and being allowed to stay that would prove the most difficult. In the America of the 1980s the Nallys' case had a chance, but only if it could reach a jury. Standing in the way was the First Amendment and 200 years of history.

———

There is perhaps no more sacred document in American jurisprudence than the Bill of Rights. Topping the list of rights and protections is the First Amendment. It guarantees freedom of speech, petition, assembly, and press. It also contains the free exercise of religion clause and the establishment clause. In fact, the first freedom protected is religion. "Congress shall make no law respecting the establishment of religion, or prohibiting the free exercise of religion." Although religion is the first right addressed, the First Amendment does not rank those rights it seeks to safeguard. However, from the inception of the Bill of Rights, no First Amendment right had gone longer without any serious challenge to the absolute nature of what it protected than that afforded religion.

There are two religious protections in the First Amendment. The first is the establishment clause. In 1791 it prevented the new federal government from granting any denomination the political and governmental privileges enjoyed by the Anglican church in England. However, for most of its history America has operated under what historian Mark De Wolfe Howe termed "de facto Protestant establishment." American culture just had a Protestant "flavor." Public schools routinely used the Bible in lessons and teachers led prayers among students where no one questioned the propriety of God in the classroom. Christmas, Easter, and Thanksgiving were national holidays. Legislatures opened their sessions with prayers, legislators frequently invoked the almighty, and then both set about the work of condemning blasphemy and atheism and enforced the Sabbath with a variety of laws, including blue laws prohibiting the sale of certain goods on Sunday.

During the period from the Second Great Awakening until the end of World War II the U.S. Supreme Court decided only two establishment cases. In short, establishment was not an issue because the established religion in America was Protestant. For the most part, the concept of church and state as a source of dispute simply did not exist in America prior to the end of World War II. Thomas Jefferson's belief that the establishment clause had erected "a wall of separation" between church and state may well have held meaning for the people of his age, but it did not come to the forefront of constitutional debate until the 1940s.

In 1947 the U.S. Supreme Court decided *Everson v. Board of Education*. In ruling that a city could provide busing for parochial school children as well as public school children without violating the Constitution, the Court analyzed the historical purpose behind the establishment clause. Fear of a state-supported religious institution that would threaten religious dissent and diversity in America lay at the heart of the clause. The Court in *Everson* concluded by stating that the establishment clause required an absolute neutrality by the government both as between different religions and between religion and nonreligion. Finishing in a flurry, the majority in the 5–4 decision quoted Jefferson's phrase in his letter to the Danbury Baptists that the establishment clause had erected a wall of separation between church and state.

Everson signaled the end of Protestant de facto–establishment in America. The Court had made it clear that the establishment clause applied to the states and their political subdivisions under the Fourteenth Amendment. It was fine that government had to remain neutral among religions, among Protestant sects, and among believers and nonbelievers, but what concerned Protestantism was the notion that government neutrality signaled a belief that America was no longer founded on the premise that religion was essential to a civilized nation.

For over two decades following *Everson* the U.S. Supreme Court decided establishment clause cases by applying a two-prong test: Was the state action or conduct secular in nature? Did it have the primary impact of inhibiting or advancing religion? If either prong failed, the state action would not pass constitutional muster. In 1971 the Warren Berger Court in *Lemon v. Kurtzman* refined the *Everson* test by adding a third element. Whether a state could constitutionally intrude into the area of religion now rested on a revised application of the rule in *Everson*. The *Lemon* test required three things for governmental regulation to escape invalidation under the establishment clause: Does the governmental action have a secular purpose that neither endorses nor disapproves of religion? Does it have an effect that neither advances nor inhibits religion? Does it avoid creating a relationship between religion and government that entangles either in the internal affairs of the other?

The case law on establishment since *Lemon* is a web of jurisprudence that seems to clearly strike down governmental intervention in areas of financial aid to non–higher education. Non–financial aid cases ranged from prayer to nativity scenes to religious instruction. The test was whether the activity or law served to endorse one denomination or religion over another. What is important for this story is that when Ed Barker filed *Nally v. Grace Community Church of the Valley, et al.* in March 1980, the *Lemon* test was fully entrenched, and it threatened any governmental activity, including activity on the part of the judiciary, that would excessively entangle the government in the business of religion.

The second First Amendment guarantee is freedom of religion. If litigation was scarce for establishment prior to World War II, cases on free exercise were almost nonexistent. Only the Mormon polygamy cases, *Reynolds v. United States* (1878), appear as an isolated blip on an otherwise blank screen. However, *Reynolds* introduced a standard that would have far-reaching ramifications and would go to the heart of Ed Barker's argument in the Nally case 100 years later.

The court in *Reynolds* refused to exempt Mormon polygamy practices from the purview of state laws, forbidding such practices despite the argument that polygamy was part of the Mormon religious belief. The Court introduced the belief-action doctrine, holding that although belief was protected, federal statutes could punish criminal conduct irrespective of religious beliefs. The First Amendment did not shield religious practices that adversely affected the public interest. Belief-action endured as a viable legal doctrine for almost eighty years only because it took that long before a free exercise case again reached the U.S. Supreme Court.

In 1940 the Supreme Court in *Cantwell v. Connecticut* overturned the holding of *Barron v. Baltimore* (1833), handed down over 100 years before, and made the Bill of Rights binding upon the states for purposes of the free exercise clause. In striking down a conviction against a Jehovah's Witness for preaching and handing out pamphlets door to door based on First Amendment speech grounds, the 9–0 opinion by Justice Roberts actually relied on a religious freedom argument. Although the state could regulate speech and solicitation, the First Amendment allowed not only a "freedom to believe but a freedom to act." But religious action has limits. Within the body of the opinion is the oft-quoted phrase that whereas religious belief is absolutely protected, action is not. That distinction would go to the crux of the debate in *Nally*.

In 1943 the Supreme Court overturned its own ruling in *Minersville School District v. Gobitis* (1940), in holding that a law compelling Jehovah's Witnesses to pledge allegiance to the flag was unconstitutional. The decision in *West Virginia State Board of Education v. Barnette* held that the right to not pledge allegiance was not only an aspect of religious freedom, but was protected under the broader guarantee of freedom of speech. Although subsequent decisions would see the Court carve out specific exemptions based on free exercise of religion, it is significant that certain conduct enjoyed protection both as a form of religious belief and as free speech.

Little activity followed until the 1960s. With *Sherbert v. Verner* in 1963 and *Wisconsin v. Yoder* in 1972, both the belief-action test of *Reynolds* and the notion that a state could trample on a religious belief or action without a compelling state interest disappeared. *Sherbert* involved an unemployment benefits claim by a Seventh-Day Adventist who refused to work Saturdays, her day of Sabbath, and was dismissed. In sustaining the woman's claim to benefits the Earl Warren Court held that the government could not burden a fundamental right like free exercise of religion without showing it was protecting a compelling state interest by the least intrusive means possible. For the next ten years the Court reaffirmed *Sherbert* in numerous holdings.

In 1972, the Burger Court in *Wisconsin v. Yoder* confronted the issue of education within the context of religious freedom. The Amish sought an exemption from a Wisconsin law requiring Amish children to attend public school. They argued that sending their children to public schools beyond the eighth grade violated their religious beliefs. The state denied the exemption and on appeal the U.S. Supreme Court held that in order to *deny* an exemption based on religious freedom, the state had to demonstrate a compelling state interest.

This, then, was the legal wall that surrounded the citadel of religious freedom as Ed Barker prepared to file Walter and Maria Nally's lawsuit against Grace Church. Not only would these First Amendment guarantees serve to shield the church and its ministers as a defendant, but there was a real possibility that the First Amendment could prevent the suit from ever reaching a jury. The establishment clause stood poised to repel any assault on the church that would require the courts to become excessively entangled in religious affairs. On its face, *Nally* raised such a possibility. At its core, the Nallys' suit questioned the standards the church and its ministers adhered to in counseling mentally troubled patients. At some point a judge was going to have to determine what standards should apply to church counselors. Assuming one could fashion such a standard, there was still the issue of burdening religious freedom, the inner wall of protection. Whether one agreed with Grace's total devotion to the Bible as the source of all spiritual and mental guidance, it was "their belief," and belief enjoyed the protection of the *Sherbert-Yoder* rule.

Establishment and religious freedom, two imposing obstacles, were reinforced by yet another of the Supreme Court's World War II decisions, *U.S. v. Ballard* (1944). Walter Nally believed, and still believes, Grace is a cult, not a religion. *Ballard* made that a non-issue by precluding judicial inquiry into the sincerity and reasonableness of one's religious beliefs. Unless someone was ready to make new law, no one would be allowed to question the "reasonableness" of Grace's doctrine or to scrutinize the sincerity of John MacArthur's beliefs or those of his codefendants, Duane Rea, Lynn Cory, and Richard Thomson.

From the beginning, in almost tacit recognition of the constitutional obstacles he faced, Ed Barker maintained one concept that became the thread that wove its way throughout his entire argument and across the eight-year life of the case: "This is not about religion, or religious beliefs, it is about the minimum standard of conduct that anyone who purports to counsel mentally ill people should have to adhere to." In other words, this was action, not belief, and even under the Supreme Court's ruling in *Cantwell*, action was not absolutely protected.

On March 31, 1980, Ed Barker filed *Nally v. Grace Community Church of the Valley, John MacArthur, Richard Thomson, Duane Rea and Lynn Cory*. The suit set out the facts leading up to Ken Nally's suicide and then pled three legal grounds in support of a wrongful death claim: clergy malpractice; negligence; and outrageous conduct. The clergy malpractice and negligence counts asserted that Grace Church was negligent in failing to properly recruit, hire, and train the spiritual counselors that administered to Kenneth. The individual defendants failed to make themselves available to Kenneth for counseling, and the four pastors "actively and affirmatively dissuaded and discouraged [Nally] from seeking further professional psychological and/or psychiatric care." The third count incorporated the negligence allegations and charged defendants with outrageous conduct for teaching certain Protestant religious doctrines that conflicted with Nally's Catholic upbringing and that "otherwise exacerbated" Nally's preexisting feelings of guilt, anxiety, and depression.

Ed Barker reached back to the final days of Kenneth's life and alleged that one of the individual defendants had told Kenneth his temporarily paralyzed arm was God's punishment for his (Kenneth's) sin. Relying on Rich Thomson's statement made just eleven days before Ken finally ended his life, the Nallys alleged that the defendants' conduct was further outrageous because they taught Ken, whom they knew to be depressed and entertaining suicidal thoughts, and imbued him with the notion that if he had accepted Jesus Christ as his personal savior, he would still be accepted into heaven if he committed suicide.

In 1980 outrageous conduct represented a catch-all legal remedy for conduct that did not neatly fit within any other recognized theory of recovery. In California outrageous conduct was actually an element within a claim for intentional infliction of emotional distress. As a separate ground for recovery it required a showing that a defendant's actions recklessly disregarded the health, safety, and welfare of the plaintiff. The conduct must be so reckless that it rises to the level of an intentional effort to harm. Under this theory, the Nallys alleged that although there was no intent to kill Ken or to cause Ken to kill himself, Grace Church and its counselors were aware of Ken Nally's suicidal state of mind. To impress on him that suicide carried no spiritual penalties and was in fact one of God's ways of helping lost souls was so reckless as to rise to the level of intentional conduct designed to injure.

Walter Nally had always maintained his goal was to stop the killing at Grace Church, meaning to prevent any more suicides, yet his suit had no request for injunctive relief. According to Nally, Ed Barker never mentioned the possibility and an injunction was never discussed. Perhaps Barker realized that just suing the church was going to push the boundaries of state entanglement in religion to its outer limits. An injunction would actually require the court to define specific conduct that would be prohibited and then monitor the church to be sure that its injunction was honored. As the case was pled it already raised obvious establishment clause problems: an injunction would have made an already monumental task even more difficult.

By the time the suit was filed Barker knew he had a contender. What he feared was that he might not get to court. His fear was justified. It would not take long for Grace Church to step up to its own defense and an integral part of that defense was the imposing wall between church and state erected by the establishment clause and supported by the very broad and equally formidable protection afforded religious freedom. For Ed Barker it "wasn't about religion." But for Walter and Maria Nally to have their day in court they were going to have to make the California judiciary understand that this was not about religion. This task was made more difficult by the presence of the church's lawyers, two men who had never met one another but would now form quite a "team" in their own right: one a native Californian, battle-tested through years of defense work in the California courts, the other a man with a real and personal stake not only in the case, but in the church and its leader.

CHAPTER 4

Defining the Issues

It did not take long for news of *Nally* to become public. The day after Barker filed the complaint, newspapers throughout the San Fernando Valley carried the same message. "Minister Sued in Wrongful Death," "Church Sued for Malpractice," and "Parents' Suit Charges 'Malpractice' by Clergyman and Church in Suicide of Son" were but a few of the headlines that greeted readers on April 1, 1980. The articles summarized the facts and allegations of the petition and indicated neither the church nor its ministers had any comment. At least one article reminded readers that this was the same church that made headlines the year before with John MacArthur's statement that the Bible indicates the husband should be a family's sole breadwinner. Apparently MacArthur and Grace's forty-five-member, all male, board of elders had even contemplated firing a half-dozen female secretaries who worked at the church, but later decided not to. Within a week the church issued a short statement to the effect that "counseling at Grace was handled consistent with Biblical principles and the allegations of wrongdoing are false."

News of the suit quickly spread as newspapers, religious publications, and legal journals picked up the story. Reactions were mixed. The *Philadelphia Daily News* proclaimed, "Malpractice Fad Hits Clergy," but most news coverage resisted the temptation to comment, and took a wait-and-see attitude. Grace Church and its ministers, however, could no longer wait. They were faced with the legal requirement to file an answer to the complaint and that required finding an attorney. Finding a lawyer turned out to be the easiest part of the ordeal. Their trial lawyer would come courtesy of the church's liability insurance policy, which, much to Grace

Church's surprise, provided coverage for this type of suit. For its other lawyer Grace and its ministers had to look no further than its own congregation.

Preferred Risk Mutual Insurance Company wrote the general liability policy that covered Grace and its ministers. For the previous thirty-two years Preferred Risk had been the client of the small firm of Cooksey, Coleman and Howard in Tustin, California. The case showed up on David Cooksey's docket like any other insurance defense case that his firm had been retained to handle. Cooksey was in his thirties with a quiet but engaging personality when the *Nally* case came across his desk. The son of a lawyer, Cooksey was born in Des Moines, Iowa, raised in Colorado Springs, Colorado, and moved to Irvine, California, as a teenager. He finished high school in southern California, attended UC–Irvine, and graduated in its first class in 1969. After college he went on to Hastings Law School in San Francisco. Upon finishing in 1972 he passed the California Bar Exam and went to work in his father's firm. David knew nothing of the Nally suicide until the case came to him shortly after the church and its ministers were served.

Grace's other counsel, Sam Ericsson, came to Cooksey by way of a referral from the church itself. Ericsson had been a partner in the downtown L.A. law firm of Overton, Lyman and Prince. In 1976 he had taken a leave of absence to work at Grace full time and when the suit was filed Ericsson was on staff at Grace. Ericsson was perhaps the most prestigiously educated of all the attorneys, having graduated from Harvard Law School. His duties included attending to routine legal matters, doing work for Christian Legal Aid, and serving as an active member of the church community, including counseling some of its members. Ericsson's counseling was more informal, but it did bring him into contact with Ken Nally in the years prior to his death. In fact, it was Sam Ericsson who, at least in part, convinced Ken to pursue a legal career. Cooksey would later characterize his collaboration with Ericsson as a "perfect fit." "I did the trial work, Sam did the scholarly research."

Equally important to Cooksey, Ericsson's role as director of the Christian Legal Society would bring a vast array of monetary, legal, and political support. Ericsson also brought a devout, almost fanatical, personal belief in the case. He was not just a lawyer, he was a Christian lawyer and a devoted follower of John MacArthur. To an objective observer he may have been too personally connected to the case to act effectively as an attorney. However, his Christian beliefs allowed him to see the potential danger of the *Nally* case for all religion, and his personal connection to Grace for whatever detriment it caused also brought with it benefits.

Ericsson had foreseen problems from the outset. He began taking witness statements almost immediately after Ken committed suicide. He sent a blank cassette tape with a list of written questions to everyone he could think of who knew Ken at Grace. Each responding witness signed a form retaining Ericsson as his or her lawyer to avoid confidentiality problems. Ericsson believed that within two to three weeks following the suicide, he knew "the story." He was so sure he knew the facts and that a reasonable person would understand Grace and its pastors were blameless that he went to see Ed Barker right after the suit was filed.

For over two hours he laid the story out to the Nallys' lawyer. Barker admitted that some of what Ericsson told him he had not known. But then Barker asked one question: "Are any of your counselors licensed professionals?" Ericsson said, "No." That was probably the closest to a settlement discussion that was or would ever be held in the case. Ericsson had tried to stop the case before it really got started and failed. Now there was nothing to do but go to work.

If the church and its ministers were not talking, Ericsson had no such reservations. In the first months after the suit was filed he had been deluged by calls from concerned clergyman and from the start articulated his theory of the case. Contrary to Barker's insistence that this was not about religion, Ericsson maintained it had everything to do with religion. Because it was about religion, the First Amendment precluded the suit from going forward. "For 2,000 years—even longer—pastors, rabbis and priests have been meeting with people who have problems of a number of different natures. When you start talking about counseling by the church, spiritual issues are inextricably entwined and for the court to become entangled in spiritual issues is improper." Ericsson believed that asking the courts to "second guess" the counsel of pastors, priests, and ministers was a violation of the First Amendment.

Although Ericsson continued to do the talking for his client, within the month Grace Church felt compelled to issue a stronger statement than its initial disclaimer to the members of its congregation. In a carefully worded, two-page letter addressed to "Members and Friends of Grace Community Church," Thomas Lovejoy, chairman of the Grace Board of Elders, articulated the church's position. "The lawsuit hangs like an ominous cloud on pastors who seek to shepherd their flocks," wrote Lovejoy. Grace had an obligation to reassure other churches and to refute the plaintiffs' accusations. The letter then addressed the allegations within the complaint that the church had dissuaded Ken from seeing professionals, that the ministers failed to make themselves available, and that John MacArthur had exerted control and influence over Ken. Lovejoy denied each allegation and told the congregation that Grace had neither prevented Ken from seeing professionals nor ever turned its back on him. He ended by assuring the congregation that the Grace elders were "proceeding with efforts to dismiss this unconstitutional and meritless attack on the Church and will take appropriate action to guaranty that churches, pastors and other spiritual counselors in the United States need not fear litigation of this kind." That is what the suit was really about. From the beginning, people in religious circles everywhere understood that this case was about more than Grace Church.

It would not take long for the issue to reach the court. David Cooksey filed a demurrer, a procedural pleading that argued that the church and its ministers should not even have to file an answer because the suit, as a matter of law, violated the First Amendment. The decision as to whether the Nallys could even pursue such a suit would fall upon Superior Court judge Thomas Murphy. Murphy, himself an Irish Catholic, was in the latter part of his judicial career. He had a reputation as an outgoing judge, saying hello to everyone as he made his way down the hall, and never hesitating to stop and ask someone wandering by, "Can I help you?" He wasted little time in making what would be the first of several decisions on the *Nally* case.

On June 13, 1980, Murphy dismissed the defendants' demurrer and ordered the case to proceed. Stating that he did not feel the church had an "absolute privilege" in the case, Murphy ruled that the case was not constitutionally barred. "As I view the complaint, they're alleging tort liability—period. California Superior Courts can listen to any grievance then take the wheat from the chaff, issues raised in the case should be determined by a jury." However, Murphy warned that the plaintiffs still had to show a duty of care at trial that would make the church liable to them for Ken's suicide. The judge gave the defendants thirty days to file an answer. No trial date was set, but Walter and Maria Nally's case was still alive.

Neither side had been able to show Murphy legal precedent for a clergy counseling situation, and with no prior example to fall back on, Murphy let the case proceed. The reactions were predictable. Cooksey and Ericsson were disappointed. Ericsson had filed a lengthy, 105-page brief with the court and he did not attempt to hide his feelings. Conceding that fact issues existed, Ericsson could not restrain his personal beliefs and insisted "the issues were so entangled [with religion] that the courts should stay out. We are playing games when we try to say mental health and moral health are different." Ericsson's view on moral and mental health issues as indistinguishable was not the legal view of the time, and it certainly would not have qualified as expert testimony in a mental competency hearing. But judicial decisions encompass more than just black-letter law. An attorney's moral views can find their way into judicial opinions when those views mirror those of the judge or for some reason strike a sensitive area with the court.

If Cooksey was disappointed, he did not express it, at least not publicly. This was just the start. He accepted a demurrer for what it was, a first shot that in extreme situations might take a case out, but not likely. He would go on with the business of preparation.

Barker was pleased. He had slid by the first impediment. He was still in court and he continued to harp on his theory, a theory that Murphy seemed to grasp. "We have an action alleging wrongful death, which is based on traditional concepts of duty and foreseeability of harm. We are not suing John MacArthur because of his religious beliefs. They had some special responsibility to handle him [Ken Nally] and I believe they handled him wrong, with the result that he ended up killing himself."

The written answers for the church and the four individual pastors were essentially the same. First came a general denial, "defendants deny each and every, all and singular, the allegations in plaintiff's Original Complaint and demand strict proof thereof." Then the defendants listed eight affirmative defenses. These are claims made by the defendants that must be raised so as to allow the plaintiffs to understand why the defense claims it is not liable. By law, a defendant can only present evidence in support of such defenses if he or she has specifically pled them.

The first claim would be the basis of most of the defense's pretrial efforts: The plaintiffs had failed to state a cause of action and the facts set out in the complaint do not entitle them to legal relief. The next three were First Amendment defenses. They claimed the suit violated religious liberty, the establishment clause, and the free exercise of religion clause. The defendants then alleged that Ken Nally and his parents had contributed to Ken's death by not exercising ordinary care on his and their own behalf. The last three were an allegation that the plaintiffs had waited too long to sue, which proved groundless, and two allegations that the suit violated the First Amendment guarantee of free speech. Both sides had staked out their ground. Now came the hard part, proving their respective cases. Each side would need to establish the facts of the case, and the parties wasted no time.

———

Then began the discovery portion of the case. Cases are often won and lost at this stage even though the general public has little understanding of what happens and rarely sees it develop. Litigation in 1980s America was not the "trial by ambush" that Americans were so fond of watching on television, in which any of a number of prime-time legal heros pulled the surprise rabbit out of his briefcase. In reality, by the time most cases reached trial there were no real surprises, just a genuine debate as to what the facts meant. To say that surprise does not occur ever would be wrong. To say it seldom happens would be accurate.

Discovery at its simplest and least expensive form involves questions one side requires the other side to answer, or wishes the other side to admit that certain facts are uncontraverted. The most beneficial form of discovery is the oral deposition. It allows the attorneys and the parties to see each other in a setting that most closely resembles trial. Not only does one glean facts as attorneys ask questions of parties and witnesses, but there is ample opportunity to learn something about one another. One's demeanor becomes impossible to hide as attorneys, witnesses, and parties interact. Facial expressions, body language, and nervous reactions to questions and stress of both the parties and the attorneys are on display. Between the plaintiffs and defendants there would be over twenty-five depositions taken in the case. Walter Nally went to all but two depositions. He remembers his own deposition being long, a fact David Cooksey would attest to. "The longest deposition I had ever taken," Cooksey would recall later. "It went from 10:00 A.M. to 9:00 P.M. without a break." There was just so much to tell, so much family history, so much turmoil within the family that Cooksey believed was totally unconnected to Grace Community Church. He left Nally's deposition feeling there was so much conflict between father and son, but to this day is not sure just how much of a role it played in the lawsuit itself.

Sam Ericsson knew all of the individual defendants. They were his friends and the pastors of his church. However, Cooksey did not meet any of them until after the response was filed in the case and his clients had to appear for their respective depositions. The church and its ministers were outraged at having been sued, but their anger remained controlled, both during discovery and throughout the trial of the case. Client control was never a problem at any stage of the case. Cooksey remembered MacArthur never really getting too excited, as if this was just a test and it would have to run its course, however long it took.

In nine months both sides pulled what facts there were out into the open. Cooksey remembered a few fireworks in deposition, but for the most part the process was rather businesslike. However, during John MacArthur's deposition the lawyers, either inadvertently or perhaps intentionally, left MacArthur alone in the conference room with Walter and Maria Nally. After a moment of uncomfortable silence, MacArthur spoke, perhaps in an attempt to resolve what had already gone further than he could have imagined. "What we have here is a misunderstanding," John said. "Johnnie, there may be a misunderstanding, but it is on your side," replied Walter Nally. That was enough for MacArthur: he got up and walked out of the room. That would be the last time either man would speak to the other.

The case was clearly personal, if not between the lawyers, then definitely between the clients. In a profession of give-and-take negotiation, where settled cases outnumber trials by nine to one, there was never really an offer to settle in *Nally* other than the formal offer made by the plaintiffs as required by the California Rules of Civil Procedure. The Nallys offered to settle for $1,000,000, an offer the church and its pastors completely disregarded. Cooksey never made an offer on behalf of the church. From the outset the church and its pastors understood the long-term ramifications of the case. Walter Nally had opened the door to widespread liability for clergymen everywhere, irrespective of their religion or particular denomination. The church felt it had to slam the door. A settlement would only give hope to others considering following Walter and Maria's example.

After deposing the fact witnesses, Barker had three or four experts and Cooksey deposed them all. Years after the suit was over Cooksey would recall not knowing how Barker financed the litigation. Plaintiffs' work can be expensive and experts seldom work for free. What Cooksey did not know then was that Walter Nally financed the lawsuit. Barker agreed to work on a contingency fee arrangement, but Walter paid all costs as they were incurred. Walter Nally spent in excess of $100,000 over the eight-year life of the case. In addition, he acted as a law clerk, gofer and general assistant.

One of the tasks Nally undertook came out of one of Barker's more novel and, as it turned out, ingenious ideas. Unlike auto accidents or medical or legal malpractice, clergy malpractice cases did not enjoy an established battery of expert witnesses waiting to testify. If Barker wanted experts he was going to have to find them on his own. His solution was to cast his net as wide as possible and see what he found. He did it by having Walter Nally go to the library and pull the names and addresses of every licensed psychiatrist and psychologist in California. Then Barker prepared a flyer describing the litigation, asking for expert assistance, and attached to it a copy of an article written about the case in *Los Angeles Magazine*. The entire packet was mass mailed to all the professionals Nally had located. Juan Barker, Ed's wife, was a new associate at the time the case was tried. She recalled that a lot of people did not respond to the flyer and some responded, but were too "fringe" to use. However, from the entire mailing the plaintiffs found four or five good experts. Good is probably an understatement, considering the unknown character of expert testimony for such a case. Not only did Barker get psychiatric and psychological experts, but two were either present or past members of the Protestant clergy.

Expert testimony would be crucial to establish what Judge Murphy considered to be the plaintiffs' real burden: a standard by which to measure the conduct of the defendant church and its pastors. Without a standard of care it would be impossible to create a duty owed by the church to the Nallys. Without a duty, there could be no liability. Ken's death would be "injury without fault." Applying a standard of care to clergy or pastoral counseling would not only pose constitutional problems, but practical problems as well.

Grace's counselors were not professionals. As Duane Rea had admitted to Walter Nally, they held no degrees, professed no particular expertise in psychiatry or psychology, and for the most part rejected any notion that they needed any kind of professional accreditation to do God's work. However, Grace Church was not alone. In medical and mental health jargon Grace's pastors were "indigenous, para-professional, mental health counselors." Translation: They were part of a vast and growing army of people without professional training that counseled others at the community level. Outrageous? Perhaps, but the average American did not think twice about the qualifications of counselors at YMCA camps, schools, businesses, or other community institutions that offered some kind of counseling services as part of their total package. Even had most Americans bothered to consider the problem of nonprofessionals, in most instances their choice would have been a nonprofessional or nothing.

———

Paraprofessional counseling grew out of a trend that began in the latter part of the nineteenth century. Its genesis was an effort by concerned individuals to meet the needs of a part of society that was unserved by the resources of family and friends or by the woefully inadequate institutions that existed. The amateurs of the late 1890s and early 1900s did what they could and tried to convince their local communities to pitch in with money or other resources. The early paraprofessional was most obvious in the social work field and could be found in places like Hull House in Chicago and other settlement houses that sprung up during the Progressive Era. In the early years of nonprofessional mental health, the major criteria for filling the void left by professionals was personal knowledge of a community situation, familiarity with the lifestyle and culture of the people to be served, and sympathy and empathy for those one sought to help.

In the decade following World War II what was once a beleaguered group of amateurs developed into a career field of its own. By the end of the 1950s manpower studies predicted that America's future mental health needs would never be met by professionals alone. There were simply not going to be enough Ph.D.'s or M.D.'s to meet the increasing need. As the 1960s came into full swing the manpower shortage among mental health professionals became a reality.

The paraprofessional movement took its place among the many movements that dominated the tumultuous 1960s. Statistical studies showed that the demand for mental health counseling outstripped existing professional help by as much as seven to one. An article in a professional journal in 1973 flatly stated, "The plain and simple truth is that future delivery of more appropriate mental health services to the general population will be ultimately related to the mental health professional's ability to make maximum and judicious use of nonprofessional manpower in direct services roles." There was no longer a debate of "can we use" non-professionals, but only a question as to "how to use" them. Non-professionals were here to stay, and delivered "a significantly large portion" of the actual direct health services in America by the mid-1970s. In 1976, when Ken Nally first sought out Grace's counselors with his emotional problems, paraprofessionals were the single largest category of personnel providing direct services in the nation's 3,300 mental health facilities. With so much paraprofessional support in institutions devoted specifically to mental health, it is little wonder that non–mental health institutions such as churches that provided some type of counseling services met their staffing needs with nonprofessionals.

The debate became more complex as both professionals and laymen grappled with issues of competence. Were nonprofessionals more likely to do harm than good? Were they a godsend, capable of rectifying the manpower problem by adequately filling all the holes in the field of professional mental health counseling? Although there was no consensus, the answer to both questions seemed to be "no." Nonprofessionals did not appear to be per se more dangerous and they could provide substantive therapeutic guidance. Even professionals had to admit that paraprofessional counselors made meaningful contributions to the improved mental adjustment of their clients. Some, although not all, studies of paraprofessional counseling concluded that lengthy professional training was not necessary. People with the right traits of warmth, empathy, interpersonal sensitivity, and genuineness could be as effective as professionals in bringing about constructive improvement to a client's mental health and well-being.

On the other hand, most professionals conceded that paraprofessionals were far from a panacea to the manpower shortage, and as appealing as it might be to believe, not everyone could be an effective paraprofessional counselor. Some studies cautioned against allowing paraprofessionals to counsel people with sexual problems, marital strife, or pathological conditions. One area of particular concern was suicide prevention. However, despite professionals' fears, suicide prevention suffered from the same problem that plagued the mental health field in general: insufficient manpower. Paraprofessionals found themselves confronted with suicide risks as a routine part of their work experience.

The manpower shortage helps to understand the rise of the paraprofessional, but staffing concerns alone do not explain the presence of pastoral counselors like those at Grace, nor the appeal of a less "professional" approach to mental health care. The 1960s saw the emergence of the "third revolution," a movement characterized by an abandonment of traditional individual therapy and an embracement of a greater community-type approach in an effort to reach more of the general population. This effort to reach more people also brought with it the resurrection of "moral treatment," an approach made popular in the late nineteenth century. Moral treatment emphasized helping a person through emotional crisis by addressing his or her environment as a component of mental health. The modern version that reemerged in the 1960s stressed group therapy, local support systems, and a generous dose of self-help. Not only was this methodology well suited for the exploding field of paraprofessionals, but it was ideal for clergy and pastoral counselors who saw people on a community level and relied on self-help as a key component of problem resolution.

Paraprofessional counseling begged the question, "What standards of care should be applied?" The answer was that there were no clearly defined standards. The clergy and pastoral counselors also brought with them another set of problems. Not only were there no generally accepted mandatory standards, although the American Association of Pastoral Counselors purported to have some voluntary guidelines, but clergy counseling raised questions about the propriety of religion in any part of the counseling realm.

Most people did not see the debate raging, but within the many psychology and psychiatry journals that permeated the field, issues of religion and counseling played out. For religious leaders the notion that ministers counseled their congregations seemed natural and hardly posed a problem. However, for a medical field that had increasingly defined itself in a secular context, the interplay between religious issues and counseling posed significant problems. How does one cope with sin? Is the example of perfection set by Jesus Christ too high a standard for people to meet who are trying to work through difficult problems, problems they may never completely master?

Most secular psychiatrists and psychologists recognized that a person's religious beliefs could not be ignored. To deal with the whole person meant dealing with feelings of guilt and sin, emotions driven by religious beliefs. Although studies on the importance of religion in America tended to be contradictory, some psychiatric and psychology professionals perceived waning religious interest by the late 1970s. Regardless of the national trend, noted religious historian Martin Marty was quick to point out that religious roots remained important to a large segment of American society. Many mental health professionals agreed and cautioned against ignoring a person's religious beliefs in trying to counsel people in crisis situations. Faith in God, faith in humanity, and the positive aspects of support from religious communities were all resources that a good mental health counselor could and should tap into when trying to resolve people's emotional problems. Many stressed that Christianity's notion of forgiveness offered one of the most useful aids to a counselor. This concept could be extremely helpful in the context of suicide counseling because a particular quality of God's forgiveness was not only the ability to forgive others, but to forgive one's self.

Like most debates, the opposition was equally vocal and there were those who felt religion might hinder rather than help the counseling process. If a counselor or a client allowed their religious beliefs to become a part of the counseling process, these beliefs might impede the honest evaluation of a person's problems. Some secular professionals criticized denominational religion in general because of its hypocrisy and tendency toward narrow moral absolutes. Religion and some of its traits were deemed contradictory to the entire philosophy of counseling. The most glaring shortcomings were the desire to convert souls interfering with resolving the client's problems, conflicts caused by notions of sin, original and otherwise, problems raised by religious ideas of morality and virtue, the tendency of religion to control human behavior rather than accept it, and separating matters of faith and belief from the client's emotional problems.

By 1980, a small number of clergymen began to see the clergy/counselor as an inherent conflict of interest. One clinical psychologist, Richard L. Krebs, later entered the Protestant ministry and had very definite ideas on clergy counseling. Krebs argued that the clergy has a vested interest in winning souls and that proper counseling might require the clergy to subordinate that role to effectively work a client through a mental or emotional problem. Krebs believed that sometimes a counselor must be a faceless, anonymous individual, and a pastor simply could not be such a person. He argued that clergy counseling resulted in a "confusion of functions." The potential counseling client might have seen the clergyman in a variety of roles as teacher, worship leader, and role model, and yet expect the clergyman to subordinate those roles to that of counselor, with all the objectivity and confidentiality counseling requires. Krebs contended that most clergymen could not do this.

Despite these concerns, Ken Nally's search for help within his church was consistent with the conduct of many Americans. Studies in the late 1970s showed that in the United States people were most likely to seek help, at least initially, through their pastors or other religious leaders before trying another avenue. The discovery conducted in the case confirmed this, both as to Kenneth himself and the general trend in America. The clergy and pastoral counselors thus found themselves on the front lines of suicide and other chronic mental illness, a task many churches, including Grace, did not shy away from. Even professional counselors recognized that religious conviction might make suicide less likely. Religion itself involved complex issues, which made people with strong religious beliefs more intellectually and emotionally mature. Religion also required an element of integrity, since failing to meet God's standards required more effort, not the rejection of God or his standards.

Despite the benefits of religion in counseling, the most accepted approach was to integrate religious beliefs and secular methods. As one study argued, "The use of religious resources may be very effective in dealing with suicidal individuals. However, religious factors may be at least partially involved in the crisis itself. The accountable counselor in any situation is obligated to explore a variety of possibilities." Integrated mental health practitioners, whether professional or paraprofessional, rejected the notion that the Bible was a guide to everything: "To use a complex text, spanning two millennia as a source for all of life's problems was an evasion of responsibility." However, the fact that modern secular mental health professionals saw the Bible in that light did not mean that such a standard should apply to the clergy and pastoral counselors.

The crux of the Nallys' case lay in Grace Church's belief that the Bible was the answer to all of man's troubles. The depositions of Rea, Thomson, Cory, and MacArthur left no doubt where scripture stood within the church's theology. The depositions of Ed Barker's experts reinforced the point that although no readily identifiable standard existed, the clear consensus was that religion could be helpful, but only as a component of an integrated approach. Many counselors, even pastoral counselors, conceded that religion and religious principles could be and often were misused tragically in that a particular religious practice might prove to be dysfunctional to the total physical and emotional makeup of an individual. Inordinate amounts of guilt and the perceived abdication of personal responsibility were the most common manifestations of this misuse.

One of the major concerns that emerged in the secular-religion counseling debate would play a huge part in the Nally suit. Religion, particularly Judeo-Christianity, which taught life after death, contributed to a notion among believers that, in the words of an old gospel hymn, "This world is not my home, I'm just passing through." The concern was that taken to the extreme, such beliefs could become a form of escapism and actually serve to condone conduct that mental health counselors seek to prevent. Richard Thomson's deposition and his training tape were both in evidence. It would be impossible to de-emotionalize the reverberating statement: "Suicide was just another way God calls his errant flock home."

Walter and Maria Nally's lawsuit had become more than a simple conflict of church versus state: It threatened to alter not only the fundamental position of religion under the Constitution, but could conceivably undermine the ability and willingness of non-professionals to provide a service that most Americans could no longer get along without. The issue would come to a head in Judge Thomas Murphy's courtroom, and for Barker and the Nallys, it would take place much sooner than expected.

As soon as discovery was completed the constitutional assault on the *Nally* lawsuit resumed. On July 2, 1981, Cooksey and Ericsson filed a motion for summary judgment on behalf of the church and the four individual defendants, seeking to have the *Nally* suit again dismissed before it could reach trial. Unlike the demurrer that failed the year before, this motion now had the benefit of all the facts that had been extracted over the course of the year-long discovery process. The defendants contended that given these facts, the religious character of the defendants, and the mandates of the First Amendment, there was simply no issue to be decided by a court.

CHAPTER 5

The Long Road

On the morning of October 2, 1981, the parties and attorneys prepared for what would be the first of many days in court. As Walter Nally sat waiting for Judge Murphy to appear and announce his verdict, he reflected back over the eighteen months since he and Maria had filed their suit against Grace Church. During that time both sides had not only conducted extensive discovery, but the debate the suit raised about religion, counseling, and the First Amendment took center stage in the court of public opinion. Both sides had found a willing platform for their respective positions and as Judge Murphy prepared to render his decision, the lines were clearly drawn. The public debate did more than simply define the respective positions of the parties, it opened a door into an aspect of American religion and business that until *Nally* had operated in relative obscurity. It was a world driven more by fear than actual harm, but actual harm did exist. The fear alone had been sufficient to generate a multimillion-dollar industry by 1980.

Clergy malpractice might have appeared novel and remained a legal uncertainty, but there was more to it than most people realized, and without most Americans even knowing, clergy malpractice insurance had become a reality.

John Cleary worked as an attorney for Church Mutual Insurance Company of Merrill, Wisconsin. Church Mutual had insured churches for a variety of property-related risks since 1898. In the spring of 1979 it became the first carrier to offer clergyman who counseled parishioners professional liability insurance. Cleary offered this explanation of the growth and prevalence of clergy malpractice insurance in a society that was still not sure that the clergy should or could be sued. "Forty years ago, most people wouldn't have thought of suing their church, but I can tell you from experience that these lawsuits are now being brought quite regularly." Why had they not been made public? Why was *Nally* considered to be the first? Cleary pointed out examples of suits prior to the *Nally* case, and explained that most are thrown out of court and those that are not die at the hands of juries that refuse to award damages.

Elder DeWitt Hill, a pastor of the Greater Trinity Church of God in Little Rock, Arkansas, was sued in December 1978 by Charles Washington, a member of his congregation who alleged that Hill's preaching had caused Washington's wife to lose her affection for him. The case was tried and the jury found for Hill, but the pastor had spent $2,500 in legal fees defending himself. Hill was "shocked," he did not think Washington would carry the suit that far. Even more troubling to the pastor was Washington's assertion that it was Hill's interpretation of the Bible that made Washington's wife look upon him as a "sinful and ungodly creature."

Hill's case was the only instance Barker, Ericsson, and Cooksey could find where a suit against a clergyman had not been simply thrown out. Despite some speculation that the case never existed but had been invented in an effort to generate a market for clergy malpractice insurance, media coverage of the time indicates that Hill's ordeal was genuine. Had the parties looked a little harder they would have found an even older case, *Carrierri v. Bush*, a 1966 Washington State Court of Appeals case.

In *Carrierri* the court refused to allow a clergyman a qualified privilege for exercising his religious beliefs in a suit filed against him by a husband for alienation of his wife's affection. Married in 1953, the Carrierris had moved into a community where Arnold Bush had started a church. They began to attend and over time Mrs. Carrierri's attitude toward her husband changed to the point that she claimed to no longer love him and told him so. Evidence adduced at trial demonstrated that when Mr. Carrierri confronted Arnold with the dissension he was causing between husband and wife and told him to stop, Bush had replied, "No, you're full of the devil. I've got the gift of discernment, I know all your sins." Bush then told Mrs. Carrierri, in front of her husband and children,

"Don't listen to him, I've told you many times before, don't listen to your husband." The appeals court rejected any argument of privilege based on free exercise of religion and stated that where ill will, intimidation, threats, or reckless recommendation of family separation existed, the pastor could not hide behind the shield of the First Amendment.

The *Carrierri* case seemed to slip into the abyss of legal precedent and was never raised, nor apparently ever appealed to the Washington Supreme Court. However, Cleary knew of the case, as did other malpractice carriers. The fear of such a possibility and the reality of what DeWitt Hill had experienced prompted clergyman all over America to secure insurance protection. By 1980 Church Mutual wrote clergy malpractice coverage in twenty-seven states. Over 1,500 Lutheran congregations signed up for a nationwide malpractice policy. Atlantic Insurance Companies, Inc. of New York added clergy malpractice to its coverage in 1980. The Episcopal Church pension insured its eighty affiliated churches through the Church Insurance Co. of New York, its wholly-owned, nonprofit subsidiary. Preferred Risk Mutual covered the Presbyterian Church and the Church of the Nazarene in addition to Grace Community Church of the Valley. Chad Hensely of Preferred echoed the spirit of the times: "We seem to be becoming a more litigious society day by day. Everyone sues everyone, and the cost of defending malpractice lawsuits is astronomical. People buy malpractice lawsuits not because of judgments but because of defense costs."

Evidence of the cross-denominational impact of clergy malpractice surfaced when Rabbi Mordecai Simon, director of the Chicago Board of Rabbis, offered malpractice insurance to the 200 members of his group in a letter that stated:

In response to several inquiries and much discussion, the Chicago Board of Rabbis is offering a professional liability program exclusively for the CBR. Many factors were carefully considered before deciding to offer this program. However, the work and duties of today's rabbi place him in a sometimes vulnerable position. There is always the possibility that the rabbi may be held personally responsible for some alleged malpractice error or mistake arising out of the performance of his professional services, regardless of training and experience.

For many clergymen insurance represented an evil in itself. Some came to the idea only reluctantly. The chief concern lay in the possibility that although insurance offered protection, it might also serve as a lightning rod or beacon and encourage malpractice suits because potential plaintiffs saw the possibility to actually recover damages.

The debate over *Nally* did more than simply expose the existence of clergy malpractice insurance, it offered ministers and laymen alike the opportunity to expound on why the clergy had become legal targets. The answers revealed the growing division of opinion among the clergy itself.

Edmund Perry, a Methodist minister and chairman of the Department of History and Literature of Religions at Northwestern University, believed the fault lay with the clergy. "Ministers have become too promiscuous in playing counselor. Too many have usurped the responsibility that really should be left up to professional psychiatrists." Perry added that "It's one thing to be trained in counseling; it's another to take on the responsibility of therapy." Lynn Buzzard, a fellow Methodist and minister in Oak Park, Illinois, did not see it that way. "It would be a sad day," he said, "if a minister had to consider the possibility of a suit before he tried to help someone, or if a priest had to issue a disclaimer before giving a sermon." Historian Martin Marty carried Buzzard's suggestion a step further, advocating that clergymen sign over their assets to another party and distribute cards to prospective counselees saying, "I have no malpractice insurance and have no assets. If you would like my services on these terms, please sign."

Laymen had their opinions too. William Tippner of Jamesburg, New Jersey, wrote *Time* magazine asking, "Malpractice suits against ministers? Why not? It is the next logical step for an increasingly litigious society that has decided to by-pass old fashioned dialogue, communication and reasonable negotiation. But what has happened to the legal profession that accepts such cases, and the judicial system that hears such suits?" Paul Michener of Waynesville, Ohio, spoke from personal experience and offered a contrary opinion. "Why shouldn't clergymen be responsible for what they say?" Michener explained that he was the victim of a faith healer as a child and was prevented from receiving medical help when his left leg was severely burned. "Thirty years later I am still trying to repair the damage. If medical doctors are legally responsible for their deeds, why not the clergy?"

In the aftermath of his trial, DeWitt Hill offered an analysis of why he and others like him had become legal targets. "Ministers have become very involved—in politics, on golf courses, in activities they didn't used to be involved in, so people start looking at a minister as a person, not as one that deals with spiritual aspects of a person's life." If ministers were going to go beyond what ministers do, if they were going to become active in politics and take up the sword, so to speak, in an effort to change America, then perhaps people and the courts would be willing to forsake the shield offered by the First Amendment and place the clergy on the same grounds as everyone else.

Closer to the Nally's home, Rabbi Ben Zion Bergman published an article in the *San Fernando Valley Law Review*, "Is the Cloth Unraveling? A First Look at Clergy Malpractice." In words that must have encouraged Barker and the Nallys, Bergman got to the heart of the clergy malpractice issue. Counseling had been a traditional function of the clergy of all denominations. However, like other traditionally religious functions and rules, like Sunday closing laws, mental and spiritual counseling had become secularized. As soon as counseling became secularized the obvious question arose: Could the clergy counselor be held to the same standards that a secular counselor is held? Bergman, who was not only a rabbi but an adjunct professor at Loyola School of Law, answered emphatically, "yes." Bergman even went a step further and argued that far from having a chilling effect on the clergy-counselee relationship, standards and regulations would enhance clergy counseling by providing the parishioner with a sense of security in the clergyman's competence. Bergman concluded that "Both considerations of justice for the victim of

incompetence and the enhancement of the clergyman's effective-
ness would seem to militate in favor of clergy liability."

Walter Nally hoped Bergman was right. If not, he already knew
where things were headed. "If they [clergy] can get out [of liabil-
ity] on the grounds of religious freedom, then doctors won't need
malpractice insurance anymore. They can just send away for a $2
ordination certificate, hang it up on the wall and say, 'Oh, I wasn't
practicing medicine. I was just doing the work of the Lord.'" Sitting in Judge Murphy's courtroom on October 2, 1981, Walter was
about to get the first of many, and sometimes contradictory,
answers to his question.

———

When both parties finished oral arguments, Murphy asked, "Anything further? Does it stand submitted?" Both sides agreed the case
was submitted. Then Murphy ruled. He wasted no time. His decision was both unequivocal and brief and began with what must
have been his favorite quote from Harry Truman, "Gentlemen, let
me remind you that the buck stops here."

After conceding that everyone was entitled to his or her own
opinion he quickly gave his. In Murphy's opinion there was no triable issue of fact. The case was closed, end of story:

> You have furnished the court with reams of affidavits and reams
> of facts and positions. I have to sort them down. I have spent
> considerable time on it. I have listened patiently to you today.
> It is a tragedy, but there is a limit to what a court can or can't
> do. There is no one that I know of that can extend their hands,
> although I have heard some claims that hands can be extended
> and they at least heal the sick, but nobody, and I'm not being
> facetious, can raise the dead in this room. Ken is gone. There
> is nothing we can do to bring him back. The best the court can
> do and I have done it, is give those who have a grievance, under
> the law and fitting it within the facts, a chance to come forward
> and state that, period . . . I see and I find no triable issue of fact
> in this case at this particular time . . . This is a question of
> law . . . there is no need for equity here. You got justice. Grace

got justice. Mr. MacArthur got justice . . . Mr. Nally probably feels that justice was not reached. That's too bad, Mr. Nally. As I said to them, I'm not here to do their laundry. I'm certainly not here to do yours. I feel much aggrieved about the boy, but that's my ruling.

In a matter of minutes it was over. Ken was dead and the Nallys had no claim. For Ed Barker eighteen months' worth of work was down the drain. For David Cooksey, Sam Ericsson, and their clients, it was a year and a half well spent. Exoneration, or at least relief.

Again, the reactions were predictable. Sam Ericsson wasted no time in expressing his pleasure with the decision. Now a full-time attorney with the Christian Legal Society in Fairfax, Virginia, Ericsson claimed, "This ruling removes a veiled threat that was hanging over the clergy and churches and their right to counsel."

Sam had not reckoned on Walter Nally's commitment. As far as Nally was concerned his lawsuit was no mere threat and it was far from gone. He would appeal. Ed Barker made that clear within a week following the decision. "I believe Judge Murphy made a very incorrect decision," adding that Murphy's ruling came "much to our surprise."

The Nallys would appeal but an answer would not come soon. One of the realities of American jurisprudence is that resolution through the courts takes time, a lot of time. It took eighteen months to reach the summary judgment stage. Walter and Maria Nally did not know it when they filed their appeal, but it would be almost another three years before the California Court of Appeals would hear the case. In the meantime all they could do was wait.

Murphy's ruling would be difficult to live with not only because it was adverse, but because like many summary judgment rulings, there was little of the judge's thought processes to analyze. Murphy had looked at all the facts presented by the parties through affidavits, documents, and audiotapes. Reams of deposition testimony from fact witnesses and experts alike provided substance to what had been bare allegations eighteen months before. He had concluded that regardless of the evidence, Walter and Maria Nally had not alleged a claim that would allow a jury to find in their favor. With all of the evidence in twenty-five depositions, tapes, letters, and other proof, a jury could not possibly find for the Nallys? Not according to Judge Murphy. If there is no legal basis to recover, it does not matter how egregious the facts may seem.

In general, the law views summary judgment as a harsh remedy. To grant a summary judgment is to deprive the losing party of its day in court. To assure that summary judgments are granted only when they are absolutely appropriate, the law has erected a set of standards for granting such motions to dismiss a case. All evidence must be viewed in the light most favorable to the nonmoving party. In this case, all evidence that supported the allegations of negligence, clergy malpractice, and/or outrageous conduct had to be construed in the Nallys' favor. But what if the evidence isn't clear, or facts are in dispute? Any disputes or ambiguities are to be construed in favor of the nonmoving party. Once again, if there was doubt, the doubt was to be resolved in favor of the Nallys. The affidavits of the parties, John MacArthur, Lynn Cory, Duane Rea, and Rich Thomson, could serve as evidence, but only if what they testified to was clear of any inconsistency and could not be contraverted or refuted by other testimony. With all the evidence alleged by the Nallys against Grace and its ministers taken as true, a summary judgment could be granted only if there was no disputed issue of fact. Under the law as it stood at the time of the motion, the nonmoving party, in this case the Nallys, could not raise a legal cause of action. The Nallys did not have to show that they would win, they just had to show that there was enough of a dispute that a jury should determine whose story to believe. Murphy determined that the facts as presented by the plaintiff did not fit into any existing standard of care so as to give rise to a duty on the part of the church and its pastors.

How could this happen? Ken Nally was dead. He had committed suicide when he was under the care of Grace Church's ministers and counselors. Grace had told Ken that he should not seek outside medical help and even if that was disputed, for purposes of this motion it was assumed to be true. The church taught that suicide would not keep one out of heaven and that it was just another way that "God calls his errant flock home." Again, for purposes of the motion all these facts were deemed true. The church counselors had no professional training, and admitted as much. Expert testimony offered by the Nallys indicated the church's practices were inconsistent with both lay standards and religious standards. The evidence showed that Grace and its ministers not only knew that Kenneth had tried to commit suicide before his attempt in the Nally home, but had been told by Ken when he was recovering in the hospital that he "would try again." Despite knowing that he expressed an intent to try again the church pastors and counselors told no one.

In Murphy's analysis, even though Kenneth clearly died under circumstances where the church may have even been negligent, committed theoretical malpractice, and perhaps engaged in conduct that may have outraged the sensibilities of some people, there was no liability. Kenneth's death was injury without fault. To find the church and its ministers responsible for Ken's death under a tort theory there had to be a recognized standard to evaluate the conduct of clergymen engaged in pastoral counseling. Ed Barker had presented at least four experts that testified in deposition that they disagreed with Grace's methods and that those methods may well have caused Ken's death, but none of that testimony rose to the level of a clearly articulated, generally accepted standard to evaluate religious counselors. More important, Murphy seemed to believe that any effort to establish a uniform standard applicable to all religious counselors would not pass muster under the First Amendment guarantee of religious freedom. To impose such a standard would require the courts to judge a person's religious beliefs and Murphy simply did not believe that could be done consistent with the mandates of the U.S. Constitution.

Barker filed the necessary paperwork to appeal the ruling. There was nothing more to do but wait. Everyone returned to their lives. For the Nallys that meant not only coming to grips with Kenneth's death, but having to live with the idea that the people and institution they felt were responsible might never have to answer for their conduct. Walter Nally continued to work at Ed Barker's law office. It kept him busy and allowed him to keep his hand on the pulse of the case, even if little was occurring.

Lynn Cory, Rich Thomson, and Duane Rea went home to places far removed from Grace. Although Cory and his wife remained in southern California, Duane Rea now lived in Washington state, and Rich Thomson had moved on to Houston, Texas. John MacArthur returned to his calling at Grace Church. For the present he and the church could and did feel a sense of vindication and relief shared by other members of the clergy who followed the case. The lawyers also went their separate ways. David Cooksey slid back into the routine of his insurance defense practice, Ed Barker returned to life as a solo practitioner, and Sam Ericsson went home to Washington, D.C.

America seemed to fall back into a routine. The intense media coverage that characterized *Nally* since its filing now all but disappeared. Not even the legal community seemed interested in the questions that only months before had stimulated everyone. Prior to Murphy's ruling in October 1981, Sam Ericsson found the time to write an article for the *Valparaiso Law Review* that set forth the legal and constitutional arguments he had argued. Perhaps the most interesting aspect of the article came on the first page and should have provided fair warning for everyone that *Nally*, although subsumed in the appellate process, was far from over. Centered directly under Ericsson's name at the top of the page appeared William Prosser's statement that "torts is the battle-ground of social theory." In June 1984, Ericsson, Grace, and the rest of the United States would discover that Judge Murphy's ruling did not end the battle.

———

On June 28, 1984, the three-judge panel sitting on the California Court of Appeals handed down its decision in *Nally*. The vote was 2–1, not unanimous, but all the Nallys needed to get back in the race. Justice Vincent Dalsimer wrote the majority opinion, joined by Justice Gabriel Gutierrez. The majority concluded that the defendants failed to demonstrate the absence of any triable issue of fact, and that having failed to do so, the case should be remanded to Judge Murphy for trial. Dalsimer's opinion hung on one cause of action and one piece of evidence: the allegation that the church and its ministers engaged in outrageous conduct and the counseling tape of Rich Thomson whose words now came back to haunt Grace: "Suicide for the believer is the Lord saying, 'Okay, come on home. Can't use you anymore on Earth.'"

Dalsimer concluded that based on the evidence of Ken's condition in the months preceding his successful suicide attempt and Rich Thomson's counseling tape, that a reasonable inference could be drawn that Grace Community Church and each of the individual defendants either followed a policy of counseling suicidal persons that, if one was unable to overcome one's sins, suicide was acceptable and even a desirable alternative to living, or recklessly caused such persons extreme emotional distress through their counseling methods if those persons did not measure up to the pastor's religious beliefs.

The majority opinion tied the factual basis of its conclusion to California law. First, Dalsimer reminded the parties that all doubts as to the propriety of awarding a summary judgment against a nonmovant are resolved in favor of the nonmovant and can only be granted where there is no triable issue of fact under any legal theory pled in the complaint. Next, Dalsimer reasoned that in California a wrongful death suit like the Nallys' could be sustained on the theory of intentional infliction of emotional distress as a substantial factor in bringing about the suicide of the decedent. Dalsimer cited *Tate v. Canonica*, a 1960 California Supreme Court case, in which the court had concluded that if a defendant intended to cause serious emotional distress, even if the person who committed suicide knew what he was doing when he killed himself, it would not relieve the defendant of liability. The court in *Tate* had not dealt with reckless disregard, only intentional conduct, and had in fact held that where the defendant had not intended to cause injury, no cause of action would exist. Dalsimer pointed out that the court in *Tate* did not have the issue of reckless disregard before it, and therefore had not addressed the possibility of sustaining a wrongful death suit on the outrageous conduct of the defendant.

Drawing on the 1979 California Supreme Court case of *Agarwal v. Johnson*, Dalsimer set out the elements of a cause of action for intentional infliction of emotional distress as established in *Agarwal*: outrageous conduct by the defendant; intention to cause or *reckless disregard of the probability of causing emotional distress* [the court added the emphasis]; severe emotional suffering; and actual and proximate causation of the emotional distress. Dalsimer then tied *Tate* and *Agarwal* together and stated that the Nallys did plead an adequate cause of action for wrongful death arising out of intentional infliction of emotional distress by the allegations that the defendants, as agents of the church, knew that Ken was depressive and had suicidal tendencies, exacerbated his feelings of guilt, anxiety, and depression with reckless disregard that their conduct would increase the likelihood that Ken would commit suicide.

Dalsimer held that MacArthur, Cory, Rea, Thomson, and Grace Church had failed to establish the absence of a triable issue of fact on the outrageous conduct theory. He pointed out that the California legislature viewed the encouragement of suicide as dangerous and had provided a law that stated, "Every person who deliberately aids, or advises, or encourages another to commit suicide, is guilty of a felony." Dalsimer conceded that no such allegation was contained in the *Nally* suit, but he implied that the conduct alleged by Walter and Maria Nally had been deemed to be socially unacceptable, and as such could be construed as outrageous and reckless.

Having established a legally triable issue of fact, Dalsimer then pierced the apparent protection afforded to Grace's counseling as being the expression of a religious belief. Dalsimer couched the question in terms of whether clergymen and churches should be immune from liability for intentional infliction of emotional distress caused by their counseling simply because the counseling had a spiritual aspect. Citing *Cantwell v. Connecticut*, the same 1940 U.S. Supreme Court case that applied the freedom of religion clause to the states under the Fourteenth Amendment, Dalsimer unequivocally said "no." The First Amendment embraces two concepts, "freedom to believe and freedom to act." The first is absolute, but in the nature of things, the second cannot be. Counseling, Dalsimer concluded, fell within the latter category.

Dalsimer then drew upon two cases that did not deal with the tort of intentional infliction of emotional distress, but did address the larger issue of suing clergymen. *In re Edward C*, a 1981 California case, sanctioned the removal of children from the custody and control of parents whose religiously motivated discipline had detrimental physical and emotional effects on the children. The parents had argued that the U.S. Constitution imposed severe limitations on the state's right to interfere with parental rights of child rearing based on religious beliefs. The court agreed, but stated that "Mistreatment of a child, however, is not privileged because it is imposed in the guise of freedom of religious expression . . . The severe, repeated beating for such childhood infractions as . . . the inability to remember a Sunday school lesson amply demonstrates the father's pitiless and unreasonable approach to discipline." The court not only allowed the child that had been the subject of the beatings to be removed, but also removed two boys that had not been beaten, stating that either one or both would become the object of the father's "ruthless drive for religious perfection."

In *Nelson v. Dodge*, a 1949 Rhode Island case, the court imposed a constructive trust on property turned over to a church minister under circumstances where it deemed undue influence on the donor had existed. In *Nelson* the defendant minister repeatedly threatened the plaintiff donor with eternal damnation. The plaintiff became so physically and emotionally ill that he asked the minister if there was any hope for him. She replied that God wanted him to strip himself of all his worldly possessions and donate them to her.

Dalsimer recognized that the cases were not directly on point, but concluded that they demonstrated "the principle that remedies should exist for harm caused by extreme and outrageous conduct even when the expression of such conduct involves the expression of religious beliefs." Dalsimer had crossed the point that someone in the judiciary would have to cross if the Nallys' suit was to continue. It was not a question of "was there legal precedent" to support this suit, but "should" there be? More than just a legal argument, Dalsimer had fashioned a social argument for clergy malpractice and he had found the basis for it within the allegation of outrageous conduct.

Dalsimer cited case law from other jurisdictions that established liability against religious institutions for intentional infliction of emotional distress. Both *Lewis v. the Holy Assn', etc.* and *Christoffsen v. Church of Scientology, etc.* had been decided after Judge Murphy's 1981 ruling. *Lewis* was a Massachusetts case and *Christoffsen* came out of Oregon. Neither was absolutely determinative of the facts in the *Nally* case and both cases had refused to find liability. However, they stood for the proposition that liability was possible, and that is all the Nallys needed.

The majority opinion concluded by stating that under the law and the facts, the free exercise clause did not license intentional infliction of emotional distress in the name of religion and could not shield the defendants from liability for wrongful death for a suicide caused by their conduct. Having found one triable issue of fact, the majority did not have to address the other causes of action. The entire suit would return to Superior Court and be tried before a jury.

L. Thaxton Hanson presided over the Second Circuit Court of Appeals and he filed the dissent. In a thirty-seven-page opinion Hanson recited the procedural history of the case, recounted the long chain of factual events leading to Ken Nally's suicide, and then focused on several key issues. First, he argued that under the case law in California, the relationship that existed between Ken Nally and the church, its counselors, and its ministers fell far below what was necessary to create a legal duty between the defendants and the decedent. No duty, no liability, even if there is injury. Second, Hanson argued the majority opinion had found a cause of action where none had been pled. There was no allegation within the Nally complaint of intentional infliction of emotional distress. The majority had created the cause of action from the plaintiffs' pleading that alleged "outrageous conduct."

Judge Hanson's argument turned on duty, and he offered a well-established body of case law to support his argument. California law held that in order for a relationship to give rise to a duty under a negligence or malpractice theory to take affirmative steps to prevent a suicide, the relationship must be "special." The requisite special relationship had been held to exist and had initially been limited to where a patient was in a hospital for psychiatric treatment and had committed suicide. Subsequent case law in *Vistica v. Presbyterian Hospital* (1967) and *Meier v. Ross General Hospital* (1968) had allowed both the hospital and the treating physician to be held liable.

In 1978 the California Supreme Court extended this duty to outpatient psychiatrists, holding that the necessary "special relationship existed." In *Bellah v. Greenson* (1978) the court held that ". . . the requisite special relationship does exist in the case of a patient under the care of a psychiatrist, and a psychiatrist who knows the patient is likely to attempt suicide has a duty to take preventive measures." However, the court refused to extend the doctrine in *Tarasoff v. Regents of University of California* (1976). *Tarasoff* imposed a duty on a psychiatrist to warn a specific victim of a patient's potential assault. The court in *Bellah* refused to extend that duty to circumstances where the assault would be the self-inflicted injury of the patient himself. In other words, there is no duty to warn anyone that a person is going to kill himself.

Hanson pointed to the evidence that showed Ken had been living at home when the suicide occurred. If the law did not impose a duty on a psychiatrist who is paid for analyzing, evaluating, and treating patients for serious suicidal tendencies, how could it impose such a duty on lay counselors or ministers? Hanson was also aware of the social issues. "Morever, in a practical sense, to hold otherwise would pose a dangerous threat to federal and state constitutional guarantees of religious freedom and freedom of speech and could seriously inhibit ministers, priests, and rabbis and other ecclesiastical persons of various religious denominations from seeking to help a person overcome suicidal tendencies through spiritual guidance." In Hanson's view, the issue did come down to belief and he felt the majority had taken isolated excerpts and statements out of context in order to breathe life into an otherwise dead claim.

Having dispensed with the first two grounds of negligence and malpractice by finding no duty, Hanson assailed the majority opinion that found support for the allegation that the defendants had not only failed to prevent Ken's suicide, but had actually caused his death through their outrageous conduct. In his opinion the majority completely misstated the law in *Tate*. The court in *Tate* had expressly limited its holding to instances where the defendant had intentionally caused injury, and the injury was a substantial factor in bringing about the suicide. Hanson adamantly argued that not only was there no evidence to support an intent on the part of Grace Church and its ministers to inflict emotional injury on Ken, but the majority knew that to be the case. That is why it fashioned the extension of *Tate* by arguing that *reckless* conduct could be substituted for *intentional* conduct.

In Hanson's analysis the majority had completely undermined the law. Although all plaintiffs should be entitled to bring actions and be given full and fair opportunity to present their cases, the law had an obligation to defendants as well as to prevent the continuation of unmeritorious claims. Hanson summed the entire case up in one short paragraph:

> In the final analysis, the tragic story that develops is one of a youth who prior to and subsequent to becoming affiliated with Grace Church was suffering from emotional problems stemming from his relationships with women and his family. He constantly sought advice from people he respected prior to his affiliation with Grace Church as well as persons in the medical and psychiatric field, yet consistently rejected such advice. His parents, the plaintiffs herein, were clearly aware of Kenneth's suicidal tendencies and his consistent rejection of help from all sources, and took no steps to have him committed for psychiatric hospitalization against his will.

Hanson saw no evidence that the church had tried to dissuade Ken from seeking professional help, nor any evidence that Ken was not allowed to seek professional help. Hanson feared that to hold otherwise in the *Nally* case would be to open a "virtual Pandora's box of litigation by subjecting all the various religious faiths and their clergy to wrongful death actions and expensive full-blown trials" just because they had been unsuccessful in preventing someone predisposed to killing himself from actually doing so.

Although Hanson conceded that there might be facts under which a church could be held liable, *Nally* was not such a case. The founding fathers had placed a high emphasis on freedom of speech and religion and the facts of this case did not justify the infringement of either sacred right.

Hanson fashioned a sound argument and in some places, particularly with regard to duty, it might have been the stronger of the two. It is hard to ignore his contention that the majority opinion had fashioned a cause of action where none had been pled and in direct contravention of existing law. Hanson had interpreted the law strictly and despite the tragic situation, found no legal basis to afford the Nallys any relief.

Members of the local community where Walter and Maria Nally lived expressed outrage and disbelief at the appellate decision. Charles Miller of Tujunga wrote a searing letter to the editor of his local paper. In Miller's opinion the appellate court had defined malpractice as any harm caused to someone when performing one's duties. The court had accused the church of conspiring unknowingly to destroy a life, its motive, retribution. Miller described all of Grace Church's charitable acts in the last thirty years, ministering to the sick and dying, caring for the handicapped, providing food for the hungry, jobs for the "luckless," and aid for earthquake victims, famine-stricken Africa, and the innocent people caught up in the revolution in Central America. To argue that the church knowingly or unknowingly led Ken down a path to his own death was to mete out "a judgment by its own inference of malpractice that must shock many even as it defies the truth."

Dalsimer and Gutierrez had taken a different road. Their approach looked beyond where the law was and in view of the harm tried to take existing law to another level. In one sense, that is what appellate courts do. They take existing law, consider the evolving social and cultural environment, and allow the law to grow. As opposed as people like Charles Miller had been to the court's ruling, other citizens supported the court's willingness to allow the law to grow and meet social and cultural changes. They found comfort in the knowledge that the law was willing to take steps to prevent religious freedom from becoming fanatical fervor.

Joan Francis wrote the editor of the *Leader*, a southern California paper, in response to a statement by John MacArthur in the paper's coverage of the *Nally* suit. Francis was concerned with MacArthur's statement that he was "a teacher of the bible, not his own opinion, and that all anyone did at Grace was preach the bible." Francis's objection seemed to be that all Christian churches are Bible-teaching churches and that Grace Church and its ministers might not be willing to admit that they were not the only ones teaching the Bible. She acknowledged, "our desire to follow our own consciences and adhere to the highest principles we can imagine is good." But the desire of any one group to impose its views on everyone around them was "terrifying to free Americans." She pointed out that when "a belief" becomes "the belief," the historical result had been events like the Crusades, the Inquisition, the witch trials, European conversion of Western Hemisphere peoples, and Hitler's attempt to exterminate the Jews. To Francis, the issue was whether America would continue to stand for "everyone's right of religious freedom or whether it will encourage one set of believers to impose their perceptions upon the rest of us." In a sense Francis missed the point. The issue was not whether a church was Bible teaching, but whether its teachings should be taken literally or not.

Nally was headed back to trial. Ed Barker and the Nallys would have their day in court. In a case where little seemed clear, what was becoming very clear was that Prosser had been right. *Nally* was more than a contest over laws and legal precedents, it was a battle waged over social issues with long-term and far-reaching ramifications. Still so far from resolution, the case had already determined that a small portion of California's judiciary was willing to consider suing the clergy. It had been a long road just to get to trial, but for the Nallys it was worth it. A jury was going to hear their claim.

CHAPTER 6

Voir Dire

On June 28, 1984, David Cooksey put the obligatory call in to his client. John MacArthur listened calmly as his attorney explained that the appeals court had overturned Judge Murphy's decision and it looked as if they were going to trial. MacArthur's response was characteristically stoic. "I guess we have to do what we have to do."

The California Court of Appeals reinstatement of the *Nally* case not only breathed life back into the suit, but allowed the parties to address the court of public opinion. "I said my 'Our Fathers and Hail Marys' and swore to my father that I would find out what happened to his grandson," Walter Nally told the *Los Angeles Times*. "Some clergymen think of themselves as being so close to God that they blur the distinction between who's doing the talking." It was clear that regardless of any far-reaching ramifications for the clergy in general, for Walter Nally this was about one clergyman in particular. "I get more determined every day to see it through. I don't know whether they [church officials] lack confidence, but I hope they realize that I don't. The devil had my son by the tail and he couldn't shake him. Now I might have the devil by the tail, and he will probably have a hard time shaking me."

By this time even John MacArthur realized that the suit had become personal and he spoke out. "There's a certain amount of identification with Christ when we suffer reproach in his name. He too was falsely accused. If we have to go through this, if this is what the Lord has chosen for us, I guess he has a purpose in it. I just believe my life is in the Lord's hands—I serve him." But MacArthur also refused to accept the blame for what happened. "As a congregation we did everything we could possibly do, including bringing him [Ken] into our lives as closely as he would allow himself to be brought."

Cooksey reiterated what he had maintained throughout the case. "What comes ringing through all the testimony is the fact that the boy would not listen to his pastors, he would not listen to his parents, he would not listen to his doctors, and he went off and committed suicide against the wishes of everyone who knew him." Cooksey then took the obvious next step and on August 6, 1984, he appealed the court of appeals decision to the California Supreme Court.

On August 30, 1984, the California Supreme Court issued its decision refusing to hear the case. Chief Justice Rose Bird indicated that she had been willing to hear the case, but the majority of the court voted against her. Bird had received a thirteen-page letter from the International Society for Krishna Consciousness urging her to hear the case. Perhaps Cooksey's brief had struck a nerve with the Krishnas when he stated as ground for the appeal that to allow judges to regulate clergy spiritual counseling would be to make them "The Big Brother to whom clergy must look to as they counsel their members." Although the brief (or the letter) may have swayed Bird, it did not convince her colleagues.

From a practical standpoint the refusal to hear the appeal made sense. The court had nothing to gain by taking on such a volatile issue at such an early stage in the case. To uphold Judge Murphy's summary judgment decision would deny the plaintiffs access to the courts and require an overturning of the lower appeals court. To take the case and affirm the appeal would decide nothing more than that the case should go to trial and at the same time run the risk of approving new law with regard to elements of intentional infliction of emotional distress. There was also the danger of establishing a cause of action for clergy malpractice without the benefit of all the facts. The easy and safe course was to refuse to hear the case, let it be tried, and then deal with it on appeal after a full and compete record had been amassed.

The supreme court did, however, take a significant step, and using a peculiar procedure in California, "decertified" Dalsimer's court of appeals opinion. American law is governed by the concept of stare decisis. Its literal Latin translation means to abide by, or adhere to, decided cases. As a legal doctrine it holds that once a court has laid down a principle of law as applicable to a certain set of facts, it will adhere to that principle and apply it to all future cases where the facts are substantially the same, regardless of whether the parties or the property at issue are the same. The message sent by the California Supreme Court was not altogether clear. An obvious interpretation is that the court did not want a clergy malpractice opinion floating around in the body of California case law as precedent that such a claim was valid. Another less obvious interpretation is that clergy malpractice aside, the court was not willing to adopt Dalsimer's legal interpretation that reckless or outrageous conduct could be substituted for intentional conduct in a claim for intentional infliction of emotional distress, where in earlier cases the supreme court had clearly stated that such a cause of action could only stand if the defendant intended to injure the plaintiff. For whatever reason, it decertified the opinion. If clergy malpractice was to become a matter of legal precedent it would have to happen on the next appeal.

That was enough for Cooksey. He made it clear there would be no further appeal to the U.S. Supreme Court. "We are going to the trial court and try the case." Other lawyers in the legal community were not so composed. Tom Brandon of the Legal Aid Society in Oak Park, Illinois, found the California Supreme Court's refusal to hear the appeal "unfortunate and alarming." Brandon feared that appellate courts could now fashion causes of action where none had been pled and that in this case, it would allow judges to determine what religious orthodoxy is and what heresy is, matters he deemed "forbidden."

Ed Barker was disappointed the court decertified the opinion, but he was thrilled with the court's decision to let it go to trial. With virtually all of the work already done, it would take only a couple of months of preparation once a trial date was set. In November 1984, the Nallys got their date, April 23, 1985. With that, Barker went to Bhopal, India, in January 1985. Walter Nally could not believe he had left, but Barker had to make a living and the case was all but ready to go. The chemical disaster in Bhopal offered an opportunity for U.S. plaintiff's lawyers to pick up significant business and he was going to take a look.

Barker was back in time for the pretrial conference set for January 29, 1985. In addition to the matters normally decided at these conferences, this one brought an unexpected surprise. The attorneys showed up at 7:00 A.M. to avoid press coverage. Judge Thomas Murphy handled several routine matters, including requiring both sides to disclose their witnesses by February 28, 1985. Then he announced to both sides that he was recusing or disqualifying himself from the case. Murphy claimed that the bench must maintain its integrity, and that his feelings were so strong about the case that he did not feel he could properly sit as judge. He so disagreed with the appeals court decision that good conscience required him to step down. His replacement was Judge Joseph R. Kalin.

In contrast to Murphy, Kalin was reserved and shy. The son of a coal miner and steel worker in Pennsylvania and Ohio, Kalin brought a practical background to the bench developed through years of labor relations work. Prior to law school he had worked as an electrician and had become involved in labor arbitration and mediation. He continued his interest in labor after becoming an attorney, taking union locals on as clients and representing individual members in a wide variety of general legal matters. He had come to the Glendale Superior Court after seventeen years as a general practitioner in Huntington Beach, a stint on the Glendale municipal bench, and as a superior court judge in Pasadena. Kalin thought of himself as a collaborative judge, one who worked with the parties and attorneys to solve problems, even after the case reached trial. Kalin's reputation among the local bar was that of a judge who believed in a more relaxed atmosphere, but with enough formality to command the respect needed to keep both lawyers and clients in line.

Kalin found himself drawn to the growing and evolving body of tort law. He recognized the impact that new causes of action would have and not only did not advocate impeding new theories of recovery, but was not bothered by their creation. Kalin believed "that if there is responsibility or a duty there, it may be that

{ *Clergy Malpractice in America* }

nobody's seen it for 100 years, but it is still there. We have nothing to look forward to but new areas and new theories. . . . I don't know if this is good or bad, I have some concerns about that." Murphy's disqualification brought Kalin face to face with as new a theory as he had ever seen, and the opportunity to judge for himself whether it was good or bad.

Ericsson's first reaction was disappointment. Given Murphy's feelings about the case, it is easy to understand why Ericsson was sorry to see Murphy withdraw. However, his sentiments were tempered by something that happened six weeks before the pretrial hearing in January 1985. Sam got a phone call from Dennis Dalsimer, the son of Judge Dalsimer, who had ruled against Grace Church and sent the case back to trial. Dalsimer was active as a Christian lawyer in several of the same organizations that Ericsson worked with and had called to discuss the *Nally* case. He assured Ericsson that his father genuinely felt there were issues that needed to be resolved at trial, but cautioned Ericsson that his case had only one problem: Judge Murphy. Ericsson could not believe what he was hearing. Murphy was for them. He had granted summary judgment in 1981. True, Dalsimer admitted, but Murphy was too flamboyant and unpredictable. What this case needed from the defense perspective was a hardworking, scholarly judge. Dalsimer told Ericsson he would pray that Murphy not try the case. The younger Dalsimer's prayers were apparently answered when Murphy stepped down. Ericsson could only wait and see if Dennis Dalsimer had been right.

Neither Cooksey nor Barker seemed particularly disturbed by the change in judges. Cooksey in fact immediately set out to test Kalin's willingness to try the case and the judge wasted little time in putting his own beliefs into practice. Cooksey took a last shot at dismissing the case, as he and Ericsson again argued that the appellate court had taken the taped lecture by Thomson out of context. Kalin listened to the church's argument and on March 8, 1985, denied Grace Church's motion to dismiss the case. In ruling that there were sufficient issues for trial, Kalin refused to overrule the appellate court, stating that the "appeals court has indicated there are issues to be tried and did not intend to limit issues in the case to the one lecture," but added, "I think there is no question that the plaintiff has many mountains to climb in this case." Barker did not care if he had to climb the Himalayas: he had gotten over a huge obstacle that threatened to never let him try. His reaction was simple: "We're ready to go."

———

On Monday, April 22, 1985, jury selection began. Seated beneath the chandeliers of the Burbank Holiday Inn banquet room, 150 people wondered whether this was to be a trial or a convention. The unusual forum for jury selection had become necessary in light of the publicity the case had received since its filing. Prior to his self-recusal, Judge Murphy had determined that a large jury pool would be essential to the selection process. After the potential jurors found their seats Kalin addressed the group and asked them to bear with the publicity and the surroundings. His Glendale courtroom was too small to accommodate everyone and he had chosen to allow press cameras into the courtroom because the press's access was an inherent part of democracy. The venue did not seem to faze Kalin, perhaps because he had once used a banquet hall to try a products liability case where it had been necessary to bring two completely assembled automobiles into court.

In what was expected to take as long as three to four days, Kalin began questioning the jurors. They were taken in groups of sixteen, with twelve designated as jurors and four as alternates. The alternates would sit throughout the trial, but only vote if a member of the panel had to leave during the course of the trial. Kalin's questioning followed general lines: "Had they heard of Grace?" "Did they know any of the witnesses on the list?" One person was excused from the panel because there were ministers in her ex-husband's family. Another was excused from the general pool because his son was a Christian youth counselor.

Ed Barker then took over the questioning. In a deliberate but calm voice Barker inquired of the panel: "Can you find a clergyman accountable if it were determined that he violated the law?" "Does it make you uncomfortable to judge a clergyman?" "Do you feel churches and ministers should have special treatment?" "Does anyone have strong feelings on fundamentalist churches, suing clergymen, biblical counseling, or other biblical issues?"

By late Monday afternoon the gravity of the occasion began to dawn on the jury pool. The sound of knitting needles that had been so obvious early in the morning slowly subsided as everyone turned attention to the matter at hand. Killing time gave way to understanding the issues, as everyone realized that some of them would be called upon to pass judgment over men of the cloth. Those in the general pool listened intently as sixteen of their peers on the first panel handled questions that became progressively weightier.

Most people denied having any specific knowledge of the case, but half of the sixteen member panel admitted to having heard of the case generally. The same number conceded they had attended Grace Church at least once in recent years. Two people admitted to knowing someone who committed suicide. One woman, Juanita Fernandez, was excused when she admitted that she was from a religious family and might tend to favor a pastor's testimony. However, fifteen people stated that they could use the law to decide if the church was negligent. Barker probed into the religious affiliation of jurors, a tactic that offended Sam Ericsson. Barker asked each member of the panel, "Are you a born-again Christian?" Four answered yes, and of the four two were stricken, but two would remain and eventually serve as jurors on the case. Ericsson claimed Barker's questions were inappropriate, saying there could be no religious test for any juror and that they (defendants) were comfortable with anybody evaluating the case.

On Tuesday morning the defense took its turn at quizzing the jurors. Cooksey made it clear that he did not care about a juror's religious background. All that he cared about was the ability of a juror to "give a person a fair and impartial trial if [a pastor] expressed a view that was repugnant to you." Cooksey also asked if anyone had a friend or close relative involved in the field of psychiatry, psychology, or mental health care. Like Barker, he asked if anyone was uncomfortable sitting in judgment of a pastor. One potential alternate was excused because she admitted to strong feelings that might prejudice her ability to fairly decide the case. Outside the courtroom, the woman, a management consultant whose identity was kept confidential, admitted to a reporter that she was a plaintiff in a pending lawsuit involving psychiatric issues and said, "I do not believe that any man can be blamed or held responsible if he's counseling someone who commits suicide. I don't care who he is. I don't think we can play God."

Before concluding its questioning the defense distributed a press kit containing the church's annual report and statements refuting the Nallys' allegations that Ken was "effectively prevented from seeking professional help with regard to his personal problems." The packet also had a statement saying, "Grace Community Church, its elders, members and friends, look forward to the opportunity to finally clear the air concerning the issues raised in the Nally lawsuit."

Almost lost in the process, Walter and Maria Nally sat in the rear of the courtroom with their son, Walter Jr. Wally was now twenty-three, almost the same age Ken had been when he took his own life. Seated several rows in front of the Nallys, John MacArthur and his wife Patricia watched the selection of the sixteen strangers who would decide their fate. For a man totally resigned to the final judgment of all men by God, the prospect of having his conduct judged by the people in that room was somehow unsettling.

On Monday Barker had estimated the selection process would take a week. By Tuesday afternoon the two sides had selected a jury of three men and nine women. The process had taken one day of court time and required questioning nineteen people. Barker liked the jury. Years later, Cooksey would say that it was an "O.K." jury, but clearly one he was satisfied with going into battle.

Voir dire literally means "to speak the truth." In modern trial procedure it is a term of art and refers to the examination of a witness, or in this instance, a potential juror, to ensure that he or she is competent and has no self-interest or other bias that would prevent them from objectively weighing the evidence. It is impossible to overestimate the importance of this preliminary process. By the time *Nally* went to trial in 1985, an entire industry had developed that offered technical trial support for jury selection.

Experts had bodies of data on how age, gender, occupation, family background, ethnicity, and other factors affected jury voting and prejudices on cases ranging from products liability and domestic relations to criminal and quasi-criminal prosecutions. No such data existed for clergy malpractice.

Cooksey had been adamant that religious preference was irrelevant. All he wanted was for people to be fair. Barker had probed deep into religion, perhaps aware of the sentiment felt by many Americans that fundamentalism threatened basic freedom, and wanting to make sure he could draw on the social stigma attached to the Radical Right, the Moral Majority, or both. Maybe he just wanted to be sure that anyone who believed God could do no wrong did not also believe God's servants were equally free of any culpability. Fundamental religious beliefs did not appear to completely bar one from serving; Barker left two people on the jury who admitted to being born-again Christians. The truth was that despite all the questions and scrutiny, trying to decide which characteristics were best suited for each side was a shot in the dark. Cooksey's gut feeling was probably right: just be fair, even if you hear things that are totally repugnant to your own beliefs.

In some civil jurisdictions legal experts estimated that as high as 75 percent of jury trials are over by the time the jury is selected and the attorneys make their opening statements. What this means is that the impressions jurors get of the parties and their lawyers, coupled with the degree to which each side is able to explain its case, is so great that many jurors literally make up their minds in the early stages of the trial. Obviously, not all jurors decide so early and some cases clearly turn over the course of the trial itself. However, what is clear is that the early impressions and prejudices formed as a result of the selection process itself stay with jurors throughout the trial.

Everyone was surprised that the process in this case went as quickly as it did. None of the attorneys felt pressured by time, nor did they feel that they had failed to ask anything important of the prospective panel. Perhaps the case and controversy were so novel that most people were genuinely unsure how they were going to react to certain evidence and the idea that at its core, the case required them to judge ministers. Similarly, the novelty of the suit left the attorneys wondering just what kind of jury they wanted.

————

Any doubt that this case would be anything but a dogfight from start to finish disappeared at 9:25 A.M., Wednesday, April 24, 1985. The attorneys were already in Judge Kalin's chambers minutes before opening statements to argue a motion *in limine*. The motion is routinely made by one party to limit or exclude a piece of evidence or oral testimony, before the jury hears or sees it and is forever prejudiced by the knowledge. This motion addressed the "albatross" that hung from the neck of the defense since the inception of the case and threatened to drag it under: Rich Thomson's counseling tape with the suicide reference.

Cooksey and Ericsson sought to prevent any mention of the tape during opening statements on the grounds that when Barker tried to offer it later in the trial the court would have to rule on its admissibility. Grace Church's lawyers explained that the tape was made eighteen months after Ken's death, he could not possibly have heard the tape, and that therefore it was not only irrelevant, but would be prejudicial. Barker maintained that the tape, although made later, had relevancy in that it demonstrated Grace's belief system, a belief system that Ken Nally had thoroughly accepted. Evidence that suicide was either encouraged or deemed acceptable, Barker argued, was highly relevant.

In chambers Kalin first made it clear he would not rule on the admissibility of the tape at that time. That being the case, to mention the tape in opening statements could hurt both sides. If Barker referred to it and later it was excluded, he might look bad having promised evidence and been unable to deliver. On the other hand, if the tape were mentioned and excluded, a juror might also reason that it was kept out because it hurt the defense, thus prejudicing the church and its ministers anyway. Barker agreed not to mention the tape and Kalin ruled that he could mention other tapes that his experts had listened to in preparation for their testimony, so long as he avoided any specific reference to "Thomson's tape." With the first of many in-chamber discussions over, the attorneys stepped into the courtroom.

After welcoming the jury, Kalin covered a few administrative matters and then he explained that what followed would be the opening statement of each party wherein they would explain their case. Kalin cautioned the jury that nothing either side said in opening statements was or should be construed as evidence. It was only a road map to lead the jury from the start to the end of the journey.

Over the next hour Barker took the jury through the steps that brought them to court: Ken's death and the family's anger that led to Walter Nally's investigation and to filing the lawsuit. Point by point Barker walked through the sequence of events in the years leading up to Ken's suicide.

Opening statements are supposed to be unemotional introductions: directions, as opposed to argument. At one point Barker slipped into emotional argument as his voice slowly got louder. Finally, Cooksey objected and the court cautioned Barker that he was straying into argument. It was hard. He had waited so long. He had lived with the case until he knew it in his sleep. Regaining his composure, Barker explained what evidence he would present. The gist of his opening statement was that the church and its ministers had undertaken to counsel Ken Nally. Having accepted that responsibility they had an obligation to do so in a competent manner. There were standards that apply to everyone, clergymen and laymen alike, who purport to counsel the mentally ill, and the church and its ministers had failed to abide by those standards. Equally important, when the Nallys finally understood the seriousness of their son's condition, the church withheld crucial information at the precise time when Walter and Maria Nally were trying to decide whether to involuntarily commit Ken. Information that, had it been made known, would have swayed their decision. As a result, Ken Nally was not committed and he is dead. For Barker, this case was not about religion, it was about simple legal duty that applied to everyone.

Sam Ericsson opened for the defense. He introduced the church and its ministers, explained how Grace had developed since the

1950s, how much it had grown, and how important a part of the community it had become. Ericsson focused on all the help the church and its ministers had provided. He drew attention to the church's sincere religious beliefs as to the use of the Bible and how it held the answers to all of mankind's problems. He concentrated on the last days of Ken's life, how much medical attention Ken received, and that Ken committed suicide when he was living at home, under circumstances where both his parents and his doctors had access to him, tried to help him, and were unsuccessful.

Judy Gabriel sat quietly in the gallery and listened to both lawyers lay out their respective road maps of where this case was going. She had seen many things in her life. As a reporter and foreign correspondent for several newspapers over the course of her career she had witnessed natural disasters and wars. Years later she would recall that nothing she covered before or after ever felt quite as intense as this courtroom and this case. She had recently resigned her position on the staff of the *Daily News*, the local newspaper serving the San Fernando Valley, to return to what she loved, covering the news. As a reporter she would cover every day of the trial. Looking around the packed courtroom she realized she was lucky to have a seat; there were none to spare, and over the course of the next few weeks every seat would be taken.

Most of the spectators were members of Grace Church, people who had come to witness the spectacle of their minister, church, and beliefs on trial. They were an audience with a vested interest in the outcome. With a congregation of 20,000, only a small segment would actually see the trial and the same people were rarely there every day. Most would be like Pat Rotisky, who made time in an otherwise busy day to go to court. Pat was and is today John MacArthur's secretary. She still remembers the trial and what it felt like. "We all felt like we were on trial. The trial brought a fear of the unknown, and an uneasy feeling that the government and legal system that we had a deep respect for may be chastising us."

CHAPTER 7

He Didn't Need a Friend . . .

Barker's first three witnesses testified to the Ken Nally they knew growing up and the transformation he underwent upon converting and joining Grace Church. They painted a picture of a vibrant boy, always upbeat, zealously into athletics, who as a young man somehow changed. Mark Stanners, a childhood friend who also knew Ken at UCLA, testified that once Ken converted he was a completely different person. "Religion, religion, religion, and that was kind of a turn-off for somebody like me who was involved with my Catholic religion." Cooksey did not cross-examine the first two witnesses and asked Stanners only a few questions.

Next Barker read the testimony of Ernie Hauser into the record. Hauser did not testify in person but his deposition was read into evidence. Generally lawyers hate this. Deposition testimony is dry and juries often tune it out or miss its significance. Barker had no choice; Hauser could not attend, so he read the questions and David Cooksey read the answers.

Hauser had found Ken dead in his apartment. They had been friends, attended church and Bible study together, and Barker's questioning brought out Hauser's observations of Ken's growing depression in the two years leading up to his suicide. Hauser established Ken's commitment to Bible study, his routine listening of tapes made by John MacArthur, and the counseling he received from Duane Rea, Lynn Cory, and Rich Thomson. In the two weeks following his failed suicide attempt and hospitalization at Verdugo Hills, Hauser had noticed Ken had been much more depressed and despondent. Over the course of his testimony Hauser revealed that Katie Thayer, Ken's girlfriend, may have known that Ken threatened to try to kill himself again, but he did not know if anyone else knew that. Hauser spoke of Ken's conflict that his family had not embraced Jesus Christ and might not be saved. Finally, Hauser recounted the details of discovering Ken's body and the police investigation that followed immediately thereafter.

Although not spectacular testimony, Barker had begun to establish Ken's state of mind in the years leading up to his death, his depression immediately preceding his suicide, the connection between Ken, the church, and its counselors, and the circumstances of his suicide. Hauser still offered no proof that anyone other than Ken's girlfriend might have known of his intention to try again.

Day two started slow but quickly intensified. After admitting Ken's high school records into evidence, Barker began the medical portion of his case. He called Dr. Christine Evelyn, the staff physician on call when Ken Nally was admitted to the Verdugo Hills Hospital intensive care unit on March 12, 1979, following his drug overdose. Immediately after Evelyn, Barker called David A. Hall, the staff psychiatrist at Verdugo Hills who interviewed and examined Ken prior to his release on March 16, 1979. Both provided small but important pieces in Barker's case.

Evelyn confirmed Ken's depressed state and testified that in her medical opinion, he was a clear suicide risk. She was so concerned of the risk that despite Ken's immediate desire to be released, she insisted he see Hall as a precondition to his release. Ken wanted to see his "school psychiatrist." Evelyn did not know who that was but Barker hoped to use it later as an expression of Ken's unwillingness to consult secular mental health professionals, an unwillingness caused by Grace Church. Finally, Evelyn testified that had she known Ken had expressed an intent to commit suicide again upon his release, such information would have definitely affected her willingness to release Ken.

Hall's testimony followed. He possessed impressive credentials and testified that the decision to keep Ken in the hospital against his will could only come from the psychiatrist and Ken's parents. According to Hall, effective methods for treating mental illness existed in 1979 that could have cured Ken. In addition to the wide variety of drugs available to treat mental illness and depression, verbal counseling methods, cognitive therapy being one, had

proven effective. Hall saw Ken on March 16 for about ninety minutes. Walter Nally was present and Ken denied having any suicidal intentions. Hall determined Ken was depressed enough to
require medical treatment, but not a threat to commit suicide. Ken
claimed his overdose had been an attempt to temporarily escape
life's problems and not to end his own life. Although Hall felt Ken
should be hospitalized, Ken had refused, and neither Hall nor
Walter Nally felt the circumstances were strong enough to warrant involuntary commitment.

When asked by Barker, Hall unequivocally stated that had he
known Ken had expressed an intent to try and kill himself again,
Hall would have involuntarily committed Ken. He also confirmed
that no one ever told him that Ken had expressed such a willingness. Ken had been resistant to secular treatment and not only
asked Hall if he were Christian, but wanted to consult the church
and its pastors regarding issues of his own mental health treatment.
Ken had agreed to see Hall on March 23 but canceled, deciding to
see a Christian psychiatrist instead. Hall admitted to being a fundamental Christian himself and knew that pastors and secular
counselors could work together. He expressed concern that Ken
did not feel he and Hall could work together.

Although the constitutional issues of whether a church could be
held liable at all never disappeared, Cooksey could not rely on such
an argument at trial. He had to establish that if the church was held
to a standard of care, that it and its pastors had met that standard.
Cooksey's problem was that no such standard existed. Would the
church and its pastors be held to the standard of a psychiatrist, a
psychologist, an ordinary rational man, or a lay church counselor?

In a short cross-examination of Evelyn he did a good job of
establishing the opportunity to keep Ken hospitalized, and he
confirmed that the Nallys found it hard to accept that Ken had
tried to kill himself. He also established that the drug Ken overdosed on had been prescribed by another psychiatrist, and thereby
hoped to show that the church had not prevented Ken from seeking and receiving professional help.

Cooksey's job was to show that all the opportunity the family
needed to save Ken had existed and that their own unwillingness

to commit Ken against his will had killed him. During his cross-examination of Hall, Cooksey established that on March 23 or 24 Walter Nally had been told by a Dr. Parker, the doctor Ken had chosen to see, that Ken should be hospitalized. Walter Nally had rejected that advice. Hall admitted that a psychiatrist cannot predict suicide and further admitted that Ken had denied any previous suicide attempts. Cooksey finished strong as Hall admitted that Dr. Parker, a doctor referred to Ken by the church, had suggested involuntary commitment one week before Ken committed suicide, and Walter Nally had refused.

Barker had established that both the Nallys and Ken's doctors lacked important information that might have swayed the decision to commit Ken, information he would later show the church had and withheld. Cooksey had shown that the family had the opportunity to commit Ken and had refused. Hall had distinguished between involuntarily admitting someone and keeping them there against their will, but Cooksey had held his own.

The day ended with Dr. Richard Mohline on the stand. Mohline served as the dean of administration at Rosemead School of Psychology and had an appointment in practical theology at Talbot Seminary at Biola University in California. His experience lay in pastoral counseling and the integration of pastoral counseling with psychology. He actually saw Ken once, as a pastoral counselor, but his testimony went more to his own beliefs than his personal observations.

Mohline provided the groundwork for a key component of Barker's case: the duty of a pastoral counselor to refer someone to a more qualified person if the problem or condition was beyond his or her training and ability:

Q. In the course that you teach on emotional problems, do you teach anything about the duty to refer?
A. Yes.
Q. What you teach then as I understand is that a pastoral counselor who is dealing with the severe mental problem has a duty to refer that person to someone who has different training?

A. Unless he's had the training, experience himself which he may well have, some pastors do have that experience—

Q. Excuse me, such pastors are psychologists or are psychiatrists?

A. That's correct, right.

Mohline added later in his testimony that in his classes he taught that cooperation between pastoral counselors and professionals was absolutely essential. Mohline had seen Ken after he left Verdugo Hills. When asked if he wanted to commit suicide, Ken avoided the question, saying only that "he was looking for answers." Mohline believed Ken was looking to God and did not push the suicide issue further. But he added that had he believed Ken was suicidal, he would have initiated an intervention to have him involuntarily committed. He also confirmed that no one had told him that Ken was contemplating suicide. He had seen Ken, evaluated him, and made a referral, sending along all the information he had been given, information that did not include Ken's prior suicides, nor his promise to try again.

Cooksey's cross-examination took less than two minutes. He established that Grace had sent Ken to him, that he had seen Ken and referred him to Fullerton Psychological Services, a service that relied on counseling techniques other than just the Bible. Cooksey continued to stay the course: Ken had received all kinds of help and ignored it. His parents could have committed him and did not. Still, Barker had done well. He had introduced a theologian that believed "good" counseling required an integrative approach and that part of the process involved not only referral to more qualified people but a complete sharing of information. Barker ended the day with a custodian from the coroner's office who authenticated Ken's death records.

———

Monday's testimony started fast. After establishing the facts of the suicide through an L.A. police officer, Barker called Fred Barshaw, a pastor at Grace Church for the last twelve years. Barshaw had been counseling coordinator just prior to Rich Thomson assuming the position. Using two pages from Grace's 1979 annual report, Barker established the size and breadth of the Grace counseling program.

Barshaw testified that in 1979 Grace Church held over 1,000 counseling sessions, of which half were members and half were of the "unsaved community," those members of the local area who did not belong to the church. The report stated that one of the unique characteristics of Grace Church's counseling was that emotional problems were really all spiritual problems at their root. Grace counselors routinely counseled people over the phone in crisis situations where they called looking for help in an emotional state. Barshaw objected to the use of the term "counseling staff," insisting they just had pastors who counseled. Fred Barshaw never counseled Ken "formally" but did interact with him and discussed with other members of the Grace community who knew Ken, including Lynn Cory, the possibility in 1976–1977 that he might try to commit suicide. Barshaw admitted he never sent Ken to a psychiatrist or a psychologist and insisted that with biblical counseling and a strict adherence to the instructions of the Grace counselors Ken's long-term problems could have been resolved. Barshaw insisted Ken would not follow the biblical advice of his counselors.

Following Barshaw, Barker called Duane Rea, the first of the defendants to testify, and in many ways the most important. Rea had been the one pastor that had a formal counseling relationship with Ken and his testimony would take most of two days. Barker had him designated as an adverse, or hostile, witness, meaning he could be cross-examined using leading or suggestive questions, even though Barker had called him in the plaintiffs' case. From the very beginning one thing became clear. Neither Grace Church nor its pastors would attempt to hide or otherwise tone down the nature of their beliefs or the actions that followed.

Barker immediately established that Rea counseled Ken formally in 1978 and informally in 1979, that he routinely counseled depressed people and even suicidal people, and that the Bible was his sole source of guidance.

Q. And the counseling that you gave was essentially biblical; is that correct?

A. That's always my intent, so I would have to say yes.
Q. And your belief then and now and all your life has been that the Bible holds answers to emotional problems; is that correct?
A. Absolutely.

Barker also established Rea's counseling credentials or lack thereof.

Q. Do you have a license in psychology or psychiatry, or any of the mental health professions?
A. No, I do not.
Q. Have you taken any graduate study or graduate courses in psychology?
A. No. I read.
Q. Have you had any undergraduate training in psychology?
A. No, I have not.
Q. Have you had any formal training in psychology or psychiatry?
A. No, I have not.
Q. How long have you counseled people for emotional problems?
A. I have been working in dealing with people's emotional problems since I was nineteen, from the early time when I was working with youth groups in a church in Burbank.

Rea's training amounted to "reading a lot and experience."

When Rea stepped out of the witness box on April 30, several things were clear. Rea had never told Ken to seek any other source of help other than God. In Rea's opinion Ken's problem lay not in getting counsel, but in following it. Rea admitted that as Ken lay recovering in Verdugo Hills Hospital that Ken promised he would again try to kill himself when he got out. Rea admitted he never told the Nallys or anyone else what Ken said, despite believing that Ken was serious and that he had not threatened to kill himself as a ploy for attention. When pressed as to why, Rea responded that, "I presumed that they [Nallys and doctors] were all fully aware of why he was there, and it would be pure redundancy for me to speak of such matters."

Rea testified he knew how badly Ken was suffering. A year prior to the March 1979 attempt in one of their last sessions Ken had told

Duane that he could not live his life. Poor grades and the demise of his relationship with his girlfriend had made him despondent. Throughout he early part of 1978 Ken repeatedly expressed an inability to cope with life. Rea's response was to cite Ken scripture.

Barker and Rea covered the fine lines between despondency and depression and between formal counseling and discussions they had as "friends." Rea had seen Ken one week before his death when Ken came to his house and helped his family trim trees. Barker probed into Rea's relationship with Rich Thomson and questioned whether he had received any training from Thomson. Rea admitted he had listened to some of *The Principles of Biblical Counseling.*

At times Barker referred back to Rea's deposition when the pastor strayed from testimony he had already given. Although it slowed the questioning, it was important for Barker to expose inconsistencies in Rea's testimony. Barker need to undermine Rea's moral authority and make him appear less than truthful in the eyes of the jury.

After four sessions, some as long as three hours, spread out over four months, Rea admitted that he told Ken in 1978 he could no longer counsel him because Ken refused to do his "homework." Ken continued to want to deal with the same "ground," as Rea called it, the same problems. Rea believed that as a steward of God's time, if no progress was being made, he had an obligation to cease formal counseling, but his door always remained open as a "friend." Barker pressed and Rea conceded that once Ken left his care Rea never suggested any other avenue of counseling. Barker offered Rea the opportunity to embrace an integrated approach to counseling. Rea refused.

Q. You don't have any religious conviction against psychiatry and psychology; is that right?
A. When they parallel what God says is his word, more power to them, but where they counter it, whether it's a psychologist or whatever -chologist, I would have to say, "Don't take advice."

Rea claimed that he and Ken had "tremendous accord."

Two days of testimony ended in a flurry as Rea conceded that there were no codified standards for dealing with people who expressed suicidal tendencies and that he had continued to admonish Ken that his emotional problems could be solved by accepting God's teachings. Barker took Rea through every element of suicidal ideation. Rea admitted he knew and recognized each element and then conceded he had seen each element in Ken. Still, he had not referred him to anyone else even after he refused to continue seeing him on a formal basis in 1978.

Cooksey's cross-examination of his own client lasted only a short time. He concentrated not so much on Ken, but on Rea's counseling of Maria Nally. His purpose was clear, to show that the many problems Ken had came directly from his own family situation. He also demonstrated from Rea's notes that Walter Nally's alleged affair had been known to Ken, despite Maria's attempt to keep it from her son. During direct examination Barker had raised the possibility that Rea had breached Maria's confidence by telling Ken of his father's affair: this line of questioning was designed to show that Ken discovered the affair from a source other than Duane Rea. Grace Church's defense to the allegation that Ken's prior suicides and his threat to try again were improperly withheld was based on that information being confidential. If Rea breached a confidential relationship with Maria, it would be more difficult to argue the church was protecting the sanctity of such a relationship with Ken. Cooksey could not rehabilitate Rea's theological position on counseling. Win or lose, that was his belief. What he could do was try and prove what he had always maintained: Ken got lots of advice from a variety of people and ultimately committed suicide because he could not cope with deep-seated problems that came from his family situation.

Immediately following Rea, Barker called Dr. James T. Long, a psychiatrist with a lengthy list of impressive credentials, including membership in the American Association of Pastoral Counselors. Long had experience working with interdenominational pastoral care programs. He had read Rea's, Barshaw's, and Thomson's depositions in preparation for his testimony. A short time into his testimony Cooksey and Ericsson stopped it with an objection that went to the heart of their constitutional argument. Neither Long nor anyone else could constitutionally testify to standards of pastoral or religious counseling that Grace Church must adhere to. Kalin excused the jury and counsel went into his chambers.

Harkening back to Judge Murphy's early admonition, if the defendants could destroy Barker's ability to establish a standard of care or conduct, a legal duty, then no matter how bizarre Rea's counseling methods might seem, there could be no liability. Sam Ericsson had been relatively quiet throughout the trial. Litigation was Cooksey's bailiwick and he was happy to leave it to him. But this was constitutional law and Cooksey let Ericsson lead.

Citing *Cantwell, Ballard,* and relevant California law in *Tarasoff* and *Bella,* Ericsson argued that it was impermissible under the First Amendment to allow anyone to claim that Grace Church had to meet a particular standard of care. This was belief, not action, and Grace Church's beliefs were beyond scrutiny. Kalin agreed. He would not permit any expert or psychiatrist to testify that Grace Church's teachings or religious-based counseling would have to fit a standard of care. However, Kalin would allow, in light of the evidence so far and the court of appeals decision, testimony as to standards applicable to counselors in general, religious, secular, or otherwise. That is, if one accepts the responsibility of counseling, one must meet certain duties that are not peculiar to any religion. Testimony would also be allowed on a duty to refer, such a duty being common to any counselor beyond his abilities. Kalin excluded testimony as to basic educational requirements. To allow it would be to set standards for a particular church and he refused to do that. Finally, Kalin saw no duty to cooperate with family or other psychiatrists other than to warn if they are suicidal. Kalin would allow testimony on outrageous conduct. For example, did the church's failure to refer breach a duty common to all counselors and become outrageous? However, he killed Barker's argument that the church dumped Ken, so to speak, by stating he saw no duty to continue to counsel Ken once Rea determined Ken would not follow his instructions.

Ericsson realized Kalin had made up his mind, at least for now, but continued to push his main theme. The beliefs of Thomson, Rea, Cory, and MacArthur were so interconnected with their counseling practices that they were inseparable, and as such, could not be attacked or standardized. Emotional problems for Grace Church were indistinguishable from spiritual problems. Kalin agreed that a church never lost the right to save a person's soul, but he seemed to be leaning in Barker's direction, saying ". . . look, I think you should go to a psychiatrist; this is beyond me . . . you may have problems that are beyond my capacity and I still want to counsel you and still want to bring you to God and the church." There were two cases going on: one before the jury, the other in chambers. Barker was beginning to make headway with the jury. The defendants were going to have to win the battle in chambers. Right now, Barker seemed to be winning that one too, or at least doing well enough to keep his case alive.

Long's testimony established a set of standards that would or should apply to anyone engaged in counseling, irrespective of religious belief or denomination. In his opinion, Rea had violated every one of them. Rea failed to investigate the seriousness of Ken's suicidal ideation, not just in 1979, but as far back as 1977. Rea failed to refer Ken to someone more qualified, he failed to inform the hospital psychiatrists and the Nallys of Ken's promise "to try again," and thereby severely prejudiced Dr. Hall's ability to accurately evaluate Ken's condition.

Cooksey did what he could. He established that Long had been involved in the case only six weeks, that he had read only three of the twenty-five depositions, that he testified as a paid expert of the plaintiff, and that he himself had lost 3 people out of about 400 suicide cases. Cooksey then took issue with Long's belief that had Rea acted properly the outcome would have been different. He also established that Grace had not purposely tried to destroy Ken's self-esteem. As a whole, a good job, considering what Long had said. This should have been it but Ericsson, perhaps still emotionally charged from the session in chambers, took it upon himself to address some "areas Mr. Cooksey did not cover."

Ericsson drew Long to the fact that Rea had allowed Ken in his home, and Ericsson desperately wanted him to admit this was a good thing, a caring attitude. Long, however, disagreed. All lawyers know that the key to effective cross-examination is control. Do not allow a witness to elaborate: force him to give short, yes-no answers. Ericsson blundered:

Q. Isn't that [taking Ken into his home] an effective way to maintain an established rapport with somebody that's reaching out for help?

A. It may or may not be.

Q. Could you explain your answer?

A. I sure can. Ken called [Rea a week before his suicide] wanting to talk . . . and Pastor Rea made a specific conscious intent not to talk, but simply to trim trees and work. This man did not need to trim trees. He needed somebody to talk with, he needed that avenue open up to him which Pastor Rea was shutting out and Pastor Rea had a very special opportunity to do something, to grab him by the scruff of the neck psychologically and say, what is going on with you. We need to help you . . . the man wants to come over and talk to him and he's going to trim trees. Now that's ludicrous.

Q. He was available as a friend, right?

A. He didn't need a friend, he needed something more than that. He needed a counselor, someone who could help him take charge of a devastating situation. Friends you can get, he needed a counselor.

Q. Pastor Rea remained available, open to Ken the entire—those last three weeks of his life?

A. I just mentioned to you, he did not. He made a specific attempt and said he decided not to talk to the man on the very day that he came over and said he wanted to talk, according to what I read.

Q. He was available?

A. He was physically available, that's all I saw.

In a few short minutes Long had said things on cross-examination that he had not said even during direct examination in response to Barker's questions. He had undermined Cooksey's efforts and had severely tarnished Grace Church's notion that friendship and fellowship were as useful as professional help. Ericsson went on for a few minutes more, but it's doubtful the jury heard anything else. The damage was done and it would be Ericsson's last cross-examination. Cooksey tried to limit the damage but ultimately let it go.

Long had been a good witness. Subsequent efforts to narrow the standard to pastoral counselors would not be so successful. Barker next called Scott Sullender from the American Association of Pastoral Counselors (AAPC). Cooksey and Ericsson again vehemently objected. In chambers the debate raged, fueled in part by having Sullender give his testimony out of the jury's presence before Kalin would consider allowing him to testify before the jury.

Sullender testified out of the jury's presence that the AAPC tried to fill a regulatory void. The state would not and could not regulate pastors, so the AAPC offered itself as a quasi-regulatory organization. It could not punish, but offered some basic rules and guidelines. Over Barker's objection, Kalin refused to allow Sullender to testify that the AAPC's guidelines should govern Grace Church's conduct. In his opinion an organization with 2,500 members had not risen to the level of being generally accepted. Sullender was allowed to testify as a counseling expert and respond to hypothetical questions as to how he would handle a suicidal person, but he could draw no connection to the AAPC or to Grace Church. As a result of Kalin's ruling, Sullender added very little to the case. This in-chambers round went to Cooksey and Ericsson.

The second week closed out in a rush with brief testimony from several witnesses. Barker put on Alan Bullock, a physician who had examined Ken's injured arm three weeks prior to his death, at the request of Rich Thomson. The gist of the testimony was that Thomson had mishandled the situation by not paying closer attention to Ken's depression and needs. Bullock had spoken with Evelyn and shared her belief that the church had restricted Ken's medical options.

Julies Milestone, the doctor who had prescribed the Elavil to Ken, followed Bullock. He testified to its lethal qualities if taken in excess. Two witnesses from the coroner's office established the facts of Ken's suicide, but the most important witness was Maria Nally.

Maria's testimony recounted her sessions with Duane Rea and provided insight into Ken's steadily declining state. However, her most important contribution was for the jury to see her suffering, with the sincerity of a woman who had lost her son and honestly believed that this church and its pastors had been responsible. Unlike Walter Nally, who had distanced himself from Ken's church, Maria tried hard to embrace Ken's new faith and simply could not. She also offered a different and personal perspective on the family's internal problems. She particularly dispelled any notion that Ken's mixed ancestry posed an emotional problem for him as the defense had suggested during discovery. She also put a different spin on the alleged affair, explaining the woman Walter had become involved with had serious problems, among them a child addicted to drugs.

The most important factual evidence lay in her testimony that Rea had told Kenneth things that she shared during counseling and that Ken could have only learned from Rea: a breach of a confidence, the same type of confidence the church clung to as one of the reasons why no one had ever revealed Ken's promise to try and kill himself after Verdugo Hills. Judy Gabriel recalled Maria Nally as almost majestic, answering each question in her clear but broken English, struggling with some questions because she did not understand, but always honest.

Maria Nally was so compelling a witness that Cooksey had already decided to take a very hands-off approach with her. What he did manage to do was establish that an ongoing dialogue occurred in the last weeks of Ken's life between the Nallys and several doctors and that Maria Nally did not want to see Ken hospitalized. Walter Nally had spoken with Hall and Parker after Verdugo Hills. Walter explained to Maria that Hall was considering hospitalizing Ken. Maria recalled, "I said no. That's a crazy hospital. He's not crazy."

After almost two weeks of trial the parties confronted an issue that plagued Grace Church from the beginning and now had to be addressed: Richard Thomson's counseling tape. The court of appeals had fixed on the tape as the source of the outrageous conduct claim, and that claim alone had kept the *Nally* suit alive when it seemed destined to die four years earlier. Thomson was up next and the tape offered Barker a chance to play Thomson's own words to the jury, that suicide "is just another way God brings an errant believer home," and then argue that he and Grace encouraged Ken to kill himself.

In a hearing that took up most of the afternoon on May 2, 1985, Kalin listened intently to both sides and heard Thomson's testimony on how and when the tape was made. He ruled the tape was inadmissible, even as evidence of the church's doctrine on suicide. Barker could ask Thomson about suicide, but he was not going to be allowed to use a tape made eighteen months after Ken's death, that he could never have heard, even if that doctrine was taught by Grace and it might reflect Grace Church's biblical counseling approach. The tape was not relevant because its contents did not reflect a one-on-one discussion between Ken and Thomson. To admit it would be to put the church's beliefs on trial without addressing whether the church was negligent or acted outrageously. The tape was an expression of belief, not an action relevant to the case. Kalin believed the case was not about religion, it was about counseling. Although Barker may have lost the evidentiary issue, he had to at least be happy with Kalin's mindset. Barker had argued for years the case was not about religion and it seemed the trial judge now agreed.

––––––

The tape was gone, but its maker remained, and on Monday morning, May 5, the third full week of trial, Barker went back to work. Juan Barker recalled that Barker only went after two people during the course of the trial; Duane Rea was one, Thomson was the other. His testimony actually started the Thursday before, but the evidentiary hearing took up most of the afternoon. Thomson remained on the stand the rest of the day and to a great degree it was the same story as Rea's.

Thomson had been head of counseling at Grace from 1978 to 1980. He believed the Bible was the best book for understanding man as created by God. Although he had no formal counseling education, he majored in English Bible at Talbot Theological Seminary.

Thomson indicated that the Grace counseling ministry had not only been open to everyone, but treated all kinds of emotional problems, from severe depression, alcoholism, and sexual problems to phobias and schizophrenia. Sin lay at the root of these problems and each had a corresponding biblical answer. Thomson had suffered from deep depression at one point in his life and had apparently found the answer to his problems there (in the Bible).

Before Thomson's testimony resumed on May 6, counsel were back in chambers debating the admissibility of Thomson's book, *Principles of Biblical Counseling*. Ericsson contended the book was teachings, beliefs, and that all that was relevant was what the defendants actually told Ken. Barker wanted it in as evidence that the pastors preached or advocated that suicide was an alternative that would not threaten a believer's salvation, proof of the outrageous conduct the court of appeals had identified.

If Ericsson had withdrawn into the shadows during trial after his cross of Long, he was beginning to find his stride in chambers before Kalin. Ericsson insisted that not only was Grace on trial, but that all church counseling was threatened. Churches all over America and in foreign countries watched these proceedings, anxiously awaiting the outcome. Kalin struggled to understand Ericsson's position. The judge understood belief, but questioned when belief became action. To teach psychiatry is bad is belief, to actively discourage psychiatry crossed the line into action. Ericsson was adamant that the two could not be distinguished. Religious belief by its nature required that conduct follow belief. To condemn the conduct was to judge the belief and under the First Amendment the courts could not do that. Kalin allowed Thomson's book into evidence, but Ericsson's point began to trouble him. Particularly his concern that legal liability might chill pastoral counseling and prevent people from receiving help who were badly in need.

Thomson's testimony served to emphasize Ericsson's concerns because Thomson was even more dogmatic than Rea. Barker questioned him by direct references to pages in his book wherein Thomson answered counseling questions by direct reference to the Bible. In front of a jury made up predominately of nonbelievers, Thomson's religious beliefs could easily begin to sound ridiculous in the face of a claim that he and his colleagues had negligently caused a man's death. The jury's perception of Thomson stood to decline even further, based on perceptions of Ken Nally. Ken was a twenty-four-year-old adult when he committed suicide, yet by the midpoint of the trial, even Judge Kalin had begun to refer to him as "the boy."

Thomson did not help himself by arguing with Barker over issues that most people involved in the case had already resolved. Thomson refused to admit that he had any type of secular legal duty. Thomson insisted his obligations and any standards he had were between him and God. Finally Kalin told Barker to move on, the jury could make its own call on the issue.

Thomson insisted he had not had a close relationship with Ken and that his actual input had been peripheral to that of Rea and Cory. Barker did finally get him to admit that Grace Church believes that "once saved, always saved," and that he had told Ken Nally that. He also admitted that in the sessions he had with Ken that suicide had actually been discussed. In most respects Thomson's testimony mirrored Rea's both in content and duration. Like Rea, he was on the stand for the better part of two days. Like Rea, he argued that Ken got good advice but he refused to accept it. Church pastors had encouraged Ken to seek other help in 1979 and even Thomson thought going to Mohline was a good idea. He admitted that in the only discussions he had with Walter Nally prior to Ken's suicide, he had expressed encouragement in Ken's condition. Thomson's testimony ended without Barker ever being allowed to use the counseling tapes. It had been a long two days.

What followed was more medical testimony. Barker called Dr. John Parker, a medical doctor who saw Ken a week before he died. Ken came to Parker as a referral from Pat MacArthur, John's wife. Parker thought Ken was emotionally in trouble and recommended hospitalization. He testified that in conversations with Walter Nally that the father was receptive to the idea. Parker conceded, however, he knew nothing of Ken's promise to try again and that such information would have been important to know at the time.

On cross-examination Cooksey emphasized Parker's recommendation of hospitalization and the fact that despite Walter Nally's apparent willingness to do so, it did not occur.

What was beginning to develop was that the last month of Ken's life had been a whirlwind of medical care; many people saw Ken, some did not communicate with one another, and despite some real concerns for Ken's continued safety, he never returned to a hospital after leaving on March 16, 1979. Each side had its own perspective on this situation. Barker argued the medical attention had been too little, too late. He tried to place the blame on Grace Church, focusing on the fact that only Grace's pastors and Ken knew that he had promised to try to kill himself again. Cooksey tried to paint a picture of everyone earnestly trying to help a man and his family, and they both refused to take advice. Any confusion was not the church's fault.

Thomson and Grace Church refused to articulate a standard of care. Barker would establish one without them. One of the experts who answered his mass mailing was Bill Adams, a psychiatrist and Methodist minister. Adams actually knew MacArthur and Grace Church. He expressed a deep respect for MacArthur's father. Part of his professional work involved lecturing pastoral counselors. He heard Thomson testify, read his deposition and his counseling book.

In Adams's opinion Grace Church violated no standards because it had none to violate. As far as the standards that apply to all counselors, Thomson had wholly failed to adequately investigate Ken's suicide and had completely failed to meet the standards set for anyone that counsels suicidal people, religious or otherwise.

According to Adams, Grace Church needed to be able to integrate its approach with secular psychiatrists, and it did not. Adams posed a difficult problem for the defense. He not only purported to respect the church and its ministers but testified he would be "privileged" to be a member. His attack was against its counseling ministry. Cooksey did the best he could, but Adams proved tough. Even under a strong cross-examination Adams refused to bend.

Ken's resistance should have been handled not by pushing him away, but by finding the means to treat him. That is what counselors did, in Adams's opinion. The confusion that existed in Ken's care toward the end of his life, and by now had to be apparent to the jury, Adams blamed on Grace Church and its staff, saying, "it was handled in a very sloppy manner." Adams did admit what Ericsson had claimed, that separating psychology from spirituality was impossible. In the end the impression Adams left with the jury was one of Grace and Thomson wholly failing Ken.

Q. [By Cooksey] Doctor, from everything you have read about this case, it's fairly obvious, isn't it, that everyone was trying to help this boy?

A. I would not agree with that at all.

Q. You don't think Pastor Thomson was sincere in his efforts to help this boy?

A. I think he was sincere, but so was Hitler. It's not a commitment to helping. He should have qualified himself. What he did fed that young man's depression. It set impossible standards for him. He [Thomson] was not only depressive, he had an intractable self-defeating style. In setting high standards, he only fed his sickness. That type of counseling would drive that young man to suicide.

Adams even disputed whether Thomson was doing biblical counseling. "Lifting a verse out of context and saying this is an answer, I would not call that Bible counseling."

Q. [Cooksey] In other words, doctor, you don't agree with Rich Thomson's interpretation of the Bible; is that right?

A. Probably I agree with a lot of it, but not when he uses it to hide behind to be an authority and treat a young man that is desperate for help and can't even integrate what he is saying. All he can do is use it to defeat himself over and over again. The kid was constantly being defeated by these high standards.

For the defense the best part of Adams's testimony was when he left the stand. His testimony had not been a high point for Grace and its ministers.

CHAPTER 8

Over the Wall

In the final week of trial the jury heard from several more experts and each echoed Adams, and although they were both damaging or helpful, depending on which side one was on, none hurt as badly as Adams had except to the degree they added to the weight of what Adams had already said. Walter Nally Jr. testified about life at home after Ken converted and the attempts to help Ken in the last days of his life. He affirmed that his parents had a close relationship and admitted that they had some problems. As he had with Maria, Cooksey steered clear of Walter Jr., a victim whose testimony could not help the church and might hurt it if he appeared sympathetic to the jury. Even Lynn Cory, the youngest of the individual defendants, offered little else to add to the story already told. Cory readily admitted that Ken's situation in 1976 had reached a point where he needed help beyond what Cory could provide. That was when he suggested Ken seek out counselors at Grace. Cory also admitted he had been present when Ken told John MacArthur that he would try again to commit suicide.

Barker painted a picture of mass confusion with regard to Ken's care. A failure to address severe problems that went back in time years, not months before Ken's death. Referrals that came too late and the disclosure of crucial information that never came at all. Painting from the same pallet, Cooksey portrayed a young man unable to take advice, who received secular, religious, and family counseling, yet rejected it all. A family unable to accept that its son needed help, help for problems that grew out of the family itself and began long before Ken found Grace Church.

As the trial progressed the issues surrounding mental health that dominated professional discourse for twenty years came to the forefront: Is counseling spiritual or emotional? Where does spiritual counseling fit in the realm of secular mental health? What is the best approach to take? What standards govern or should govern the clergy in their counseling role? Kalin had refused to allow evidence of a standard for "pastoral" or clergy counselors, but had been willing to admit standards that all counselors, irrespective of background, should have to follow. Is pastoral counseling religious belief, or is it action? Can the two be distinguished? Barker said yes; Ericsson and Cooksey pounded away at Kalin during in-chamber hearings that they could not be separated.

Kalin seemed to be willing to accept broad standards almost in an affirmation of Barker's belief that the case "was not about religion." What those standards would be remained unclear, but with the plaintiffs' case drawing to a close and the defense case slated for only four or five days, Kalin's task of defining standards and submitting those standards to the jury in the form of instructions loomed just over the horizon. Kalin knew he was crossing unplowed ground and told the lawyers, "We are in a new and different area, and there are no rules, and we are making it up as we go along and that's the problem."

On Thursday, May 9, 1985, the moment many individuals had waited for finally came: John MacArthur took the stand, followed by Walter Nally. For MacArthur the worst part of the entire eight years of the lawsuit came with the realization that the twelve strangers sitting on the jury would judge him and yet knew nothing about him, his beliefs, his work, or his life, other than what they had been told in the last three weeks. Like the trial itself, it was something that had to be done and MacArthur handled it like a man accustomed to the limelight, adept at speaking and in command of his own thoughts and beliefs. But Barker did not make it easy. He depicted MacArthur as a man in charge of a large organization that had gotten terribly out of control.

Preferring to be called "Mr." as opposed to Pastor, MacArthur admitted that Ken had promised "to try again" and that he had not shared that information with anyone. MacArthur had concluded on his own in the week Ken stayed at his home that Ken was deeply depressed and encouraged him to seek psychiatric help. He denied that there was any theological prohibition against Ken seeking psychiatric or psychological help. He claimed that a Christian background, at least in the short term, was not essential; Ken needed help. MacArthur believed the Nally home was the worst place for Ken and that Ken had come to the MacArthurs' house because he did not want to go home. MacArthur claimed that "common sense" said do not let Ken out of your sight and he was never alone the entire week. Barker pressed MacArthur, and both Cooksey and Ericsson became upset with the line of questioning. At a side bar (at the judge's bench out of the jury's hearing) Ericsson called the entire examination the epitome of "the Monkey Trial."

On the counseling issue MacArthur was a bit more evasive. As to the formality of the program, the extent to which it represented it could handle any problem, and the policy of referring extreme cases, his testimony was not nearly as unequivocal as Rea's and Thomson's. He initially denied knowing of any other suicide cases at Grace Church but qualified that statement, saying that there are no official records kept of such things and that he may have heard of some. MacArthur had watched everyone else testify and observed the jury. Perhaps his demeanor in some ways was his recognition that the jurors were strangers and that the extreme nature of fundamentalist dogma might or had alienated them. But there is no reason to believe he was ever untruthful. There were only a few occasions when Barker used MacArthur's deposition testimony to point out any inconsistency in his trial testimony, leading one to assume his posture at trial was consistent with his position all along.

MacArthur claimed his wife, Patty, actually called the Nallys and told them to watch Ken and his medication for fear Ken would try again. Walter later denied any call. In general, MacArthur came across far less dogmatic than Rea or Thomson. He clearly claimed to have had very little personal contact with Ken until the week Ken came to his home. He admitted Ken's situation was not kept under control, but refused to accept the blame for his death. As Barker's examination came to a close he pressed MacArthur on the issue of the church's finances, implying that it was successful. He then asked MacArthur if his flock had gotten out of hand. MacArthur responded:

> No. Not at all. You mentioned earlier that the church is successful, that might be your evaluation. From my evaluation we're far from being successful in the sense we live in a society that has not yet come to understand the things we believe to be living changes. We live in a valley where many problems are unresolved. If there are two million in our vicinity, and two thousand come to church, that means a staggering number of people who are left unaffected.

In one answer, probably without knowing it, MacArthur summed up the entire case: "So many unaffected." Not just in his area, but across America. A secular America was now ready to entertain notions of religious liability and to question the extent of the First Amendment protections afforded religion. Whether its judges agreed or this jury represented that portion of America was still unclear. But it was clear that in this part of America people were willing to listen to such ideas.

Cooksey and Ericsson used cross-examination to personalize both MacArthur and the church. In recognition that Grace Church's doctrines were actually on trial, at least for the present, the lawyers allowed MacArthur to explained the church's origins, its theory on counseling, and explained that biblical scripture limited how much time you spend on someone who refused to respond to "admonishment." Pastoral counseling was not something someone could be licensed to do, one had to be gifted to do it. MacArthur and his staff not only had that gift, but MacArthur routinely met with pastors and ministers from over fifty denominations to discuss such issues, proof not only of his qualifications, but of the breadth of pastoral counseling in general.

Walter Nally took the stand and told the story of his family's odyssey that brought them to this point. Ken had been raised Catholic, had always attended Catholic school. For Walter, Ken's conversion was a rejection of his heritage. His was the story of a family that like most families had its problems, but remained close.

He admitted that as Ken moved away to college he became more distant emotionally as well. The realization that Ken changed came at a father and son dinner in 1973 after Ken's conversion but before he joined Grace Church. As the group began to pray Walter started to cross himself, and Ken said, "don't."

Nally and his family knew nothing of Ken's suicidal past until after his death. Every indication from the church and its pastors was that "Ken would be fine." Ken even said he would be fine. Walter Nally admitted speaking with Parker, and acknowledged Parker's recommendation to hospitalize Ken, a recommendation that did not seem consistent with what the church was saying and Ken's own representations. His testimony stopped briefly as the lawyers argued the admissibility of the statement Ken made about his arm being punishment from God. It may have gone to Ken's state of mind at the time, but there was no evidence that the church had told him that. Kalin excluded the statement.

The most effective part of Walter Nally's testimony came in Barker's depiction of what the Nallys knew at the precise time when they had to decide on whether to involuntarily admit Ken to a hospital. Ed Barker drew a chart. On one side he put all the information in favor of involuntary hospitalization, on the other side, he put the information that weighed against involuntary hospitalization.

Against Hospitalization
    Walter's personal observations of Ken
    The representations of Cory, Thomson, and MacArthur
    Ken's own statements
    Walter's trust of Ken and Ken's truthfulness

In Favor of Hospitalization
    Nothing.

"I didn't have it," Nally said. He testified that had he known of Ken's prior attempts, or his promise in the hospital made to the church pastors to try again, that alone would have swayed him to hospitalize Ken, even against his will.

On cross-examination Cooksey drove home his contributory negligence theme. Walter Nally and his family knew Ken was troubled, they had the ability in the end to have altered the course of events, and did not. He also went into Nally's personal life, his unemployment, and the fact that problems within the family were at the source of Ken's troubles. Maria Nally saw it in February 1979 when she took Ken to Milestone, the source of the Elavil he used to try to kill himself. She took him to her acupuncturist, Dr. Oda. Even Evelyn had told Walter Nally that Ken was at risk. Parker called to warn him that Ken was a suicide risk. How much information did Nally need? Nally and Cooksey battled it out for several hours on the issue of whether the family knew all it needed to know and just failed to act. Nally steadfastly denied it. Cooksey sat down having at least raised the possibility.

The plaintiff's case ended with a flurry. Barker called two witnesses who testified to other suicides among members of Grace Church, contrary to MacArthur's initial statements. Two more experts testified. One, Dr. Stephen Wilson, added support to Bill Adams's testimony. He claimed that Grace had gone beyond not helping Ken, it had made his situation worse. Barker put Katie Thayer on the stand, who testified to specific conversations between her and Ken on the weekend Ken died, where he talked of going into the woods and killing himself with a shotgun. They even went to the mall together, the trip that Ken apparently used to buy shotgun shells. In a bombshell of her own, she claimed that Walter Nally admitted to her that he knew Ken was suicidal and refused to hospitalize him. That statement forced Barker to have Walter deny the allegation.

The plaintiffs' case ended with a videotape of the Nally family. The jury watched in the darkness as images of twelve-year-old Ken and his younger brother raced across the screen playing football with their dad. They saw pictures of an eighteen year Ken, laughing with his father and brother outside their family home. They saw a family that looked like any family in America. The plaintiff rested, after twenty witnesses and almost four weeks of testimony. The defense case was due up next, but before that Ericsson and

Cooksey took one last shot at ending the suit and their motion to dismiss would provide the next bizarre twist in a case that had redefined the unusual.

———

The court had hinted at a possible defense motion to dismiss on Monday, May 13. Such motions are common, but they are seldom granted. A motion to dismiss after the plaintiff's case argues that based on everything the plaintiff has put into evidence it still cannot win. Normally they are denied because having gone this far, most judges let the case run its course. However, this case was different. Two weeks before, Kalin had told both sides the case was not about religion, it was about a general set of standards that anyone counseling suicidal people should have to adhere to. As Barker fired away making points with the jury, he may have been losing the judge. Ericsson had never let up. Every in-chambers session or evidentiary hearing brought the same argument: Under the First Amendment, you cannot do what the plaintiff is asking the court to do, establish guidelines by which to judge Grace's conduct.

On Monday, May 13, Ericsson gave Kalin a 700-page document asking him to read ten cases of the material. He also gave him a 300-page brief the Christian Legal Society had prepared. By Wednesday Kalin had read every page. If Barker let his guard down at any stage of the trial it was in the area of constitutional law. As a solo practitioner Barker's nights were spent preparing for the next day. But he had received copies of what Ericsson submitted to Kalin, and if Barker was delinquent at any stage of the case, it was in not adequately responding to Ericsson's legal arguments. As Kalin ingested all of the material Ericsson gave him, he had nothing in opposition to review.

On May 15, before a courtroom packed with reporters out of the jury's presence, Ericsson argued a two-hour motion to dismiss. In a well-constructed and -delivered presentation he reiterated the position Grace Church had maintained throughout the four-week trial and over the course of the last five years. Regardless of what anyone thought about the competence of Grace Church and its pastors, the First Amendment precluded the court from establishing any guidelines for judging its biblical counseling practices, either as to the way the church counseled or how it trained its counselors. At the core of pastoral counseling lay religious belief and the belief could not be separated from the action. Freedom to believe includes the freedom to express, communicate, and disseminate that belief. To apply judicially created standards to Grace Church's counseling program was to put its beliefs on trial in violation of the Constitution.

Ericsson cited the judicially created tests for free exercise and establishment set forth in *Cantwell, Ballard, Everson, Lemon,* and the well-established body of law that had developed in the previous forty-five years. The plaintiffs' case required the court to question belief, establish standards, and become excessively involved in church matters without a compelling state interest. Therefore, counts 1 and 2, alleging negligence and clergy malpractice, had to be dismissed. As far as the allegation of outrageous conduct was concerned, there was simply no evidence to support that count, and it too needed to be dismissed.

Barker's response also followed his position from the inception of the case: This is not about religion. More important, he argued that the church had not raised the very defense Ericsson was urging. They did not say, this is my belief, this is why I did it, end of story. To the contrary, argued Barker, they claimed "we did refer, we did not necessarily have a prohibition against psychologists and psychiatrists." Barker pointed to MacArthur's testimony and asserted that when asked directly if secular professionals were absolutely precluded under church doctrine and theology, MacArthur said "no." Thus the case is about the accountability of a professional who undertook a particular job, in this case the job of counseling the severely mentally depressed person. It wasn't eight professionals who saw Ken, Barker argued, it was twelve, the four pastors of Grace were professionals who represented they could competently handle the full spectrum of mental and emotional problems and then did not do so in a competent manner. The First Amendment should not protect that kind of conduct.

After Ericsson briefly responded to Barker's remarks, the court asked a question of both sides, but clearly directed it toward the plaintiffs. The appellate court raised two issues with regard to count 3, intentional infliction of emotional distress or outrageous conduct. One was the counseling tape made by Thomson, the second was the statement made by Ken about his lifeless arm being punishment from God. The court excluded the tape and the statement. "What is your case at this point based upon the evidence before the court?" Kalin asked Barker.

Barker had to admit it was much weaker, but would not concede it was destroyed. He argued expert testimony, particulary Bill Adams's, had shown that the counseling had actually made Ken worse by establishing standards he could not meet. David Cooksey could sense where the court was going and argued flatly, "It's gone." There is no evidence to support the outrageous conduct claim. With that the court adjourned.

Barker seemed confident the case would go forward. These motions are a matter of routine. The defense had only four or five days of testimony and it simply made good sense to let the trial finish. The plaintiff had put sufficient evidence to allow a jury to decide the case. The question now was, did Judge Kalin agree?

Kalin wasted no time in ruling on the motion. The next day, in a calm, deliberate voice he welcomed the parties back into court and out of the jury's presence he ruled. In less than fifteen minutes he brought an end to five years of litigation, including four intense weeks of trial testimony.

After restating the elements of the Nallys' claims, Kalin traced the origins of pastoral counseling back to biblical times, long preceding any modern concepts of psychology and psychiatry. He alluded to the California Business and Professional Code provisions that regulated all professions, which specifically excluded the clergy, religion, treatment by prayer, and any clergy figure in any denomination when performing counseling services as a part of their pastoral duties. Sitting in the courtroom, both sides could see what was coming. There were no laws in any state regulating pastoral counseling and no standards had been provided governing pastoral counseling. Thus, Kalin said, "if there is to be any standards and resulting duties in this field, they must be judicially imposed and inserted into the existing vacuum." Kalin would not do that.

He retraced the development of religious freedom dating back to Moses, followed it to the shores of America, and then repeated the maxim that the founding fathers intended the wall between church and state "to remain high and impregnable to prevent history of both the abuse of the state by the church and abuse of the church by the state." To interfere in church counseling as the Nallys were demanding would require the courts to set standards of competence, training, areas appropriate for counsel, distinguish between moral and mental problems, and "monitor counseling for all time to come." It was not for the court or any court to question the beliefs of Grace Church, and "There is no compelling state interest to climb the wall of separation of church and state and plunge into the pit on the other side which certainly has no bottom." The court held there was no legally recognizable duty to investigate Ken's suicidal tendencies, to inform the family or other professionals, to refer Ken to secular professionals, to train counselors to secular standards, or to make counselors available to Ken. If such a duty did exist, the Nallys failed to show the church or its pastors breached them as a matter of law. Thus counts 1 and 2 were dismissed. As to count 3, the court held that the Nallys had presented no evidence to support the claim of outrageous conduct or to show that any conduct of the defendants proximately caused Ken's death, and it too was dismissed. On the very brink of storming the cathedral walls, Ed Barker and the Nallys were denied once again. In Kalin's words, "That's the price we pay for religious freedom."

CHAPTER 9

Far from Over

"Used and frustrated": the words of several jurors describing their feelings upon hearing of Kalin's decision that cut them off at the halfway point. An informal poll of the twelve jurors taken by a reporter from the *New York Times* revealed a 10–2 split in favor of the Nallys. Hardly a complete verdict, it demonstrated the degree to which the jurors felt Baker had presented a valid case. The defendants later reasoned that the poll and jury sentiments were understandable given the time they invested and the fact that they heard only one part of the case. True in part, but all four individual defendants testified, which was at least part of the defense case, and some had made an indelible impression on the jury.

The jurors were open about their feelings. Some wanted to picket the courthouse in protest, but most were a little more subdued. "A waste of time and money," said one. Audrey Anderson, an alternate, felt the Nallys definitely "had a case." Scott Schreiner of Burbank echoed Anderson, and conceded, "I felt Barker and the Nallys had a strong case, I wish I could have been allowed to decide." Juror Carrie Porragus of Tujunga also claimed to be leaning toward the plaintiffs. Cheri Ashcroft left the courtroom in tears, saying, "I felt very strongly the plaintiffs should have won. I really believe the counselors were practicing psychiatry without a license. I don't care what their religion is. But they said they could treat even schizophrenia and I'd say that is practicing without a license." Francis Lewis of Glendale agreed, "They are not capable of helping what is a medical problem."

Bob Reece, who lost his job because of jury service, and Lavon Lommen were the only two that leaned toward the church. Reece did so on the issues of religious freedom, but was ready to find against at least one of the individual defendants as being "narrow minded." It was clear that most of the jurors failed to understand why Kalin dismissed the case. Angela Wentrup agreed that the majority of her fellow jurors leaned toward the plaintiff, including herself. She was Catholic and admitted that Grace's attitude toward Catholicism "offended her."

The reaction of the parties was again predictable. The Nallys were crushed. Ed Barker "was surprised, shocked, annoyed and upset." In his opinion Kalin's ruling "was wrong, no doubt about it." One reporter asked Walter Nally if this (the suit) was something that was now better left alone. Walter responded by asking if she had children. "Children are not easy to walk away from," he said. When asked what he would do next, Walter said, "I have been tenacious about this, haven't I? I am not the one to give up easy— and that goes for my family." The Nallys would not quit here. Barker made it clear they would file a motion for a new trial, which he expected would be denied, and then appeal to the California Court of Appeals.

The defendants were as overjoyed as the Nallys were distraught. "What the Judge did took guts," said Cooksey. "But I believe it was the right decision." In a press conference the following day, Ericsson and MacArthur fielded questions. "What does this mean for clergy counselors? Why did the jury lean toward the plaintiff? Will you change your counseling practices?" Both men felt the case removed a cloud that hung over clergymen for five years. Although it cleared the way for clergy to counsel as they saw fit, Ericsson still believed it might have a chilling effect on some. You could still get sued, even if this case meant you would win. MacArthur felt vindicated, as did his congregation. John's secretary, Pat Rotisky, remembered feeling like the entire church and its members had been exonerated.

The Sunday following the verdict MacArthur devoted a portion of his sermon to explain the outcome and had Ericsson speak as to the specifics of the case. Ericsson accepted MacArthur's praise for his work but singled out David Cooksey's efforts. He "stood upon David's shoulders" in making the motion to dismiss. A good analogy. Cooksey had tried a good case even if the jury was solidly in

Barker's corner at the midpoint. It was a case Ericsson could never have tried alone. He knew the law but not the courtroom. Cooksey had to be good because Barker had gotten everything out of the case he could and used to his advantage all of the cultural and societal factors that tainted fundamentalism in the minds of many Americans.

Ericsson actually believed, or at least said he believed, that this case would foreclose any future cases like it. Even though it did not bind other jurisdictions, it was now there to be cited if such an instance arose again. In a legal sense he might have been right. As judicial precedent, *Nally* now served as a beacon for those seeking to protect the clergy from counseling malpractice. However, Ericsson had been adamant during his motion to dismiss that courts should do more than blindly follow the law. He insisted that a nation guided by the letter of the law alone was as bad as one with no law at all. Courts in America change or affirm social policy. In a sense they mirror the beliefs, fears, aspirations, and goals of society as a whole. Despite his professed acceptance of new theories of recovery, Kalin had been unwilling to venture where the jury seemed anxious to go. However, that did not mean that a different judge in a future case might not be willing to do so. What is certain is that the decision did not end the debate. It continued to rage. Unlike what happened in 1981 when Judge Murphy dismissed the case, the hiatus between dismissal and appellate decision would be filled with media coverage, social discussion, new litigation, and political maneuvering on the issues raised by the trial.

As had been the case throughout, the issues continued to play out in the court of public opinion. Despite all of the disagreement, some of it heated, virtually every participant agreed that the intense local, national, and even international media coverage had been fair, the notable exceptions being the principals, Walter Nally and John MacArthur.

Nally felt the church's "clout" played a part. True, there was a sizable fundamentalist media in California and MacArthur had a weekly radio show. But there is no indication that the press coverage had any impact on the outcome. If anything, the religious print media took the lead in much of the debate. MacArthur's criticism found a more specific target. In his opinion, the *Daily News*, San Fernando Valley's local paper, had been prejudiced against Grace Church. Judy Gabriel, the lead reporter on the story, disagreed. There was no need to alter the story for one side or the other. The case had everything any reporter could ever want in a story. "All I had to do was lay it out just as it unfolded." Fortunately for her and other members of the media, the story continued to unfold.

The May 20, 1985, editions of both *Newsweek* and *People* magazine picked up the case without knowing when the stories went out that Kalin had dismissed the suit. Each periodical focused on different aspects, but both came back to the issue of accountability. Kalin had refused to allow evidence of standards set by the American Association of Pastoral Counselors, finding the AAPC to be too "fringe" a group to set guidelines for all pastors. However, its president, James Ewing, echoed what many people believed, "there were a lot of pastors not trained to handle their parishioners' psychotherapy."

Editorials appearing in local papers like the *Los Angeles Times* and the *Los Angeles Examiner* were mixed. Although they conceded the case may have been consistent with constitutional principles, some questioned if Kalin ended it too quickly, leaving crucial questions unanswered. Others pointed to the need for persons using clergy counselors to be their own guide as to the usefulness and competency of the help. Everyone seemed to agree that victory notwithstanding, the case awakened the pastoral community to the legitimate need for referral of severe cases.

On July 5, 1985, Kalin cleared the way for the Nallys' appeal by denying Barker's motion for a new trial. Barker estimated it would take two years before an appellate court rendered a decision. In a short opinion Kalin reiterated his findings, stressing the fact that although Grace Church had the financial wherewithal to fight such a suit, to allow these suits would potentially crush smaller churches. That issue aside, legal, psychological, and clerical journals took up the debate.

Newton Maloney, Ph.D., a professor at Fuller Graduate School of Psychology, told the *Psychologist*, California's state journal of psychology, that Kalin may have been "correct philosophically, but practically he was wrong." Some minimal standards for everyone doing mental health counseling of severely depressed or suicidal patients needs to exist. But Maloney believed Grace had shown a "minimal standard of care."

As the dust cleared from the case and the parties went back to the business of living and waiting, the real breadth and depth of the affect on America became clearer. An interview appeared in the winter 1985 edition of *Leadership*. Actually it was more of a roundtable discussion among Sam Ericsson and three ministers, including John MacArthur, discussing their experiences as defendants in civil lawsuits involving their ministries. Charles McIlhenney was pastor of First Orthodox Presbyterian Church in San Francisco. He had been sued in 1978 for firing a homosexual organist, who after being discovered, refused to "change his lifestyle." The case was dismissed in 1980. Joining the group was John Mellish of the Margate, Florida, Church of the Nazarene. Mellish was free on bond afer refusing to testify in a child abuse case against a parishioner. The discussion addressed things churches could do to prevent being sued, like requiring all employees to be members and setting out standards for membership clearly. Ericsson indicated that the number of malpractice claims against clergy had grown to 2,500, in itself proof that the problem continued to grow rather than subside.

Even Ed Barker became active in the debate. His article in the July 1986 issue of *Trial*, a national legal periodical, dissected the 1985 trial and addressed specific issues of causation, standards, and other legal matters, pertinent not only to his case but to any case. His conclusion: "In our society, accountability for social injustice is important. Church leaders, at least where their religious beliefs are not challenged, should be as accountable for their actions as other professionals."

Law review articles, scarce prior to trial, now appeared, addressing many of the unanswered questions. An article in the *Michigan Law Review* addressed the issue of intentional infliction of emotional distress. It argued that a blanket acceptance or rejection of the "free exercise of religion" defense used in *Nally* would be inappropriate. Both sides have compelling interests at stake where intentional conduct in a counseling setting results in injury or death. The article advocated a case-by-case balancing test, with the facts of each case being the deciding factor. The author, Lee W. Brooks, also argued that where malice is present, that is, an intentional effort to harm, such conduct nullifies the "free exercise" defense without really hurting the overall sanctity of the First Amendment. Kalin's decision had not foreclosed malpractice, it had created the starting point for defining the theory. One thing was certain, as Ira Rifkin, the local reporter for the religion section of the *Daily News* pointed out, "the wounds run deep." Despite efforts to understand where the law was and what society needed and wanted, the Nallys and Grace Church remained unreconciled.

The debate went beyond mere intellectual discourse. Other litigants across America, either in reaction to *Nally* or fueled by the same sense that religion should be accountable, began to sue churches and ministers. All met the same fate as the Nallys, but it was their efforts and the opinions of the courts, that although struck down relief in that particular instance, seemed to leave open the door for liability under different facts.

A Missouri couple sued their minister for divulging personal information communicated during counseling sessions. An Alabama woman sued her minister for the suicide death of her husband. The couple sought counseling for marital problems and in the course thereof the pastor and woman became intimately involved. She filed for divorce from her husband who then killed himself. Both the Missouri and Alabama State Supreme Courts refused to recognize "clergy malpractice" per se, as a new and viable cause of action.

The same result occurred in Ohio where a man sued his minister for having a sexual relationship with his wife that grew out of a counseling session. The Ohio court dodged all the constitutional issues by stating that clergy malpractice was not a viable cause of action based "on the facts before it." The court was, however, clear that its holding applied to the facts of that case only. In Colorado a couple sued its Catholic priest for sexual misconduct between the priest and the wife. The Colorado Supreme Court admitted that in all instances, the First Amendment does not protect the clergy.

It allowed the wife's claim for breach of a fiduciary duty, but then held the church not responsible because the priest's acts were committed outside the scope of his role as a priest. The court did, however, refuse to recognize clergy malpractice as a new legal theory.

Perhaps the most revealing statements as to the position of church and state in America came from the Washington State Supreme Court. In refusing to allow a husband to recover for a minister's sexual liaison with his wife during a counseling relationship, the court cautioned: "It is conceivable that a [pastoral or clergy] malpractice action would be appropriate where a counselor fails to conform to an appropriate standard of care, injures the patient/spouse, which in turn results in loss of consortium damages." No one wanted to be the first, but everyone seemed to recognize that liability was out there.

Despite the sexual nature of these 1980s cases and the fact that none mirrored the facts in *Nally*, the message that the church walls were being stormed was not lost on American clergymen. At least two monographs appeared in 1986 specifically addressing the problems and pitfalls of pastoral counseling. Neither book could assure pastors where the liability issue was headed.

In January 1987, an article appeared in the *Chronicle-Telegram* that had been picked up from a publication of the "World Wide Church of God" in Pasadena, California. In it Reverand William Seith of Goodyear Heights Ministerial Association confessed, "everyone is running scared." A seminar sponsored by the association ministers from the Akron, Ohio, area confirmed what many already believed: Despite the outcome in *Nally*, the malpractice issue among pastoral counselors was becoming a major concern.

One month later, Republican assemblywoman Marian LaFollette, from Northridge, California, sponsored a bill in the California legislature to preclude punitive damage lawsuits against churches. Although the bill would not stop the Nallys' action, it came out of the same district where Grace Church was located. The bill originated from Gary Forsch, a Sun Valley Republican activist, who although not a member of Grace, said the lawsuit did motivate his actions. The same bill failed in 1986 when the California Trial Lawyers Association and the American Civil Liberties

Union opposed it. Trial lawyers opposed anything limiting access to courts as "anti consumer." The ACLU argued such a bill served to use government to protect religion and was unconstitutional. Sam Ericsson was ready to testify. The *Nally* appeal would be heard in the next few months and he feared a reversal would require "corrective legislation." Grace had not pushed this bill, but had openly advocated the 1986 legislation. Supporters of the bill contended that as of 1987 over 7,000 clergy malpractice suits were pending across America. The number had almost tripled since Ericsson's interview in 1985. Contrary to Ericsson's belief, Kalin's decision had hardly closed the issue of clergy liability and as everyone was about to discover, *Nally* was far from over.

<hr>

The legal, social, political, and cultural debate that *Nally* had become gathered strength as it swept toward its rendezvous with the California Second Circuit Court of Appeals. Four years before the first division of the same circuit breathed life into the otherwise dead lawsuit. Ed Barker and the Nallys hoped that the seventh division would do so again. The Nallys would not have the duo of Dalsimer and Gutierrez, the narrow majority that overturned Judge Murphy. Also absent would be Judge Hanson, the lone dissenter who vehemently claimed the majority had overstepped its bounds. Manning the bench would be Presiding Judge Leon Thompson, and Associate Judges Earl Johnson and John L. Cole. In February 1987, the three-member panel heard oral arguments. Walter, Maria, and Wally, now a twenty-six year-old student at Cal State Northridge, listened from the back of the wood-paneled courtroom as Barker and Ericsson addressed the court. In one sense it seemed like all of the other wood-paneled chambers they had sat in over the last seven years. They hoped the outcome would be different than the last time they sat and listened to oral arguments.

The hearing lasted only forty-five minutes. Barker's theme was as old as the case: The suit was not about challenging religious beliefs. Church counselors should be held just as accountable as their secular counterparts when they counsel mentally or emotionally disturbed individuals. "What happened was incompetence and had nothing to do with religious beliefs." The panel was not so sure, and they questioned whether the courts should probe matters of theology and whether the church would have sought other professional help under different circumstances. Judge Thompson openly questioned Barker, asking, "Aren't you asking us to go in and examine the framework of religious briefs, and aren't we getting into matters where we don't belong?" Barker stood his ground. He admitted that religion had to be discussed at the trial, "but not because it is being questioned or disagreed with. It has to be talked about because you have to understand Ken's feelings about religion to understand what he did. That would be the same if it were a psychiatrist involved and Ken had committed suicide and what they had talked about all along were Ken's religious beliefs."

Ericsson responded for the defendants as he had the last time the case involved the appellate process. His argument was essentially the same one he made to Kalin during the motion to dismiss. "In any church, practices and beliefs are like a fabric; you can't separate them. It's a holistic thing." Ericsson added that "there is no doctrine at Grace Church that says 'thou shalt not refer,' or 'thou shalt not inform.'" He was adamant that "a church cannot entrust to a jury or others to determine what is good or bad counseling [because] a church's counseling procedures flow out of the belief system and doctrines of the church." Cole seemed to concur. At one point he stated that theology is something "the court has no business monkeying around with."

Aside from the court's questioning the potential interference with religion and theology, the hearing was unspectacular. Appellate courts often question areas simply to flesh out the issues to more clearly understand the position of the respective parties. Reading anything from court behavior in such a short time is difficult and seldom helpful. Neither side offered any posthearing speculation on what it thought the panel would decide. Both lawyers filed written briefs with the court and the parties looked for a decision around late June or early July of that year.

When July came the court had not reached a decision. Instead, it made a rather unusual request of both parties: "Come back, we have questions." Neither side knew quite what to think. Although rehearings are not rare, this one seemed strange to both sides because neither had requested a rehearing. Barker remained upbeat. "It means they're taking this very seriously. They want to write a good opinion." Sensing the court might be unsure, Barker emphasized that the First Amendment should not protect pastors whose advice leads to a person's death, "where life is at stake, even the church can't escape liability."

Ericsson echoed Kalin's earlier ruling. Kenneth was an adult who had the right to make his own counseling choices. The First Amendment is absolute for people providing counseling for the church. Ericsson also reiterated several broader issues. This case was unlike any other. The result will have far-reaching implications. "The court is creating new law here."

Then came the questions, hypothetical questions. The court asked both lawyers, but pressed Ericsson in particular, as to the application of the First Amendment in different fact scenarios. Justice Johnson asked Ericsson if the First Amendment would have applied to the Jonestown situation had the religious cult mass suicide incident occurred in California. Ericsson replied, "no." The people were ordered to commit suicide. "Jim Jones obviously did not have the best interest of the people at heart. You can't hide behind the First Amendment if there is malice," said Ericsson. But he repeated that where a religious belief is sincerely held, even if that belief is repugnant to some people, the church is protected. Barker had a different perspective on the Jonestown hypothetical. He felt it was appropriate because it illustrated that a decision about what is protected by the Constitution "can't be made in advance."

The second hearing had been unusual. The questions the court asked seemed to indicate that at least some of the justices were grappling with the First Amendment issues. There was still little indication which way they were leaning, but it seemed clear that whatever decision was being made, it was not coming easily. That alone encouraged Barker and the Nallys. Still, there was nothing to do but wait. They would not have to wait long. On September 16, 1987, the three-member panel issued its decision.

———

Once again the Court voted 2–1 to overturn the trial judge and once again *Nally* was alive. Associate Justice Johnson wrote the majority opinion joined by Presiding Justice Thompson. Justice Cole dissented. The opinion covered eighty-four pages, with the majority ruling comprising all but twelve pages, and it left little room for suspense. The first paragraph destroyed any notion that the court would stumble on First Amendment issues. "In our view this case has little or nothing to say about the liability of clergymen for the negligent performance of their ordinary ministerial duties or even their counseling duties except when they enter into a counseling relationship with suicidal individuals."

The court reversed the trial court on every ground. It reinstated the negligence cause of action, the outrageous conduct claims, and reversed Kalin's evidentiary ruling that excluded the Thomson counseling tape. The majority found that established principles of California tort law imposed a duty of care on those who undertake to counsel mentally disturbed individuals, regardless of whether they are secular or religious counselors. In some cases, counselors are obligated to refer patients to more qualified professionals who possess the power to prevent imminent suicide. A reasonable juror could have found that the counselors at Grace failed to satisfy that duty. "We then hold that the First Amendment does not immunize the Church's counselors from liability for failing to meet that standard."

The majority opinion acknowledged that it did not "write upon a clean slate." A previous court of appeals ruling had already addressed the outrageous conduct claim and held that such a claim was not barred by the First Amendment. California had a legal doctrine known as "law of the case." It held that where a previous appellate court had ruled on a matter necessary to the decision of a case, that matter was conclusively established and determinative of the rights of the parties in any subsequent trial or appeal. The earlier appeals court had decided the outrageous conduct claim could be tried. This court would not address that, except to affirm that the claim should have been allowed to go to the jury and to address the overturning of the evidence that made it possible for Kalin to dismiss that claim.

The majority overturned the negligence ruling, reviving both counts 1 and 2, because in its opinion this was simply "not a religious counselor issue, it was a non-therapist counselor issue." Acknowledging the large and growing body of legal scholarship on the trial and the larger question of pastoral counseling, Johnson and Thompson then changed the focus of the case: "At this stage we are interested in a somewhat broader question—the duty of non-therapist counselors." They defined "nontherapist" as any counselor other than psychiatrists, clinical psychologists, or other categories of psychotherapists who represented they could handle mentally disturbed people. Other than homicide, suicide was the most dangerous result that could flow from mental illness. Unlike other jurisdictions, California had addressed the duty of psychotherapists to suicidal patients. For the majority, logic and policy said it was now time to apply that duty to nontherapists and pastoral counselors just happened to fall within that broad group.

"But what does it take to acquire a duty to attempt to prevent that leap off the cliff?" asked Johnson. Owning the cliff was one way. Property owners could be held responsible if they failed to prevent people from jumping off their building where it had happened before. Citing *Vistica v. Presbyterian Hospital, Meier v. Ross,* and *Bellah v. Greenson*, the court recognized the duty of psychiatrists and hospitals to prevent the suicide of their patients. The court could find no compelling reason why a duty that attached to professionals should not also apply to nonprofessionals who hold themselves out as competent to treat severe mental illness, as Grace had done.

The majority cautioned that this duty did not apply to friends, to "Band-Aid" therapy like hot lines, or to casual advice given by pastors after a service. It did, however, attach to a special relationship, like the formal counseling relationship that Grace Church's counselors admitted they had with Kenneth Nally. Because nontherapists lacked the same training as professionals, their duty was not the same. They had no duty until they became aware someone was suicidal. Then they had a duty to refer that person to a competent professional.

Johnson and Thompson did not invent this argument. They had read the law review articles and journals, some written by the clergy, advocating a duty to refer. The majority held that in light of the extensive expert testimony the duty to refer applied to Grace Church and its pastors. Even more, where the patient, like Kenneth, proved to be resistant, the nontherapist had a duty to warn others who could prevent the imminent suicide. The defendants had argued that the priest-penitent privilege prevented such a disclosure. Even Justice Cole in his dissent argued that the confidentiality privilege between psychiatrist and patient had precluded other California courts from finding such a duty to inform on the part of a professional. The majority, however, argued the privilege problem did not exist because there was no priest-penitent privilege in a pastoral counseling setting, citing the 1965 California case of *Simrin v. Simrin* and *People v. Edwards*, a 1987 California case still on appeal, as legal precedent. The court then concluded there was no confidentiality problem with informing either the family or other more qualified professionals. True, the courts had refused to extend the *Tarasoff* duty to inform a third party that a patient might try to kill that third party to a situation where the patient might try to kill himself. But the majority saw no reason to make such a distinction. The reasoning behind not extending *Tarasoff* was to avoid infringing on a legislatively established confidential relationship. Here no such relationship existed.

The majority cited the evidence and admissions of Grace Church's pastors that they knew Ken was suicidal and that they knew he promised to try again. It concluded that by construing the evidence most favorably toward the Nallys, which a court was required to do in ruling on a motion to dismiss, a jury could reasonably conclude that the defendants breached both their duty to prevent Ken's death by referring him to competent professionals, and the church breached its duty to properly train its counselors.

Despite the argument that Grace Church and its pastors were liable for breaching a standard of care applicable to nonprofessionals, the majority nevertheless felt compelled to address the First Amendment defense. Citing *Lemon v. Kurtzman*, the majority concluded the three-prong test of establishment posed no problem. The goal was to prevent suicide, a clear secular purpose. There was no inhibiting nor advancing of religion, and applying an identical standard to nonprofessional clergy as nonclergy would require no entanglement by the state.

Freedom of religion admittedly posed a more difficult problem. The key for the majority lay in the *Cantwell* distinction between belief and action. Citing *U.S. v. Lee*, a 1982 U.S. Supreme Court case decided after *Nally* was filed, and *Braunfeld v. Brown*, a 1961 U.S. Supreme Court case, the majority addressed the four elements necessary for government action to pass muster under the freedom of religion clause.

The majority restated the test for free exercise: The state action must further a compelling state interest, the burden on religion must be essential to the compelling interest, the level of the burden must be the absolute minimum required, and finally the burden must be neutral and apply to everyone regardless of religious belief. The factors are interrelated. The greater the burden, the more compelling the state interest must be. Where the burden is slight the state interest can also be less compelling, as in *Goldman v. Weinberger* (1986) where the U.S. Supreme Court upheld a military restriction against wearing Jewish yarmulkes indoors in the interest of military uniformity.

Drawing on John MacArthur's testimony and Sam Ericsson's representations, the majority concluded there was no burden on Grace's religious beliefs. Trial testimony and argument before the court revealed Grace had no theological prohibition against referring people to secular psychiatrists. Thus, Grace Church's defense was not really rooted in religious beliefs. Any preference seemed personal, not religious. Even Rea and Thomson, who advocated Christian psychiatrists, could meet a duty to refer by referring to Christian professionals.

Little or no burden on religion stood in contrast to a very compelling state interest: preventing suicide. The California Penal Code made aiding, advising, or encouraging suicide a felony. Other

California statutes allowed psychiatrists to involuntarily commit suicidal people. The state had a clear, compelling interest, and exempting nontherapists, including the defendant pastors, would defeat this important interest. The requirement to refer did not require a "direct" burden. Grace could still counsel anyone and everyone, as well as use whatever method it deemed appropriate. No one would impose liability on Grace Church for using the "wrong scripture" to counsel its parishioners, nor would they be liable to continue to provide counseling help to suicidal people. The liability attaches for failing to, in addition, refer suicidal people to trained professionals. Grace never argued the duty to refer would be overly restrictive. The majority saw no reason to even try and fashion a standard for pastoral or religious counselors. The duty to refer applied to all nontherapists, secular and religious, as well as all religions equally, and would therefore be as neutral as possible. A jury could thus find that Grace and its pastors had breached a duty to refer that in no way violated the free exercise clause of the Constitution.

Finally, the majority addressed an issue of pure California evidentiary law: the exclusion of the Thomson tape. The law of the case doctrine said the claim for outrageous conduct should be tried, but Judge Kalin had undermined the cause of action by excluding the tape upon which the first court of appeals decision based its ruling. The tape was relevant for at least two reasons, according to Johnson's opinion. First, it went to the defendants' state of mind while counseling Kenneth. Intent or reckless disregard is a key element of the outrageous conduct claim. This tape offered some evidence into what the defendant was thinking as he counseled Ken. Second, the tape was relevant, as Barker had argued, to show the customary approach of the church's counselors. Even if made later and said differently, the tape showed how and what the church routinely counseled. Thus, the probative value of the tape outweighed any prejudice to the defendants.

Johnson's opinion concluded by reaffirming Dean Prosser: Tort law is overwhelmingly common law, developed through case-by-case determinations by the courts. They were not taking away a legislative function, they were doing what courts are supposed to do. In this case, far from creating a "new" ground for liability, they refused to create a "new" theory of clergy immunity.

Justice John Cole, the lone dissenter, saw the case differently. "In my view the majority holding simply is wrong, for a number of reasons." Cole rejected the notion that courts could make law, particularly intermediate appellate courts. Regardless of its admonitions to the contrary, the majority opinion would set standards for the full spectrum of nonlicensed therapists and the opinion would chill everyone's willingness to continue counseling.

Cole condemned the majority opinion for failing to provide any type of concrete standard. How did one become burdened with the duty? Ken could not be compelled by anyone other than a licensed professional to be hospitalized. He was twenty-four years old and could and did choose. The legislature in its wisdom had already decided the issue. No one, not even a doctor, is under a duty to take affirmative steps to prevent a nonpatient from killing himself. Who should Grace have called? For Cole every question spawned ten others.

Ill-defined standards aside, Cole found that the majority opinion violated the First Amendment. Cole had no qualms with the majority's recitation of the standard, he just could not agree with its application. To reach the majority's conclusions required ignoring the trial record and preferring the religious beliefs expressed by some defendants over those expressed by others. Although MacArthur may have wavered on the issue of referral to professionals, Cole cited long portions of Thomson's testimony wherein he stated unequivocally that for him the Bible held all of the answers to mental and emotional problems. The duty to refer created by the majority totally violated Thomson's beliefs. More important, the duty ignored the fact that the patient himself might have extreme religious beliefs that precluded referral to a secular psychiatrist. For Cole this reasoning questioned the sincerity of religious beliefs and clearly violated *Ballard*. Even the plaintiffs' own expert, Bill Adams, when asked where spirituality stopped and psychiatry began, admitted that Christ wouldn't "touch that one . . . there's no answer to such a question. They are intermingled."

Cole scoffed at the notion that the duty to refer could be

deemed "essential." There was no proof whatsoever that referring actually worked, unless one would compel the involuntary commitment of every potential suicide patient. The core of the problem for Cole found its best voice in the first free exercise case, *Reynolds v. U.S.* In striking down polygamy, the court in 1878 looked to the intent of the founding fathers and found it in a Virginia statute drafted by Jefferson that stated, "it is time enough for the rightful purposes of government for its officers to interfere when principles break out into overt acts against peace and good order." Cole saw nothing of the kind in *Nally.* Because the majority formed the opinion that suicide should be prevented, it was also up to them to decide how to do it. For Cole this was a direct burden on religious belief and he rested his argument with the maxim that only in extreme cases has such a burden been upheld and this was not such a case. He hoped the majority opinion would not ultimately prevail.

As for the evidence issue, Cole argued that Kalin had given the matter a full and fair hearing during trial and then chose to exclude the evidence. Just because the first court of appeals had upheld the cause of action based on the tape did not then force Kalin to admit it over his own sound discretion. More important, Barker never argued at trial that the law of the case doctrine precluded Kalin from excluding the tape. As far as Cole was concerned, Barker waived the objection. Cole concluded by saying, "I would affirm the judgment of the trial court. It was right the first time when it granted summary judgment; it clearly was correct the second time when it granted the motion for non-suit. There should be no third time." It sure looked like there would be.

CHAPTER 10

Religion Rallies to the Cause

Walter Nally could not restrain his elation. "We've been waiting for this a long, long time. I certainly thank those two judges, Johnson and Thompson." The church had no immediate comment. The story hit the local papers and quickly spread nationally. Cooksey and Ericsson filed an obligatory motion for reconsideration that the court denied one month later. There were only two places to go now, back to trial or to the California Supreme Court. Three years ago the state high court refused to hear the case, but that was a different court. Perhaps this one would decide otherwise.

The level of concern within the religious community had steadily increased as *Nally* fought its way through the system, refusing to die despite several close calls. With each apparent victory the nation's clergy relaxed, only to be thrust back into uncertainty as an appeals court crushed what they believed was a sound decision. With the September 1987 decision sentiments went from concern and paranoia to outright panic among some religious circles. If the California Supreme Court refused to hear the case it would go back to the trial court. Few people at this juncture doubted what would happen. The jury had been vocal in its support of the Nallys' case. The court of appeals had now given that passion a legal framework that seemed to eliminate the First Amendment as an obstacle to liability. Cooksey filed his appeal with the California Supreme Court and waited.

The California Supreme Court in 1987 was not the same court that declined to take the case in 1985. Chief Justice Rose Bird and two of her colleagues no longer occupied seats, all three having been voted out in the 1986 confirmation election. To completely understand the makeup of the court in 1987 and the California legal and political climate of the times, one must understand a case that had absolutely nothing to do with church, state, religion, or the First Amendment: *People v. Tanner.*

Governor Jerry Brown appointed Rose Elizabeth Bird in 1977. Bird seemed to epitomize "Governor Moonbeam's" liberal political agenda and followed a long line of liberal justices dating back into the late 1950s. She was young, female, relatively inexperienced as a judge, and determined, as Brown had been, to challenge the conventional wisdom and well-settled traditions of the state judiciary. She became leader of a court that could be characterized only as liberal. By the time Governor George Deukmejian took office in 1983, six of the seven justices then sitting had been appointed by Democratic governors.

California had a system that allowed voters to confirm or reject on an intermittent basis appointments to the state's high court. Bird's appointment had ruffled feathers from the beginning, including some justices on the court, specifically Justice Stanley Mosk, who many thought should have been elevated to the chief justice seat. Although Bird had served only a short time when her first confirmation election occurred, there were already internal issues that created some degree of controversy among the bar and the voters. However, the personality conflicts paled in comparison to controversy that arose on Election Day, November 7, 1978, and continued for some time thereafter.

People v. Tanner came before the Bird Court in 1978 and brought with it strong public sentiment. *Tanner* involved a California law that made jail time mandatory for any person who committed a crime using a handgun. Public opinion strongly supported mandatory jail time for such offenses. On the morning of the election the *Los Angeles Times* published a story written by two of its most experienced reporters, that the Bird Court had come to a 4–3 decision on *Tanner,* holding that the defendant need not be sentenced to jail time despite having used a gun. The article alleged the court was withholding the opinion until after the election because it would be unpopular and might adversely affect the confirmation of some justices. What followed was a legal and political maelstrom that brought a year-long hearing before the California Commission on

{ *Clergy Malpractice in America* }

Judicial Performance. Upon rehearing in 1979, the *Tanner* decision was reversed in favor of upholding the mandatory jail law. In the process not only did the Bird Court come under intense and unfavorable scrutiny, but many people questioned the ethics and professionalism of the media, particularly the *Los Angeles Times*. By 1983 two full-length books appeared criticizing both the media and the conservative political right as being on a crusade to attack the courts. Some saw the California situation as a dress rehearsal for a national attack by the conservative right. Suffice it to say that when Rose Bird and her court came up for confirmation in 1986, her fate was almost predetermined. The voters not only swept Bird out but also refused to confirm two of her liberal colleagues.

Governor Deukmejian wasted no time. In 1987 he appointed three new members to the supreme court. As chief justice he elevated his only other appointee, Malcolm Lucas, a conservative minority member of the Bird Court whom the voters had confirmed in 1986. To fill the three associate justice vacancies the governor appointed David N. Eagleson, John A. Arguelles, and Marcus M. Kaufman. These three joined Lucas and three holdovers: Stanley Mosk, who also survived confirmation in 1986, Allen E. Broussard, and Edward A. Panelli. Mosk and Broussard now represented the liberal minority of the court, much like Justices William Brennan and Thurgood Marshall did for the U.S. Supreme Court. Panelli seemed willing to follow precedent, an important consideration given the Lucas Court's willingness to begin undoing the legacy of the Bird Court, but showed signs of siding with the Lucas majority on some issues. With Lucas, Kaufman, Eagleson, and Arguelles the court now had a conservative majority capable of profoundly changing California substantive law.

Lucas and the three new appointees were all middle-aged males in 1987, all had extensive legal experience, and all but Kaufman had been trial judges with hands-on experience in the practical effects of appellate decisions. Although Kaufman had no experience as a trial judge, he had spent seventeen years as a California circuit appellate judge prior to ascending to the supreme court. As the new court prepared to go to work, legal observers in California realized that this court, despite its "conservative" tenor, seemed willing to overrule not only individual or specific death case–type rulings of the Bird Court, but to take on core legal doctrines. Through the traditional tools of judicial restraint, deference to the legislative process, and will of the people, many saw the Lucas Court as the beginning of the end for the legal liberalism that had predated Bird. Most in danger was the expansion of new theories of tort liability and the possibility that recent expansion in the area of tort liability might be undermined. This was not the kind of court most likely to uphold a novel theory of recovery against an institution that enjoyed 200 years of constitutional protection. It was just the type of court Grace Community Church of the Valley wanted.

Until the late 1970s the California Supreme Court enjoyed a reputation as an independent, progressive, and professional body. It had struck down the death penalty in both 1972 and 1976. The landmark case in reverse discrimination, *Bakke v. State Board of Regents*, came out of California. In retrospect, even some of its critics conceded that the Bird Court had not significantly altered California law. For Rose Bird the radicalness tended to be her own way of doing things and the perceptions others had of her and her methods. Bird's court was probably no more divisive than most high courts, and certainly no more than the U.S. Supreme Court at the time. However, the tendency of justices to air their disputes in public, particularly the practice of writing separate opinions and partial dissents, of which Bird was often guilty, made the situation perhaps look worse than it was. It was also more than just the *Tanner* fiasco that undid Bird and the liberal majority of the court.

Regardless of how much the Bird Court seemed consistent with prior California Supreme Courts, California in the mid-1980s was no longer the same state it had been. America in general had not only become a more litigious land by the 1980s, but it was becoming a nation weary of criminal due process and the rights of the accused.

Ronald Reagan campaigned in 1980 on the promise to change the federal judiciary. He believed the liberalism of the Warren Court had begun a trend wherein the courts made policy rather than merely exercising judicial judgment. Reagan vowed to return the courts to their more limited and proper role of administering justice. His attorney general, Edwin Meese, used the Justice Department to screen potential candidates for federal judgeships and to ensure that only candidates who shared Reagan's beliefs as to the proper role of the courts would be appointed. Reagan would eventually appoint slightly over one-half of the 732 Article 3 judges on the federal bench. He appointed four justices to the U.S. Supreme Court, and the Reagan appointees reflected the conservative beliefs of the chief executive who appointed them.

Reagan's notion of the judiciary's role trickled down into the state court systems. By the early 1980s the Supreme Court had begun the slow process of undermining search and seizure law and the expectations of privacy afforded criminal suspects, cases that most often concerned the conduct of state and local law enforcement officers. In California the Bird Court often found itself on the unpopular end of criminal cases where the public did not want to hear about criminal rights. For example, in 1985 the court overturned the a murder conviction in *People v. Alcala*. Rodney Alcala had been convicted of murdering twelve-year-old Robin Samose and dumping the girl's nude, mutilated body into a ravine. Alcala was identified from a composite sketch of a man who had approached the girl only hours before her death, asking to take her picture. He confessed to two cellmates while in a holding cell and had a record of child molestation. The Bird Court overturned the conviction on the grounds that the admission of his prior molestation crimes was improper and unduly prejudicial because the prior crimes were not "sufficiently similar" to the murder. As the confirmation election approached, the local district attorney prepared to retry the case. *Alcala* was one of many cases where conservative Californians, a group that seemed to grow larger every year, found fault with Bird.

In addition to the *Alcala* case, Bird seemed resistant to allow convicted inmates to be put to death and seemed more concerned about those convicted of driving while intoxicated (DWI) than the victims of such activity. Don Floyd was representative of the growing groundswell against Bird. "I thought I knew what the judicial system was all about," Floyd said in 1980. When his son was killed by a drunken driver and received a thirty-day jail sentence and one year's probation, Floyd reassessed his understanding of the law and formed the anti-Bird Crime Victims for Court Reform.

Bird's supporters pointed out that statistically 85 percent of people arrested for felonies were convicted, and only one out of ten appeals reaching the supreme court resulted in freeing the defendant. Once again, it may not have been Bird herself, as much as she became a symbol of everything wrong with a liberal judicial activist legal system. The winds of change were blowing and it did not bode well for Walter and Maria Nally. It was not just that Bird was gone, it was that the Lucas Court seemed to embody this new conservative judiciary and it would decide whether to hear the appeal. The Lucas Court marked a clear departure from the traditions of the last thirty years at precisely the time when the Nallys most needed the liberal legal tradition.

Christmas 1987 came and went. Three weeks into the new year the California Supreme Court made its decision. In a 7–0 vote the court elected to hear Grace Church's appeal of the 1987 court of appeals decision. Oral arguments would be held in June 1988. David Cooksey was pleased. "Our contention is that the appeals court was trying to prescribe the content of religious counseling in violation of the First Amendment." He added, "We think that kind of governmental intrusion into the ecclesiastical sphere is unconstitutional." Ed Barker could not hide his disappointment and admitted that "apparently there may be some critical First Amendment issues they want to consider." For Walter and Maria Nally it was one more obstacle that had to be overcome.

Whatever one might have thought back in 1980 when the case was filed, no objective person in 1988 could possibly believe that *Nally* would simply go away or that the case did not pose a serious threat to religious counseling. *Nally* had been heard by two trial judges, sixteen jurors, and six judges of the California Court of Appeals. The jury leaned toward the Nallys, both trial judges came down squarely for the church, and four of the six appellate judges found the Nallys' claim to be legitimate. Whatever else it had resolved or failed to resolve, *Nally* had become the hydraulic hose that Justice Holmes said defined a landmark case. It had wiped away everything people thought they knew about religious free-dom, the First Amendment, and tort liability, and left only uncertainty in its wake. No one laughed or scoffed at the notion that the clergy could be sued. It was now happening all over America, albeit unsuccessfully. Would Walter and Maria Nally be the first to prevail? Not if churches across America and the California legislature had anything to say about the issue.

The same week that the California Supreme Court decided to hear the *Nally* appeal, the State Senate Judiciary Committee approved, by a 7–2 vote, a bill proposed by state senator John Doolittle, a conservative Republican from Citrus Heights. The bill, SB1, would bar most punitive lawsuits against religious organizations and charitable groups. Unlike previous bills that may or may not have been related to the *Nally* suit, Doolittle's bill was aimed at *Nally*, and if passed, it would threaten Walter and Maria Nally's lawsuit. Doolittle said that the "proposed law would save churches from going under because of costly punitive damage suits." Walter Nally could only shake his head. It seemed everyone was trying to prevent him from getting Grace Church. "It's amazing. I guess they recognized that they can't get God's forgiveness, and it looks questionable whether they will get the court's forgiveness, so now it looks like they've gone to the legislature, and may get forgiveness." There was no doubt in his mind whom the bill was aimed at. "The way it was written, I understand it was principally aimed at us, as I read it, it would not hold them [Grace] responsible." The same type of bill had failed in each of the previous two years.

The bill had actually been severely gutted in committee. Doolittle favored full immunity for religious organizations. The bill only served to limit punitive lawsuits against charitable organizations, which included religious organizations. Punitive damages would be allowed in special cases, including instances where the defendant charity tried to hide evidence. Doolittle insisted the law was needed. He claimed there were over 2,000 suits demanding $100 million in damages nationwide. His colleagues were not so certain. Some argued there was no proof that churches need such protection from the legislature. Despite the debate, the bill looked as if it might actually pass. However, in May 1988, a little over a month before the *Nally* case would be heard by the Supreme Court, SB1 died in the Senate Judiciary Committee by a vote of 7–4. A similar bill in the state assembly likewise died. The votes were just not there. If Grace Church was to prevail it would have to be in the courts.

While the debate raged in the California legislature, churches and religious organizations across America rallied to Grace Church's side. In one sense they offered support to one of their own, but in a very real way they were stepping up to their own defense. "Every priest, minister and rabbi is in jeopardy," said professor emeritus Reverend Franklin Littell of Temple University. Littell, the founder of the Hamlin Institute for the study of religious liberty and persecution, joined James Wood of Baylor University, founding editor of *Church-State Magazine*, Gordon Melton, professor of religious studies at the University of California at Santa Barbara and author of the two-volume *Encyclopedia of American Religion*, and Los Angeles attorney Barry A. Fisher, a church-state expert, at a press conference held at the Los Angeles Biltmore Hotel on January 14, 1988. The men had gathered for a hastily called, two-day symposium attended by dozens of clergy and attorneys for the purpose of launching what they called a "counteroffensive to the assault on religious liberty."

Dubbed "Clergy, Malpractice, Religious Liberty and the Law," the conference marked the formation of an ad hoc group of U.S. religious leaders and human rights activists operating as the Congress for Religious Liberty. The sole purpose of the organization was the reversal of the September 1987 court of appeals decision in *Nally*. The conference served as a planning meeting to accomplish that goal. Littell told a crowded press room, "The recent *Nally* decision now reverts any progress that was made to turn the trend away from punishing religion and religious counselors for their attempts to succor those in need and minister to the needs of their parishioners." Barry Fisher added, "Such decisions, if they stand, open the door for more litigation against churches and ministers."

The conference organizers had two concrete objectives. The first was to organize a think tank based on the West Coast that would coordinate efforts to overturn the appeal. At the same time the conference would organize a delegation that would go to Sacramento prior to the deadline for submitting legislative proposals to the California legislature, and provide revised language for Senator John Doolittle's anti–clergy lawsuit bill. A steering committee formed at the Biltmore Conference had already drafted language to nullify any requirement for clergy to defer to secular psychiatry when dealing with the suicide-prone parishioner.

When David Cooksey filed the defendants' appeal to the California Supreme Court in October 1987, he anticipated that around fifty churches of various denominations would file some kind of brief in support of Grace Church's position. By April over 1,500 churches had answered the call, as amicus curiae briefs poured into the California Supreme Court and money and emotional support found its way to Grace Church. Sam Ericsson played a major role in this outpouring of support. As director of the Christian Legal Society in Washington, D.C., Ericsson used his nationwide contacts to ensure that any church or religious organization that had not heard of *Nally*, or somehow remained unaware of the potential ramifications of the case succeeding, understood what was at stake.

The majority of the briefs came from small, nondenominational churches, and in one way or another they all focused on the singular point that liability should not extend to counseling by clergymen. One brief purported to be on behalf of 6,000 churches. The briefs came from all faiths and from the most unusual of places. WMHR-FM, a religious radio station in Syracuse, New York, filed a brief. The station aired a regular religious counseling show and felt the chilling effect of the *Nally* court of appeals decision. In its brief the radio station stressed that "no prior court has presumed that the clergy could or should determine whether parishioners require professional care."

Barker filed the brief on behalf of the Nallys and Sam Ericsson filed the brief for Grace Church. After almost eight years of litigation the positions in each were predictable. Barker relied heavily on trial testimony, particularly that of his experts, who characterized Ken's situation as one where a likely suicide patient was pulled into a circle of fundamentalists and an extensive counseling program. Barker emphasized that the program included fifty counselors available at three services every Sunday and who offered over 1,500 sessions a year, according to MacArthur. Ken had admitted to attempting suicide and was counseled extensively by men who claimed to be able to cure mental illness, but in reality had no training.

The expert testimony established that the pastor-counselors instilled hostility toward secular mental health professionals and relied entirely on the Bible and the notion that all mental illness is caused by sin. Because of negligence, Barker argued, Ken was actively prevented from seeking professional psychiatric help. To compound the problem the defendants' outrageous conduct ingrained a belief in Ken that he had betrayed Christ's love and trust, and "otherwise exacerbated Ken's pre-existing feelings of guilt, anxiety and depression," with the knowledge that it would increase the likelihood Ken would again try to take his own life.

Ericsson's brief stressed that the appellate court decision in effect sought to regulate the content of religious ministering. "The church and its pastors seek to teach and practice a thoroughly biblical and world view, believing that the Bible is the divinely inspired word of God containing the truth that must govern Christians in their relationship with the almighty, with the world at large, and in their own personal lives." To attempt to regulate this belief system by requiring church counselors to follow judicially established guidelines "unavoidably and unconstitutionally entangles the state in matters of church doctrine, discipline and practice, inhibiting religious liberty and autonomy, burdening its free exercise without compelling justification."

With the case docketed for hearing before the Supreme Court in June 1988, differences in biblical interpretation disappeared, at least temporarily, as Catholic, Jew, Scientologist, and denominations of Protestantism took aim at the same target. Scientology had a pragmatic motive outside the general desire to see religious counseling free of governmental intrusion. In November 1987, a Los Angeles branch of the church was sued by a woman seeking to hold the church and its ministers responsible for the suicide death of her son in 1986. The $6 million lawsuit alleged that the church officials tried to destroy the close relationship she had with her son and their efforts ultimately drove him to leap off the church's building in Hollywood. The complaint alleged intentional infliction of emotional distress, negligence, and outrageous conduct. In language reminiscent of the *Nally* complaint, Irene Marshall alleged that church officials "held themselves out as particularly competent to provide the decedent with personal and spiritual guidance" to resolve his problems. Her son's problems sounded like Kenneth's: After high school he became plagued with inner conflicts, uncertain, confused, and unhappy with himself, believing his life had no purpose, direction, or meaning. In words that still echoed from the *Nally* trial, the complaint claimed the Scientologists had imposed coercive techniques on the young man and "exploited his preexisting emotional vulnerabilities and inner conflicts."

One of the briefs filed on behalf of Grace came from the Church of Jesus Christ for Latter-Day Saints. The Mormon brief was submitted by Rex Lee. Lee, himself a Mormon, had served as solicitor general during the Reagan administration and not only brought another voice to the debate, but one that carried significant political familiarity. In Walter Nally's words, the church had "clout," and it was bringing all of its resources to bear on the Nallys. Lee's support went beyond merely filing a brief. He agreed to argue the case on behalf of the defendants before the California Supreme Court.

Ericsson made this possible. One of his staff attorneys in 1988 had clerked for Lee as a Yale law student in 1984. He was supposed to have clerked for Ericsson at the Christian Legal Society, but upon presenting his dilemma to Ericsson, he took Lee's offer. It was a once-in-a-lifetime chance. After graduating, he came to work for Ericsson. In 1988 he took his boss to meet Lee at his Washington, D.C., office. Lee was happy to accept the offer, asking rhetorically, "Does Willie Shoemaker want to ride in the Kentucky Derby?" He offered to appear pro bono, but Grace Church's insurance agreed to pay his fee.

The Nallys also received support from the religious community, even if not as much or as prominent. In March 1988, Rabbi Arthur Gross Schaefer wrote Ed Barker and enclosed a copy of the article he had written in 1987. Rabbi Schaefer actually met

Walter Nally and the article, which Schaefer characterized as "generally supportive of your position," had been written as a result of their meeting. Schaefer concluded that the First Amendment protection of religious freedom should be a strong, high wall that would protect religion from unnecessary state intrusion. However, the state had a right and a duty to protect its citizens from harming themselves and others. Even if but one voice, Schaefer certainly echoed the Nallys' position.

On the eve of the June 15 oral argument Grace received yet another ally in its fight, one that came from a totally unexpected source but a source that in retrospect should not have been so surprising. The 1987 Court of Appeals opinion threatened more than just religious organizations in America. The majority opinion had attached liability to a broad spectrum of counselors that it defined as nontherapeutic, or nonprofessional. Churches and ministers fell within this group, but they were not alone. The opinion seemed to threaten secular nonprofessionals with liability, who, under existing California law in *Bella* and *Tarasoff,* had been exempt.

This fact did not escape California's county governments. In a letter dated June 15, 1988, but conceived and drafted some time prior to that date by a subcommittee of the County Counsels Association of California, every county attorney in California's fifty-eight counties was encouraged to take a form letter enclosed with the correspondence, copy it onto it its own letterhead, and send it to the California Supreme Court. The letter took issue with a single paragraph in the eighty-four-page 1987 appellate decision that implied "suicide could be prevented." The letter argued that such language, if adopted by the Supreme Court, could impose a new and unrealistic duty on "all counselors, including county mental programs." At least eleven county counsels, including those in Los Angeles and Ventura Counties, signed the letter and sent it to the supreme court. Ed Barker and David Cooksey both found out because as attorneys of record, they were copied on each filing.

Barker and Nally were furious. The letter only confirmed Walter Nally's deeply held belief that the case had now reached a point where it had become "win at all costs." Barker agreed. "The fact that someone would ask every county in the state to send a letter to the court that's identical—there's no intellectual or legal purpose to that. That's nothing but muscle." Cooksey admitted the letter seemed biased in favor of the church and the individual defendants, but denied knowing anything about it. Kitt Berman, litigation counsel for the County Supervisors Association, denied any attempt to choose sides. "We didn't think the letter had anything to do with the merits of the case . . . I'm sorry if it [the letter] ended up causing any trouble."

Not only did it seem to go to the merits of the case, but Barker condemned it as both biased and for totally misconstruing the Nallys' case by arguing that since no one can prevent suicide, finding the church counselors negligent would impose liability on county health programs as well. To the contrary, argued Barker, "Our case is that a professional counselor has to act professionally and do everything they can to prevent a suicide. If they do that then they have no responsibility, they just have to do their job right." Barker called Ventura County to complain but got nowhere. Walter Nally actually went to Los Angeles County and sat outside Michael Antonovich's office until the attorney agreed to see him. Antonovich had a female assistant with him and she had apparently signed the letter for Los Angeles County. Nally recalled she was very defensive and simply said she had been in Sacramento at a meeting, an individual with the county association asked her to sign, and she did. Berman insisted the letter was sent only out of overcaution to prevent anyone from misconstruing the language regarding suicide prevention. As far as she was concerned, county officials would pursue the matter no further.

That was fine for them. For Ed it was not merely the content of the letter, but the timing. Although the letter had its beginnings prior to oral arguments, most of the letters did not reach the supreme court until after the hearing, which made it impossible for the Nallys to respond to the argument within them. Barker suspected Rex Lee was behind the letters, but he could never confirm his suspicion.

CHAPTER II

Before the High Court

On June 15, 1988, the Nallys' nine-year struggle against Grace Church finally reached the California Supreme Court. Before a courtroom packed with journalists and onlookers, Chief Justice Lucas asked if the parties were ready to proceed. Rex Lee stood, thanked the court, and addressed the seven-member panel. Experienced, articulate, and eminently well qualified, both religiously and legally, Lee went right to the point.

"The issue in this case is whether under California common law and consistent with principles of California and U.S. constitutional law, religious counselors may be held liable in tort for the suicides of the people they were counseling." He then briefly laid out the facts of the last two months of Ken's life, in particular emphasizing that Ken saw no fewer than eight different physicians during that time, one of whom was a licensed psychiatrist, and two other mental health professionals, "none of which were defendants in the case."

Lee explained the court of appeals holding, requiring "effective referral," yet argued that the three-member panel failed to explain what that meant. In the church's opinion the case could be decided on grounds that rested firmly within well-established principles of California tort and state and federal constitutional law. Fortunately, Lee said, the parties agreed on what most of those controlling principles were.

First, both parties agreed that holding nonlicensed counselors liable in tort for the suicides of their patients would push California common law beyond presently established principles. Even the plaintiffs admitted the court would have to engage in some law making, or at least law extending to afford the Nallys relief. Second, it was common ground that this tort must be required by some compelling state interest, and that if so required, the cause of action had to be narrowly tailored to meet that need. Lee insisted the tort should not be created, and to create such a tort as fashioned by the court of appeals lay beyond *Tarasoff* and even beyond *Bellah*.

"Do you distinguish *Tarasoff* on grounds that Tarasoff had a license and your clients don't?" asked Justice Mosk. Clearly at least one important distinction, Lee quickly responded. The *Tarasoff* case had established the outer limits of liability for the death of a suicide patient and placed that duty on licensed professionals only.

Justice Panelli quickly jumped in with a threshold question, "Can this case be decided on just tort principles and avoid the constitutional question?" "Yes, of course you can," Lee insisted, "and I would encourage you to do so." Although the Constitution was relevant and in the background, the court need not reach those issues to decide the case. But, Lee added, if the court did reach the First Amendment issues, the plaintiff must show that the clergy malpractice tort, or duty of nontherapy counselors to refer, is needed to meet a compelling state interest. Furthermore, the tort cause of action must be narrowly tailored to meet that specific compelling state interest. Lee argued there was no compelling state interest and that even if there were, this cause of action was much too broad.

The court of appeals argued that the duty to refer did not seem to burden Grace Church's religious beliefs. MacArthur himself had testified that he had no personal problem with referrals to secular psychiatrists. Lee countered that such an analysis missed the point completely. Religious exercise would be severely burdened by the mere existence of the tort and the threat of litigation it posed. Tort liability could arise under circumstances where no one could predict the possibility of suicide. Grace did tell Ken to seek help and he still committed suicide. Unlike professionals, who know when their special relationship comes into existence, spiritual counseling and mental counseling are so intertwined that liability might arise under circumstances where no one knew a duty had attached. The chilling effect on a counselor's willingness to "enter the uncertain thickets" of religious counseling would lead all but the bravest and most foolhardy to avoid counseling altogether. Lee argued that it would also chill potential counselees who would know their pastor had a duty to commit them or to refer them on, even if they objected. The bottom line would be far less religious counseling. Citing *Corp. of Presiding Bishops vs. Amos*, a U.S. Supreme Court case decided just three weeks after the 1987 court of appeals decision in *Nally*, Lee argued the fear of potential liability would affect how an organization might carry out what it sees as its religious mission and that was enough to burden religion. Here, Lee argued, a core religious practice is burdened and perhaps stopped altogether.

To meet the compelling state interest requirement demanded satisfying an ends-means test. The objective, or end, must be compelling; not important, not substantial, but compelling. The state must then show its compelling interest cannot be accomplished by any other means. The compelling state interest here was an interest in preventing suicides. Such an interest, contended Lee, "just won't wash." Whether one looked at the question from the ends or the means, the plaintiffs cannot show the constitutional mandates had been met. Lee pointed out that the legislature has not adopted such liability and all public policy reasons weigh against it.

Justice Mosk interjected, "Aiding and abetting suicide is a crime, can one not do so by inaction as opposed to action?" "No, Justice Mosk, it requires intent, and we think that is important." The intent requirement of the suicide statute demonstrated a legislative unwillingness to attach liability to the conduct in *Nally*. The tort the plaintiffs wanted established was unnecessary and had already been considered and rejected for public policy reasons. The statute covers intent and thus is far less burdensome on religious belief.

Lee pointed out that the plaintiffs' case contained a serious hole. They had not shown and could not show any evidence that psychiatrists or other professionals were any more effective in preventing suicide than nonprofessionals. Absent that link, the narrowly tailored requirement, or means test, cannot be met because the court of appeals opinion burdens pastoral counseling without any showing that the burden would bring about the contemplated result. If one assumed professionals were better able to prevent suicide, the pastors in this case did encourage Ken to seek help. He was seeing a psychiatrist at the time of his suicide and still nothing stopped him from taking his own life. The court of appeals decision not only imposed a duty to refer on pastors, but actually created a duty to ensure that the professional to whom the patient is referred prevents the suicide.

Lee then briefly touched on outrageous conduct. "What is the outrageous conduct of which the plaintiffs complain?" he asked. "The plaintiffs, on page 53 of their brief say what it is, 'they, Grace and its Pastors, condoned, taught or otherwise imbued.' Teaching and imbuing alone is sufficient to require a nonsuit under *Brandenburg v. Ohio*, because they were not teaching violent conduct. What they taught and imbued was the notion that by accepting Christ, Ken would still be saved, and second, that the injury to his arm was God's punishment. Outrageous? Maybe to some. Some people would argue it is outrageous to teach that suicide would bar one from eternal salvation. Then there is a third view, which is that both sides are outrageous, because there is no God. *U.S. v. Ballard* resolved this debate forty years ago. It is not the court's job to determine if sincere belief is or is not outrageous. Any doubt of outrageousness as to speech in general was further resolved by *Hustler Magazine v. Falwell*, which held that censoring or prohibiting nonviolent speech or expression because of its outrageous emotional impact on an audience was precluded by the First Amendment."

In conclusion Lee argued that both counseling and teaching were protected by the free exercise clause of the First Amendment. There was no policy reason or any other reason to make a new tort. To extend *Tarasoff* beyond its present limits would violate both state and federal constitutions. More important, by refusing to do so, the court would never have to reach the constitutional issues.

Lee sat down, reserving the rest of his thirty minutes for rebuttal. Ed Barker rose and addressed the court.

I believe our case is much more limited than that. We are talking about a very unusual fact situation that produced tragic, terrible and not so unusual results. We are not talking about typical pastoral counseling or typical religious counseling, or as counsel [Lee] said, counseling as it normally occurs. Nor are we concerned with the teaching of a church, or any type of typical or normal teaching. We are concerned with a situation which we believe is very rare. This is a situation where some men, under the guise, and by guise I do not mean to suggest that they were insincere, but under the roof of the church, held themselves out as competent to take on the horrendous task of providing the primary treatment and primary care of the severely mentally ill. That is not your typical religious counseling. If we are going to have a chilling affect on people who have no training in psychology, holding out that they are competent to counsel schizophrenia, psychosis, suicidality, and to be the primary treaters for those people, then perhaps that is welcome.

The questions then came fast and with more frequency than they had when Lee presented his arguments. "Was there any special relationship between the church and the decedent?" "Absolutely, Your Honor, it started when the church held out that they were competent to handle such matters. They made them [representations] in the church and through classes." Ken Nally took advantage of their offer and went to the church because he was suicidal.

Barker jumped at the opportunity to address the church's representations. He knew that holding oneself out as competent is the absolute way to destroy protection enjoyed by one who otherwise has no legal duty. Having done so, the law in virtually every jurisdiction then imposed a duty, irrespective of class, religious belief, training, and experience to act "reasonably." This was not simple pastoral counseling or religious teaching; these men held themselves out as able to handle severe mental illness, and having done so, they had a duty to act reasonably. This meant they had the same duty imposed upon a professional who represented that he or she could handle such problems, and in this case that duty was spelled out in *Tarasoff* and *Bellah*. It was a duty to prevent Ken's suicide, not because all churches should do so or all nonprofessionals, but because they had represented they could do the work of a professional and having done so they created that "special relationship" between Ken and themselves that gave rise to liability.

"Did this special relationship begin with his first counseling session when they made the representation, when he joined the church, or just when did this relationship begin?" Barker narrowed his argument. It began when Ken first received counseling. Barker agreed that to hold the church to a special relationship simply because Ken joined the church would in fact create a new tort. That was not the case here. In 1976, when Ken approached Fred Barshaw, told Barshaw he was contemplating suicide, and Barshaw, as he testified, informally counseled Ken and then discussed Ken's suicidal situation with other members of the counseling staff, there may or may not have been a special relationship. But when Ken went to Duane Rea and entered into what even Rea admitted was a formal counseling relationship, where they sat down, Rea took notes, he and Ken cried together, and Rea admitted he saw signs of suicidal behavior, it was there the special relationship began. It was most definitely present when Ken, lying in his hospital bed after his March 1979 suicide attempt, told the pastors his secret, a secret he told no one else, not his family, and not the Verdugo Hills medical staff: When he got out he was going to try again. These pastors with whom he did share his secret had already formally undertaken to be his counselors.

This was important. Lee had argued that the problem with the plaintiffs' case was an overly broad remedy, because the church and its pastors could not know when the relationship giving rise to liability occurred. Here Barker attempted to answer that question. It occurred when Ken formally approached church counselors seeking help and they agreed, consistent with their representations, to undertake his problems.

Panelli spoke up, "Even if what you say is correct, it seems to me you have a difficult proximate cause situation." As Panelli understood the facts, Ken was already in the midst of the very professionals Barker and the Nallys argued he should be. "If there was a duty to refer he was now in the milieu of professional mental health people."

Barker did not waver. He was among professionals but not from a referral. Ken was there because he tried to kill himself. Emergency admission of one at death's door was not the same thing as a referral. Even if there was some debate over this issue, the jury should be allowed to resolve the question. For years the church knew he was suicidal. At the hospital he saw only one psychiatrist and there is some dispute as to how cooperative Ken was. Hall testified Ken wanted to consult the church to see if he could even speak with Hall. He told Hall he was feeling better, not that he was going to commit suicide. Hall testified that if he knew what the church counselors knew, he would have acted differently. "No, Hall was not treating him. He wanted to, he tried, but they had no doctor-patient relationship."

The evidence was clear that Ken did not see other mental health professionals. Barker went through several of the other doctors, arguing they were not mental health referrals. Even the referral to Bullock by Rich Thomson was negligent. Thomson told Bullock this is "for physical purposes only." After only one short examination of Ken's arm, Bullock was concerned enough to suggest further steps be taken, but he could not get in touch with Thomson despite several efforts to do so.

"Was he ever advised, or the plaintiffs advised to admit him to a psychiatric institution?" Barker admitted there was dramatic disagreement on this issue, but again insisted that a jury should decide the issue. No one but MacArthur ever said this, certainly no other pastor at Grace Church. The key is what was said to the family. The family admits they did not want to involuntarily admit Ken, and the information at their disposal during the critical stage of determining to involuntarily admit Ken was crucial. He told his parents he was getting better and that he was not suicidal. The Nallys had to balance what they were being told by Ken, the church, and other doctors against the potential harm and Ken's unwillingness to be committed. Had they had better information they would have made a better decision.

Panelli, obviously concerned about several aspects of the case, again jumped in. "My concern with the breadth of what you suggest is suppose a penitent goes to a confessor and admits to the confessor that he is thinking of killing himself, would that require the confessor to disclose that?" "My short answer is yes," said Barker. There may be issues of religious confidentiality, what the church feels it can or will reveal, and there may be issues of evidentiary confidentiality, what the law says is a legally recognizable confidential relationship along the lines of attorney-client and husband-wife. But Barker was emphatic that neither "is an issue here."

Panelli would not leave the issue alone. He pressed Barker that the nature of the liability he wanted to impose, even under circumstances where there was a holding out, would require breaching this confidence and with the religious confidentiality, you get into the First Amendment. Barker continued to argue that this was a narrow situation and that no such confidentiality problem existed. The Grace Church pastors admitted they spoke to each other and even their wives about Ken's problems. The two people they did not tell, however, were Hall and Nally. He conceded that the issue Panelli raised was a tough one, but stated that he hoped they would never have to confront it, and certainly did not believe it was an issue here.

The court then asked Barker the same question it asked Lee: "Did the Court have to reach the First Amendment issue to resolve this case?" Unlike Lee, Barker did not see any way around confronting the issue. "I would be very surprised if we could try the case with the evidence we have and not have to address a First Amendment defense." But even the First Amendment issues did not bar the suit from going forward.

Barker reemphasized, "This is no new tort. This is classical negligence." There is duty, overwhelming evidence of causation, and harm. Even the California Constitution, which recognized the First Amendment protections embodied in the U.S. Constitution, also recognized that those protections stop where they cause harm or there is licentiousness. Article 1, section 4 of the California Constitution stated, "Free exercise and enjoyment of religion without discrimination or preference are guaranteed. This liberty of conscience does not excuse acts that are licentious or inconsistent with the peace and safety of the state." Not even freedom of speech was absolute. Article 1, section 2 (a) held "Every person may freely speak, write and publish his or her sentiments on all subjects, being responsible for the abuse of this right."

Barker was back to what he had maintained from the outset. This is not about religion. Although one may have to address certain defenses and even discuss religion within the context of the case, no one had ever held that it could not be done. Issues of religion come up in court all the time, when discussing motives, for example. This case did not require infringing upon anyone's beliefs, it was about actions.

The court pressed Barker on the issue of causation, specifically evidence that proved causation. He insisted the evidence was clear, particularly the expert testimony. Hall testified that cognitive therapy and medication could clearly have helped Ken. Wilson testified that other forms of psychoanalysis might have helped Ken and even raised the possibility of electroshock therapy. More important, the defendants themselves said they could have cured Ken with biblical counseling. Barker hesitated to come into court as an advocate of "their kind of therapy," but contrary to the defendants' brief, which said "Ken stopped," it was the church counselors that stopped.

For Barker this was even more egregious behavior with regard to breach of duty: the unwillingness to continue to counsel him when they knew he was suicidal. He recounted Rea's testimony and his admission that he intentionally stopped seeing Ken because he refused to rejoice and "would not do his homework." The church pastors abandoned Ken. There was expert testimony that given the representations made by the church counselors they had a duty to continue, knowing his condition, and if they were not going to continue, they had a duty to refer him to someone or someplace that could competently continue. The duty was not to medicate Ken or to get him to some specific predetermined type of professional, it was a duty to act reasonably to save his life after two or three years of treating him, and after representations that they could help him.

This was an important issue. Lee had raised this point when discussing what he argued was a missing link in the plaintiffs' First Amendment argument. Barker had pointed out evidence of treatment that might have helped Ken, but some question remained whether he had produced evidence that professionals either would have or could have saved Ken. Had the plaintiffs put on evidence as a matter of scientific certainty, medical certainty, or other empirical standards that professionals were better able to help Ken than nonprofessionals?

What the church never really addressed, however, was the

intentional conduct on the part of its pastors, specifically Rea, supported by Thomson, in stopping the formal counseling sessions under circumstances where they knew he was suicidal. Justice Mosk then asked, "What should they have done?"

Barker responded that under the facts of "our case," stressing that they could only deal with these facts and not some broad or general scenario, early on Duane Rea and Rich Thomson "had an absolute duty to investigate the seriousness of this man's suicidality." They knew Ken was suicidal. On direct examination when Rea was asked about each element of a suicidal person, he knew them all and then admitted that Ken manifested them all. He and Ken wept together. Rea used the word "despondent" in his notes. Later, prior to the drug overdose attempt in March 1979, Thomson spoke with Ken and admitted on direct examination that Ken was depressed. As far back as Pastor Barshaw in 1976, the church knew Ken was suicidal and yet no one really investigated the degree of his suicidal ideation. Then, having come to the conclusion they could not help Ken, they had a duty to refer him to someone who could help. It could have been a psychiatrist, a psychologist, or even a pastoral counseling center.

"Does this discharge the duty, by referring Ken to a doctor?" asked the court. Essentially yes, was Barker's response. Except, if Thomson or whoever was doing the referring knew that Ken would not go or would not cooperate, then they had a duty to go further, perhaps even to persuade him to voluntarily admit himself, persuasion Barker believed Ken would have followed. Barker pointed out that at one point in Rich Thomson's life he had been admitted to a facility because of his own mental depression. Again, Barker insisted the church and its pastors had a duty to behave reasonably to save Ken's life under the facts they knew. This did not require them to involuntarily admit Ken, but knowing his condition and if Ken resisted, it might have required them to get an independent evaluation from someone who could seek to have Ken involuntarily admitted to a mental health facility.

Justice Panelli continued to see issues and asked Barker, "What effect would this case have on emergency hot lines?" Barker did not see any effect. This was not a Band-Aid type of service, or short-term help. It was years of formal counseling and should not apply to hot lines or 1-800 services.

Panelli clung to the referral issues. "I am concerned that you say these people are obligated to follow through." He questioned what would happen if the hot line told someone to go get help and they did not: Barker seemed to be arguing they had a duty to follow through. If so, Panelli feared, "a lot of people would stop answering phones." Panelli's concern was legitimate. In many negligence cases the issue, or one of the issues when trying to decide whether to ban or restrict something, is a balancing process. What is the potential gain or protection afforded by the ruling versus what is the potential harm? Without saying so expressly, Panelli clearly said that he might not be willing to impose the referral duty Barker argued for if it meant closing down services that in his mind provide a clear and far-reaching benefit to society.

Barker seemed to sense Panelli's concern and returned to his argument. The touchstone of negligence in California was reasonableness. Barker did not think it would be reasonable to expect crisis hot lines to refer or follow up on the people who phoned in for help. The "special relationship" that would give rise to such a duty did not exist.

Finally, Barker argued, the ultimate duty was to inform the family of the nature and extent of Ken's suicidal tendencies and certainly to inform them of his promise to try again when he got out. Immediately after Ken's drug overdose the family faced the decision as to what to do next. Involuntary hospitalization was both harsh and difficult to sustain. It was one thing to get someone admitted, quite another to keep him or her against their will. A crucial part of that decision was the information the church pastors had that they did not share. They had a duty to disclose that information, if not to the family, then to Ken's psychiatrist at Verdugo Hills, Dr. Hall. The pastors knew the family wrestled with the decision and they knew that as pastor-counselors they would not continue to counsel Ken. Again, act reasonably. Instead, Barker argued, they told the family Ken was doing fine and that he was going to be all right.

As he neared his conclusion Barker tried to put the case into a different context than Rex Lee had done. Lee characterized the plaintiffs' case as a new tort, reaching into an area where California tort and state and federal constitutional law had not ventured. Barker disagreed. For him it was the defendants asking for a new or novel protection from traditional California tort liability.

"For me the question in this case is the immunity question." He asked the court if it was going to allow persons to escape liability, persons who unreasonably held themselves out as competent to handle the severely mentally ill, who formally counseled someone for years, then when his life was in the balance failed to act reasonably. Would they be allowed an absolute immunity because the actions were done in affiliation with a church? Barker pointed out that one of the amicus briefs filed with the court was from Paradise Church, a religious institution that not only had a pastoral counseling center but was affiliated with licensed professionals. If one of those men acted as these defendants had, they would be liable.

At that point, several members of the court jumped in. "But they are licensed professionals coming to the church." "Yes, but they are operating under the roof of the church, so what is the difference?" Barker asked. He pressed further, "What about pure Pastoral Counseling centers, the state has a lot of them?" These centers had guidelines, standards, and trained professionals. Do these centers escape liability because they are pastoral counselors? "I would think not," said Barker, adding that if that were the case, every psychiatrist and psychologist would be ordained, certified as a minister, or otherwise affiliated with a church to escape liability. "Where does the line get drawn?" This is not the typical pastoral counseling situation. The pastoral role has been extended to its furthest reaches, far beyond family problems or spiritual guidance. This was a holding out of the ability to counsel the severely mentally ill.

At the court's request Barker went back through the evidence of the representations made to Ken, including church services and classes he attended. Barker pointed to Rich Thomson's book, *Principles of Biblical Counseling*, and the specific chapter titled, "Is This Problem Too Tough?" The short answer was that nothing was beyond the spiritual counselor's ability. Ken was given this book, read it, and it was available to the general public. It mentioned by name psychosis, paranoia, suicidal depression, and schizophrenia.

The court challenged Barker on this point, calling the book a teaching document and continuing to ask, "What was the holding out?" Barker went back to the trial testimony of both Rea and Thomson, where both men stated they had undertaken to counsel suicidal people and that they were competent to do so. Rea testified to having dealt with over fifty suicide cases over fifteen years. The church openly professed its competence to handle these problems through Rea and Thomson, statements they made in open court to the jury. These representations were designed to bring people in and the book was not just a teaching tool.

Barker's presentation ended with the justices pressing him on the issue of Ken having actually been referred, that he was in the care of doctors and at least one doctor had suggested commitment. Judge Kaufman seemed to believe the record reflected at least one person suggested involuntary commitment. Barker insisted there was no involuntary commitment suggestion because there was no knowledge by those making the decision, the Nallys or Hall, of the true severity of Ken's condition and his promise to try again.

Rex Lee then stood up for rebuttal, or at least it began as a rebuttal. However, as appellate work so often does, it quickly became a question and answer session as two members of the court began to focus on the notion that irrespective of religion and licensing, when people hold themselves out as competent they are then held to that standard and can be held liable for breaching such a standard. The questions came from the two furthest spectrums on the court: Justice Broussard, thought of as the most liberal member remaining, and Justice Kaufman, considered solidly in Lucas's new four-man majority.

"We simply take a different view of the record," Lee began. Ken was urged to see doctors and did see doctors. Hall did suggest commitment, the family refused. "The undisputed facts support the position that Judge Kalin was completely within his discretion to grant a non-suit in this case. We urge the Court to decide the case on clean grounds. There is simply no tort into which to fit this fact situation."

"What if there is a non-licensed, non-pastoral counselor, is there liability?" asked Justice Broussard. "No liability, Your Honor,

Tarasoff is the outer boundary," Lee responded. Broussard would not let up. "A non-licensed counselor representing himself to be competent is beyond the pale of liability?" Lee did not really answer, he simply reiterated his point that the court should not extend the liability of counselors under the common law under circumstances where the legislature has chosen not to do so based on solid policy grounds. "The plaintiff is in a dilemma," Lee began, "if this does apply to teen hot lines . . ."

"We can distinguish teen hot lines," said Boussard abruptly, "but wouldn't you be concerned if we had non-pastoral, non-licensed counselors, holding themselves out as has been alleged here, and with all the facts being the same and the result being the same, we say that there is no potential for liability?" "That is the hard case that may have to be answered someday, but that we believe does not have to be reached here," Lee answered. "It does unless we decide the First Amendment issue," Broussard shot back. Even Lee had to concede that point. If the court did as Lee asked at the beginning of his argument and forwent the constitutional issue, the question of liability based on a representation of competency to counsel the severely mentally ill would have to be addressed. If they went to the constitutional issue, they might be able to ignore the issue because right or wrong, the First Amendment precluded inquiry into religious matters.

With his time running out, Lee forged on. Even if one could distinguish the teen hot line cases, he argued, there are all kinds of informal counseling scenarios, such as those in this case. Friends offering advice, family trying to help a loved one, and the college dormitory situation with students trying to help roommates. If this new tort were to apply to all of those scenarios, "you invite Pandora into California. If not, and the tort applies only to pastoral counseling, you have very serious establishment clause problems."

"What about if it only applied to those who hold themselves out to be competent?" asked Justice Kaufman. "Do the teen hot lines do that? I don't think so. Do all the others you mentioned do that? I doubt it. What about the representations?" Lee responded the only way he could: There were no representations. The book Barker was using was simply a teaching document. That, Lee contended, was the problem. One can always allege a holding out, or misconduct or negligence. The U.S. Supreme Court had held in *Amos* that it is "this threat of litigation that poses the unconstitutional burden on free exercise of religion."

Broussard could not resist the obvious, "You told us at the outset that we did not have to reach the Constitutional issues. I don't see how you can defend this case without reaching those issues." "If so, so be it," replied Lee. Barker was right about having to decide the constitutional issues, but "only if you decide in his favor." If the court held for the church and did not extend the present boundaries of California tort law, it still did not have to reach the First Amendment issues. If the court nevertheless chose to address those issues, there had been absolutely no effort on the part of the plaintiffs to argue that the state of California had any compelling interest to establish this new tort. There had been no effort to refute the free exercise clause and establishment clause arguments.

Lee sat down and Justice Lucas dismissed the parties. With that, *Nally* had gone as far as it could in California. All either side could do now was wait. Walter Nally was not sure how he felt upon leaving. Justice Kaufman looked as if he had grown impatient with Rex Lee. That seemed good. However, there were a lot of questions about Ken having gotten all the care he needed and the church having done what Ed Barker was claiming they should have done. That felt a little unsettling.

The court clearly took the case and the issues it posed seriously. The justices pressed both attorneys, and to their credit, both Lee and Barker held his own. William Jennings Bryan and Clarence Darrow of the 1980s? Probably not. But if this was the second Monkey Trial, as Sam Ericsson insisted it had become, one thing was certain: neither Darrow nor Bryan articulated the issues in *Scopes* any clearer or with any more zeal than Barker and Lee had in *Nally*.

Deliverance

Jimmy Carter was president when Ken Nally killed himself. As the summer of 1988 stretched into fall and fall moved toward winter, Ronald Reagan prepared to leave the White House to make room for George Bush. Whatever else had or had not been decided, one thing was once again abundantly clear: The legal process takes time and perseverance.

Just like the prior appeals, there was little anyone could do but wait. As people made preparations to celebrate Thanksgiving word came to the litigants that the California Supreme Court was prepared to announce its ruling. The decision came on November 23, 1988, Kenneth Nally's birthday. He would have been thirty-four years old. It was not the gift his family had hoped for.

Chief Justice Lucas wrote the majority opinion, joined by Justices Panelli, Arguelles, Eagleson, and Mosk. Associate Justice Kaufman wrote a separate concurring opinion, joined by Justice Broussard. As many legal experts had predicted and as Ed Barker had feared, the California Supreme Court found for the defendants, refusing to expand the boundaries of California tort law and to allow the Nallys to recover against the church and its pastors for the death of their son. In what was essentially a 7–0 decision, the court not only denied the Nallys any relief but in the process it all but slammed the door on their ability to successfully appeal the case to the U.S. Supreme Court.

The majority opinion followed Rex Lee's admonition to decide the case purely on California common law tort grounds. Lucas began with a recitation of the procedural history of the case and the factual background that gave rise to Ken's suicide. Much of the factual description was based on the majority's reading of the trial record and that reading differed significantly at times from Justices Kaufman and Broussard's understanding of the record. Suffice it to say, the majority opinion did not reflect the facts as the Nallys understood them.

The first crucial distinction the majority drew went to the issue of whether Grace Church held itself out as a counseling program or counseling center. John MacArthur testified that "Grace Community Church does not have a professional or clinical counseling ministry. We don't run a counseling center as such. We aren't paid for that. We just respond as pastors, so what we do is on a spiritual level, and a biblical, or prayer level. . . ." Lucas took MacArthur's testimony on its face and refused to find that Grace Church or its pastors held themselves out as professionals. He argued that the defendants held themselves out as "pastoral counselors [only] able to deal with a variety of problems—not as professional, medical or psychiatric counselors." The factual rendition seemed to ignore the size of the staff, the nature of the problems they represented they could handle, and their professed competence to do so. Regardless, this was a crucial step. By refusing to find a holding out, Lucas avoided having to treat the church and its pastors as professionals. By relegating them back to the status of nonprofessionals and pastoral counselors, the majority could then deal with them under the existing law. Without the holding out, the court would have to create new law, or at least expand the existing law beyond its present boundaries as the court of appeals had done. This it was unwilling to do.

The remainder of the factual recitation stressed two areas. One was the number of doctors, both mental health professionals and nonprofessionals, that Ken saw in the months leading up to his death. The second area took issue with the Nallys' argument that Rea and Thomson knew Ken was suicidal. In separate footnotes the court argued that Rea did not become aware that Ken could not cope in a "physical" sense until after the March 11, 1979, attempt. They construed Rea's testimony to mean that Ken could not cope in a "spiritual" sense, in other words, lead a "Christian life." Lucas emphasized Thomson's belief that although Ken had discussed prior suicidal thoughts, that Thomson did not feel that Ken's "intimation of suicide created a serious enough likelihood where other help would be needed at [that] point."

With the facts set forth and the procedural history outlined, Lucas addressed the merits of the case. Although conceding the validity of the test that required all of the nonmovant's evidence in a nonsuit motion to be taken as true and conflicting evidence disregarded, Lucas also set out that in California, "a mere scintilla of evidence" does not create a factual conflict requiring jury resolution. There must be substantial evidence to create a question for the jury. Lucas then focused specifically on the first two counts: negligence and clergy malpractice.

The court of appeals combined the two counts and created a cause of action for negligent failure by a nontherapist counselor to prevent suicide. With no prior case law weighing either for or against nonprofessional counselors and their duty toward suicidal counselees, it was "venturing along a largely uncharted path," imposing a new and broad duty of care on nonprofessionals without any discussion of causation under the facts in *Nally*. Quoting Justice Cole's dissent, Lucas agreed that the obligation imposed on nonprofessionals by the majority was vague and loosely worded. Everything turned on a duty to refer, but refer to whom or what? Lucas identified six different variations of the duty to refer ranging from referral to persons "who possess the powers to prevent an imminent suicide" to "individuals and institutions authorized and specifically suited to prevent suicide" to perhaps the most vague, "taking appropriate measures to prevent [a] suicide." Lucas rejected the appeals court's "duty to refer."

A tort requires a legal duty, whether established by statute, common law, contract, or otherwise. Without a duty injury becomes "*damnum absque inuria*—injury without fault." Citing *Davidson v. City of Westminster* and *Tarasoff v. Regents of the University of California*, the majority argued that prevailing California tort principles imposed no obligation to prevent one from harming another or otherwise make a person responsible for another's conduct without the existence of a "special relationship." Since negligence turns on duty, the first step in *Nally* required establishing the existence of a legal obligation owed by the defendants to the plaintiffs, or by the defendants to the decedent that plaintiffs could legally assert.

Under *Meier v. Ross General Hospital* and *Vistica v. Presbyterian Hospital*, a special relationship sufficient to establish liability for failing to prevent a suicide applied only to hospitals or other in-patient facilities that had accepted the duty of care for, and attended the needs of, suicidal patients. *Meier* went so far as to impose liability on both the hospital and treating physician. The court of appeals argued that public policy and logic dictated that the duty imposed in *Meier* and *Vistica* be extended to nonprofessionals. Lucas disagreed. Relying on the lack of confinement in a professional facility, the absence of any legal control the nonprofessional pastoral counselors at Grace Church had over Ken and his behavior, combined with the fact he killed himself two weeks after leaving the confines of a professional facility against the advice of virtually everyone involved, the majority saw no reason to extend California common law to cover such a fact situation.

Because the plaintiffs and the court of appeals placed heavy reliance on *Bellah v. Greenson*, Lucas and the majority addressed what it defined as a gross misreading of the case by the appellate court. In *Bellah*, parents of a young girl who had committed suicide sued the girl's psychiatrist, who had been seeing her on an outpatient basis. The court of appeals upheld the trial court's dismissal of the suit on the grounds that it was barred by the one-year statute of limitations. In dictum, the appeals court suggested that a cause of action for malpractice might exist against a psychiatrist under the facts of the case.

Dictum is the portion of a court's decision that has no legally binding effect, but often establishes the potential for new law or sets forth principles that might later be applicable. The *Bellah* court suggested that a psychiatrist might be liable if an outpatient committed suicide. Lucas and the majority stressed, however, that even the dictum failed to create a duty to refer, but merely claimed that the psychiatrist failed to act "consonant with good medical practice in the community." In fact, Lucas wrote, the *Bellah* court specifically stated that "Licensed medical professionals simply have no duty to disclose to third persons 'vague or even specific manifestations of suicidal tendencies on the part of the patient who is being treated on an outpatient basis.'" It went one step further by rejecting the notion that the duty imposed in *Tarasoff* compelling a psychiatrist to disclose to third parties that his patient might try and harm them should apply to disclosing to third persons that a patient might harm himself. In short, no duty as suggested by the Nallys existed in California and the court saw no reason to create one.

Lucas then explained why the court refused to create such a duty. A close connection between conduct and harm might be reason to establish a duty. If one engaged in a particular conduct could reasonably foresee that harm might result from such conduct, Lucas reasoned that such circumstances might justify imposing a duty on that person. The majority saw no proximate cause between Ken's death and the actions of the defendants.

First, the church did encourage Ken to cooperate with other doctors. Two of those doctors, Hall and Parker, recommended hospitalization and the plaintiffs rejected the suggestions because their son "was not crazy." Second, the mere knowledge that a patient may have been suicidal at various stages of his life did not justify imposing a duty on all nontherapist counselors. In the context of suicidal patients the mere knowledge or foreseeability of suicide did not warrant creating a special relationship and thereby imposing a duty to refer, where such a duty might stifle gratuitous and religious counseling. For Lucas and the majority, the broad language of the court of appeals opinion not only gave rise to a vague duty, but threatened the wide spectrum of nonprofessional counselors who dominated the mental health care field, thereby depriving the vast majority of those most in need of help.

Citing *Katona v. County of Los Angeles* and *Searcy v. Hemet Unified School District*, the court reiterated that both the California legislature and courts had refused to impose a legal obligation on a person to take affirmative steps to prevent the suicide of one who was not under the care of a physician in a hospital. Under California law, a psychiatrist did not even have to accept a referral from a nonprofessional, and had no obligation to seek involuntary commitment proceedings. Finally, the legislature had specifically exempted clergy from licensing requirements and in so doing recognized that access to the clergy should be free from state-imposed counseling standards.

The court stayed completely away from addressing the constitutional aspects of the case. The closest the Lucas opinion came to constitutional questions was to state:

> Because of the differing theological views espoused by the myriad of religions in our state and practiced by church members, it would be certainly impractical, and quite possibly unconstitutional, to impose a duty of care on pastoral counselors. Such a duty would necessarily be intertwined with religious philosophy or the particular denomination or ecclesiastical teachings of the religious entity. We have previously refused to impose a duty when to do so would involve complex policy decisions, and we are unpersuaded by plaintiffs that we should depart from this policy in the present case.

That part of the opinion sounded remarkably like an establishment clause argument. Lucas even cited *Lemon v. Kurtzman*, but avoided any notion that the case turned on constitutional grounds. The plaintiffs simply failed to meet the "threshold requirements" for persuading the court that preventing suicide or the general professional duty of care should be extended to nonprofessional counselors who offer counseling to a potentially suicidal person on secular or spiritual matters. "In the present case the Court of Appeals erroneously created a broad duty to refer, and to hold defendants accountable for Nally's death based on their counseling activities would place blame unreasonably and contravene existing public policy." Ken's death had been a tragedy, but the defendants had no duty to the Nallys upon which to base liability for his death.

The court had refused to allow the Nallys' clergy malpractice claim, but it did not seem to rule out the possibility that under different facts, a clergyman might be liable. In a footnote to its opinion the majority stated that the decision did not foreclose liability on nontherapist counselors who held themselves out as professionals.

The majority had done precisely what experts predicted. Confronted with a chance to expand tort liability, the Lucas Court had refused to do so. The genius of the opinion to this point was doing so without raising reviewable First Amendment issues. By refusing to find that the defendants had held themselves out as professionals it became easy to identify the present frontiers of tort law and then refuse to enlarge the boundaries. The breadth of the court of appeals opinion made it even easier. It was no longer necessary to carve out an exception for churches: the court of appeals had literally taken the religion out of the case. Ed Barker had said from the beginning, "This is not about religion." The court now seemed to agree, and by agreeing had denied his clients' claim, at least insofar as common-law negligence was concerned. However, there remained the issue of the Nallys' third count: outrageous conduct or intentional infliction of emotional distress.

In the remaining four pages of the majority opinion Lucas disposed of this last ground of recovery. The Nallys had actually pled outrageous conduct, not intentional infliction of emotional distress. It was the first court of appeals opinion in 1984 that transformed that claim into intentional infliction of emotional distress. The 1987 court of appeals opinion addressed only two issues: Did the trial court err by excluding Rich Thomson's counseling tape? Did it err in nonsuiting the intentional infliction of emotional distress count?

Lucas and the majority went straight to the only case where a California appellate court allowed a cause of action for wrongful death based on outrageous conduct for causing a suicide. *Tate v. Canonica* was the same case the appeals court relied upon in 1984 to overrule Judge Murphy. In *Tate* the court held that a plaintiff could have a jury decide a case and survive a motion to dismiss by showing that the defendant's conduct was outrageous and that it was a substantial factor in the decedent's suicide. It need not be the sole or the proximate cause, so with that standard in mind, Lucas looked at the Thomson tape.

The tape was crucial because both the trial court and the 1984 court of appeals stated that it lay at the core of the outrageous conduct. Without the tape Kalin had nonsuited the claim in 1985. Barker's brief to the court of appeals did not address the merits of the exclusion, whether it was relevant or probative, and whether its evidentiary value outweighed its prejudicial impact on the jury. Instead, he had argued that the trial court had to accept the validity of the claim because under the law of the case doctrine the appellate court held that based on the tape, a reasonable jury could find the defendants' conduct outrageous. The plaintiffs contended that all defenses to the *validity* of the claim had been precluded. Although a jury was not bound to find in favor of the Nallys, the trial court had no choice but to allow the tape into evidence and submit the outrageous conduct claim to the jury.

Lucas conceded that in California, the law of the case doctrine conclusively established the rule of law to be followed and the substantive rights on that issue in any subsequent retrial or appeal of the case. The purpose of the doctrine was to facilitate judicial economy. It provided a degree of finality and prevented subsequent reversals by the lower court. Lucas and the majority did not believe the rule applied where a subsequent appellate court felt that a reversal was warranted on a ground not considered on the prior appeal. More important, the majority's belief that a reversal was appropriate "frees us from the compulsion that the rule of the law case might otherwise impose on us to follow a ruling in a prior appeal that we now perceive to be manifestly erroneous."

The gist of the majority opinion on the issue was very much the same as Cole's dissent in the 1987 appellate case. A ruling that the plaintiffs had raised triable issues of fact merely allowed the Nallys to present their evidence. It did not ensure its admissibility, nor did it bind the trial judge to admit any evidence, even evidence that the appeals court felt provided some proof of outrageous conduct.

Judge Kalin had excluded the tape that Thomson made eighteen months after Ken's death. Ken could not possibly have heard the tape, and the contents of the tape being of questionable relevance would have prejudiced the jury against the church. The court of appeals in 1987 argued the tape had been relevant. It showed Thomson's state of mind and it provided evidence of the probable content of the church's counseling and the customary approach to counseling at Grace Church. The majority argued this misstated the "relevant evidence."

The tape did not prove that the defendants encouraged Ken to kill himself. The trial court argued there was no evidence Thomson had been asked about salvation and suicide prior to 1980. Thomson had testified that his responses in a teaching setting would be markedly different than his responses to the same question in a counseling session. Finally, given the broad discretion a trial judge has to exclude evidence, the tape was simply too remote in time to have been relevant. In short, after exhaustive in-chambers hearings, the evidence had been properly excluded. There was really no other evidence to sustain the outrageous conduct claim and the nonsuit on the third count was proper.

With regard to the law of the case doctrine, Lucas and the majority were probably correct. To bind the state's highest court to a ruling that it believed was clearly wrong would be to destroy the purpose and power of the court. Its purpose is to review prior appellate rulings and there is no limitation on which decisions it can and cannot review so long as the case is properly appealed to the supreme court. Equally compelling is the argument that the law of the case doctrine merely got the Nallys back into court: it did not protect their evidence from a subsequent attack based on well-established rules of evidence. The appellate court ruled that the Thomson tape could support a finding of outrageous conduct. It did not assert the tape was absolutely admissible. There is no indication from the record that in considering the summary judgment motion back in 1981, Judge Murphy had excluded it or considered it. There was, however, some evidence adduced at trial that Thomson clearly believed what was on the tape and in some context may have communicated that fact to Ken. Did that make the tape any more admissible? Probably not. If Thomson said it, that is evidence in and of itself. If the majority erred it was by not considering the fact that Thomson testified to that fact irrespective of whether the tape came in or not. Was his testimony sufficient to support outrageous conduct? Apparently not.

Lucas's opinion spoke for five members of the court. However, Justice Kaufman, considered by many to be part of the Lucas conservative majority, and Justice Broussard, considered by the same observers to be the most liberal member of the court, did not join the opinion. Instead, they submitted a separate concurrence, written by Kaufman, that Broussard joined. The concurrence agreed with the end result, reversal of the appeals court and dismissal of the *Nally* case. However, it took a significantly different path to that conclusion, a path that left open the question of clergy malpractice in much the same way the majority left the door open in the future by conceding their decision was based on the specific facts of the case.

Kaufman and Broussard's position was simple: The defendants did owe a duty to the Nallys. They had held themselves out as professionals. But the Nallys had no right to recover because the church had met its duty.

During oral arguments Kaufman and Broussard remained quiet until late in the hearing. During Rex Lee's rebuttal they both came to life, particularly Broussard. The thrust of their questions went to the issue of nontherapist counselors holding themselves out as professionally competent. Their opinion reflected the areas of concern voiced during argument in June. Kaufman went directly to the point:

> I am baffled as to the basis of or the necessity of the majority's broad conclusion that "nontherapist counselors in general" do not owe such a duty [duty of care to a suicidal patient]. The evidence in the record, viewed as the law requires—in plaintiffs' favor, demonstrates that defendants (1) expressly held themselves out as fully competent to deal with the most severe psychological disorders, including major depression with suicidal symptoms, (2) developed a close counseling relationship with Kenneth Nally for that purpose, and (3) realized that Nally's suicide was at least a possibility. Thus the evidence was more than sufficient, in my view, to trigger a minimal duty of care to Nally. What was fatally absent from plaintiffs' case was not evidence of duty, but proof that defendants breached that duty, and that such breach constituted a proximate cause.

Kaufman could not understand how the majority, after chronicling the sequence of events leading up to Ken's suicide, could overlook the substantial evidence that pointed to the nature and extent of the defendants' pastoral counseling center. The only picture that could be drawn from the evidence in Kaufman's opinion was far from "a small band of simple pastors who offered occasional counseling services on minor matters to a faithful few." Kaufman pointed to the following facts from the trial record:

- At the time of the events in question, Grace Church had fifty pastoral counselors to serve a congregation of over 10,000.
- The church's 1979 annual report described pastoral counseling as "a very important part of the ministry at Grace Church."
- The same 1979 report stated that 50 percent of the counseling services were offered to nonmembers, in other words, the general public.
- Although much of the counseling was informal, ad hoc drop-in, the church offered formal counseling, with regularly scheduled sessions much like professional psychiatrists.
- The church employed a full-time secretary whose responsibilities included making and scheduling such formal counseling appointments.

Kaufman argued the majority's reliance on MacArthur's self-serving statement about not running a counseling center ignored the vast evidence adduced from Rea and Thomson about the breadth of their services and their level of expertise. By ignoring the evidence the majority was not construing it in the light most favorable to the plaintiffs and had in effect reversed the standard in California for reviewing a nonsuit order. Violations of this duty, Kaufman argued, "occurred throughout the majority opinion." He particularly pointed to the areas of the record where the majority construed the testimony of Rea and Thomson as not pointing to a knowledge of Ken's suicidal potential.

The concurring opinion pointed to specific areas of testimony and set those portions out at length, wherein Rea and Thomson had full knowledge of all aspects of suicidal potential, had identified every one of them in Ken, and further explained in detail their expertise and prior experience in handling such persons. Thomson admitted he took Ken's suicidal signs "seriously" and felt he could nevertheless continue to counsel Ken.

In light of the factual record adduced at trial Kaufman contended there was no escaping the conclusion that the defendants owed a duty to Ken Nally. To get there, Kaufman used essentially the same analysis that Lucas employed. The duty to protect another from harm arises in California only where a "special relationship" exists. The critical question, therefore, was whether such a relationship existed between Ken and the Grace pastors and counselors. To make this determination courts traditionally looked to the relationships where "the plaintiff is typically in some respect particularly vulnerable and dependent upon the defendant, who, correspondingly, holds considerable power over the plaintiff's welfare."

California recognized such an affirmative duty to protect a person from himself in *Bellah* and to protect third persons from a patient in *Tarasoff*. For Kaufman, the relationship between nontherapist and pastoral counselors and those who came to them contained the same elements of dependence and trust as those in the patient-psychiatrist setting. The reason behind the questions Broussard and Kaufman had pounded away at in oral argument became apparent: In their view the Grace pastors held themselves out as competent and Ken had relied on those representations. Although liability might be open to debate, the existence of a duty could not be questioned. The key was the "holding out." Kaufman and Broussard believed they (Grace Church and its pastors) had held themselves out as something they were not and should be held to that standard.

Kaufman insisted that the majority had totally missed the point. It was not a matter of whether the defendants should have known that Ken would in fact commit suicide. This case centered around an appeal of a nonsuit order, not the review of a jury verdict. The question was, viewing the evidence in the light most favorable to the plaintiff, could the plaintiff establish a triable issue of fact for the jury? Clearly, Kaufman argued, the plaintiffs' evidence did just that.

For Kaufman and Broussard public policy considerations demanded that the court recognize the duty owed by nontherapists to their counselees. The notion that such a duty would chill

{ *Clergy Malpractice in America* }

or prevent nonprofessionals from offering services or dissuade counselees because they knew they would have to be referred to professionals or possibly be involuntarily committed was absurd. Duty would be commensurate with training and stated mission. In most cases that would require little more than telling someone to seek competent medical help. What got Grace Church in trouble was the nature of the representation that dictated the severity of the duty. Just as he had during oral arguments, Kaufman totally discounted the threat to hot lines and 1-800 help lines. "There is simply no meaningful resemblance between such activities and the sort of counseling relationship at issue here."

Kaufman then went where the majority had not tread and addressed the First Amendment free exercise of religion issue. He really had no choice; having found a duty and potential liability he had to address the potential First Amendment defense. He began where every court that found a duty and potential liability had started, with *Cantwell v. Connecticut*.

The First Amendment bars prohibiting the free exercise of religion, but religiously motivated conduct remains subject to regulation for the protection of society. In addition to *Cantwell*, Kaufman cited *Molko v. Holy Spirit Assn.*, a 6–1 decision in 1988 wherein the Lucas Court allowed a suit for fraud arising from recruiting practices utilized by the Reverend Sun Myung Moon's Unification Church.

Kaufman repeated what the majority argued in the 1987 appellate decision, that Grace and its pastors neither objected to referring patients to professionals or using antidepressant drugs, nor did they claim their religious beliefs prohibited them from advising people to see psychiatrists. The defendants asserted, however, that tort law duties in general created an impermissible burden on free exercise. Citing *U.S. v. Lee*, Kaufman argued that where the interest is sufficient, the government can compel religiously prohibited conduct as well as prohibit religiously motivated conduct. In *Lee* the government compelled the Amish to participate in the Social Security system despite their religiously based objections. In this case the burden would be minimal. The intrusion would be the duty to advise a suicidal counselee to seek medical care and would be religiously neutral. Contrary to the majority opinion, Kaufman and Broussard found the state's interest in saving lives and preventing suicide to be compelling.

But Kaufman concluded by affirming his agreement with the majority's result. Although there was a duty, the church and its pastors met the duty. The trial record showed the defendants actively referred Ken to care providers outside the church, knew and acquiesced in his taking antidepressant drugs, and actively encouraged Ken to maintain his relationship with Hall. Hall had advised the Nallys to have him committed, even though Hall himself refrained from initiating involuntary commitment proceedings. In light of the evidence the trial court correctly granted a nonsuit since the defendants neither breached their duty nor contributed in any causally significant way to Ken's suicide.

Comparing the two opinions, Kaufman's seems more legally sound, at least insofar as the standards for evaluating evidence in a nonsuit are concerned and the issue of the defendants representing themselves to be competent to handle severe mental illness. The majority's recitation of the evidence ignored the vast majority of the trial record that detailed the size and breadth of the Grace Church counseling center. It is hard to argue the church did not hold out that its biblical counseling methods could handle any and all mental illnesses and conditions. Rea and Thomson, the two defendants in closest contact with Ken, repeatedly refused to compromise their beliefs in biblical counseling despite numerous opportunities to do so. To a layman their testimony seemed absurd at times, as they insisted in detailed explanations that their method of placing sin at the root of all mental illness offered everything one needed to counsel even the most severely suicidal person.

However, although Kaufman's legal arguments were more sound, his opinion forced the court into areas where it did not want to venture. Had Lucas followed Kaufman's reasoning and found duty but also found no breach, he would have established the tort of clergy malpractice, whether one wished to call it that or something else. The Nallys still would have lost, but other potential plaintiffs, like the woman who had sued the Scientologists under very similar allegations, might prevail. As a concurring opinion, Kaufman's reasoning provided food for thought but no legal precedent. Even though the majority opinion recognized the potential for liability for nontherapists, presumably even pastoral counselors, for representing themselves to be competent when they were not, it did not recognize a general duty.

With regard to the outrageous conduct claim the majority opinion was probably correct. Kaufman did not address that aspect of the case, leaving one to conclude he and Broussard agreed with the reasoning of the majority. Actually, Lucas did not dismiss the claim as harshly as Justice Hanson had in his dissent in the 1984 appellate decision that sent the case back for trial. Hanson had argued that the majority totally misconstrued *Tate v. Canonica*, in effect creating a cause of action where none had been pled without previous judicial precedent. Lucas's opinion ignored that problem and went to the issue of whether there was evidence to support the claim, regardless of how it arose. The one point in agreement among both sets of attorneys, the trial judge, and the three appellate courts was that without the Thomson tape the outrageous conduct claim had no evidentiary basis. During the motion for nonsuit in 1985, Ed Barker gamely tried to argue that he had provided enough evidence to support the claim, but even he conceded that the exclusion of the tape hurt.

The tape just seemed too remote. No evidence was offered to show that the message on the tape, that suicide was another way God calls believers home, had been conveyed to Ken in a counseling environment, and therefore there was no way to make the tape relevant. Did Ken believe "once saved, always saved"? No one knows for certain. But almost everyone who knew him believed that he embraced the idea. Would such a belief make it easier for someone to take his own life? Perhaps. In the final analysis the plaintiffs could never draw a close enough tie between Grace's doctrine and Ken's suicide. What Kaufman seems to have been most correct about was the lack of causation. A lot of testimony claimed that this procedure or that method "might" have helped Ken. But no one could swear that any of these methods would have stopped Ken from killing himself.

The inescapable fact in the case was that Kenneth Nally was a twenty-four-year-old adult who made choices. His choice of religious beliefs may well have increased his level of depression. It certainly increased the stress level in his life and within his family. As several experts testified at trial, God is a very tough standard, perhaps an impossible one. But no matter how hard they tried, the plaintiffs could not convince the supreme court. For the majority the nonsuit was correct. After the plaintiffs put on their case there was no evidence of outrageous conduct or a showing that had Grace Church done exactly as the Nallys maintained it should, that Ken would be alive.

Again, the genius of the majority opinion lay in the avoidance of any First Amendment issues. Kaufman's legal argument was convincing, perhaps more so than Lucas's. The *Nally* case need not decide every religious counseling case; each case must be decided on its facts. To argue that holding the church to a duty in *Nally* burdened all religion misstated the nature of constitutional inquiry. Even had the court established a duty for nonprofessionals under Kaufman's logic, the duty would be commensurate with the representation made by the counseling entity and its mission. Would such a standard have withstood constitutional muster in 1988? It is difficult to tell. Clearly, however, the Rehnquist Court has since established guidelines for regulating religious conduct or infringing on religious free exercise that are somewhat more relaxed than the standard that existed at the time *Nally* was decided. But had Kaufman's opinion represented the majority decision there would have been ample ground for review by the U.S. Supreme Court. Lucas made sure *Nally* would go no further.

What the majority avoided by finding no duty, and what Kaufman did not address, might still have created severe problems: the establishment clause argument. Assuming regulation did not pose an undue burden on religious freedom, to bring churches into court would require a certain degree of entanglement, if only to determine that the particular church had no standards or made no representations. In a sense Rex Lee's concern was valid. The fact that churches could be sued and that courts would take it upon themselves to decide if religious counseling had gone too far would require standards. Standards would vary from jurisdiction to jurisdiction as the legal system developed a body of law in the area. The process and the mere existence of standards that posed the threat of a lawsuit would chill religious counseling. Kaufman did not confront the issue. Lucas did, but only indirectly in a secular sense, by arguing standards or duties for nonprofessionals would chill secular and pastoral counselors alike.

The problem lies in the way people think, but people's opinions cut both ways on the issue. The jury in *Nally* was ready to hold for Walter and Maria Nally. Yet some jurors were not sure why, other than Ken was dead and someone should be held responsible. Others were offended by the church's dogma or the overconfident demeanor of its pastors. One woman felt they were practicing psychiatry without a license, a point that was not even an issue in the case. Under California law, Grace Church needed no license to do what it was doing. The legislature had expressly exempted the clergy from licensing requirements. In part, religious freedom and establishment protect churches, all churches, from unfounded prejudices, both by the government and its citizens. However, belief and opinion cut the other way too.

The Constitution is a reflection of the people who live under its mandates and enjoy its guarantees. To argue the founding fathers wanted it one way is easy; the difficulty comes when people and society begin to change over time and with those changes comes a change in how people and society feel about certain core principles. In 1896 "separate but equal" was the law, and most people were comfortable with that. Today, one would be hard-pressed to find anyone comfortable with the notion of racial segregation, even in parts of America where it once flourished. As a people and a society America has changed and it continues to do so. One of the most profound changes has come in how we think about religion and religious people.

In a sense the California Supreme Court decision reflected an unwillingness in America to breach the wall that separated church and state. But the voice did not reflect a unanimous will. The fact that the case finally made it to the court's door was proof of that.

The very existence of the case also demonstrated serious cracks in the wall. Jurors thought "the Nallys had a case." Among legal and religious scholars the debate raged as the case progressed. More important, even the religious clergy community demonstrated a strong difference of opinion as to the ability of the clergy to counsel the severely mentally ill. Arguably, those who felt there were areas the clergy could not handle would also find no problem with holding such people accountable where they do harm.

———

Was it the right decision? That depends on who you ask. Ed Barker and the Nallys showed the profound disappointment of people who had striven so hard and come so far for so long, only to meet with defeat. In a press conference immediately following the court's decision, Walter Nally could not restrain his anger. "The State Supreme Court gave my dead son a birthday gift. It was not a good Thanksgiving for this family." His sense of dismay grew as he found it difficult to hold back his feelings. "I cannot as a father just leave this go. No one sacrifices one of my boys to the Gods and gets away with it." There was no justice. The court made a political decision because it did not want to "take a lot of static."

Ed Barker wore the battle on his face and admitted he was "very disappointed. We had to be worried because this is a conservative court with conservative inclinations, but we thought we had both the facts and the law on our side." Barker could not believe that anyone would say that they did not have a duty to save a boy's life once they agreed to be his suicide counselor. Would the Nallys appeal? Barker did not know, but could only say that they would all sit down, evaluate the situation, and make a decision from there.

Grace's jubilation matched the Nallys' disappointment. John MacArthur said the ruling gave the church the "freedom to continue its ministry without fear of litigation." Sam Ericsson recognized what many legal observers saw, that the court's decision had made a successful appeal to the U.S. Supreme Court very unlikely. There were simply no federal constitutional issues to resolve. Ericsson characterized the ruling as a message that in noncommercial, noncontractual relations, "the court is not going to drive a wedge between you and those seeking help." David Cooksey was extremely pleased. "Church counselors can breathe a sigh of relief and can continue to do what they have been doing for centuries, without fear of being sued."

Although sharing in Cooksey's sentiments, attorney Peter Shannon of the American Association of Pastoral Counselors was a little more reserved. "We did not take sides," he said, "but the association welcomed the court's ruling because it allowed counselors to continue to assist suicidal people without risking liability." Reverend Dean M. Kelly, director of the religious and civil liberty office at the National Council of Churches, was far more blunt. "Anything that has the effect of dismissing this horrible case is a deliverance."

The fact that *Nally* met the same fate as the other clergy malpractice suits filed after it across the United States was not lost on those following not only the case, but the trend. Citing cases in Colorado, Alabama, and Ohio, Philip Harris, the solicitor for the United States Catholic Conference, observed that "the decision [in *Nally*] seems to be in line with other recent court decisions that are rejecting the so-called clergy malpractice theory." Harris was right, at least for the time being. America, at least its judicial branch, was not ready for clergy malpractice.

The Nallys took several weeks to decide the next step. In December Walter Nally made an announcement that surprised few people: They would appeal to the U.S. Supreme Court. "He was our son and we owe it to him," he said. John MacArthur expected as much, saying, "The attorney and the Nallys are so deep into this now that they cannot take the verdict at face value." David Cooksey was "sorry to hear the Nallys wanted to drag this personal tragedy along further." But when asked if he would stay on if it were appealed his answer was quick. "You betcha, I've been riding this thing for eight years, I am going to ride it to the end. I am going to see it to its resting place." He reiterated that nothing would bring Ken back, and could not understand why the family did not want to close this chapter of their lives.

In early 1989 the attorneys filed the obligatory briefs and responses. Later that year the U.S. Supreme Court refused the Nallys' petition for writ of certiorari and declined to hear the case in a one-line statement, "Writ Denied." Ten years after Ken Nally committed suicide *Nally v. Grace Community Church of the Valley, et al.* was finally over. At least the case itself.

Epilogue

David Cooksey returned to his insurance defense practice. Sam Ericsson went back to Virginia to continue his work for the Christian Legal Society. Shortly thereafter he left and assumed the reins of Advocates International, a global human rights organization. John MacArthur had a large flock to tend, one that continued to grow. Duane Rea, Rich Thomson, and Lynn Cory were no longer part of Grace Church and had not been for some time. Today Rea lives in Olympia, Washington. Despite several attempts, I was never able to speak with him about the case. Lynn Cory is apparently still in southern California, but for all the "good" phone numbers Walter Nally had on everyone, Cory's proved to be outdated and I was never able to locate him. Rich Thomson now has a congregation of his own outside of Houston, Texas. When I spoke with him in the fall of 1999 he wavered very little, if at all, from the strong position he took on the stand. For Thomson the case ended in 1988, as it did for John MacArthur, Grace Church, and its congregation.

Walter and Maria Nally returned to their home in Tujunga, California, the same house that they had lived in since moving to the Los Angeles area thirty-five years ago, the same house Ken and Wally grew up in. For Walter Nally the case has never ended. Ed Barker returned to his practice, but like his client, the case did not go away easily. For several years after the case ended both he and Nally frequently spoke at conferences, symposiums, and news programs, hit the "lecture circuit," as David Cooksey referred to it. For Barker this lasted only a short time. He succumbed to stomach cancer and died in 1991, leaving his wife, Juan, and a son.

Walter Nally continued to fight the good fight. He made a memorable appearance on the *Phil Donohue Show* as part of a panel discussion on clergy liability. Whether intentional or not, Nally found himself seated next to two members of the clergy. As the program wore on the intensity of the debate grew. Despite an obvious difference of opinion no one came to blows. As I watched a tape of the program I was surprised no one was hit.

Perhaps the most revealing aspect of the show, however, lay in what it said about America after the *Nally* suit. The case had ended but the debate continued. The comments from members of the panel that allegedly suffered from pastoral counseling abuse and the studio audience reflected a general consensus that no one is above the law, not even the clergy. One woman on the panel represented an organization from Washington trying to persuade that state's legislature to register clergy counselors for purposes of tracking complaints against them.

Despite the sincerest of beliefs, Ericsson, Cooksey, and even MacArthur had miscalculated the impact of *Nally*. They believed the clergy would be free to counsel without fear of litigation. But if Rex Lee had been right about anything it was the chilling effect of the suit. Just the possibility of being sued affected counseling. True, the clergy continued to counsel, but they did so under a new sense of fear that did not exist before Walter and Maria Nally sued Grace Church.

In 1997 Lawton Posey, the pastor of Grace Covenant Presbyterian Church in Charleston, West Virginia, as much as admitted his concerns in an article he wrote for *Christian Century*. He recalled going to the board of a Catholic hospital early in his career to be sure they had clergy malpractice coverage. He was relieved to find both that he was covered and that the board met his concerns with a "serious assuredness" that the possibilities of litigation had been discussed and addressed. As a minister he continued to feel concern over potential litigation arising from his counseling role.

Reverend Posey was not alone, nor were his concerns merely the unsubstantiated threat of being sued. Clergy liability did not die with *Nally*, it actually intensified. One year after the California Supreme Court dismissed *Nally*, the California Second District Court of Appeals, the same district that issued both *Nally* opinions, upheld the possibility that churches might be liable for conduct in connection with emotionally troubled persons. The court in *Wollersheim v. Church of Scientology* held that where a church's counseling practices go beyond acceptable counseling techniques and enter into the realm of coercion and brainwashing, constitutional protection may be denied and tort liability imposed.

Of even greater significance were two U.S. Supreme Court decisions in 1989 and 1990. In *Texas Monthly v. Bullock* the Court severely limited a state's discretion to accommodate religious practices and arguably prohibited exempting religious counselors from statutory regulation of counseling, thus reducing a state's ability to protect the religious practice of clergy counseling. Such an exemption formed a key part of Grace Church's policy argument against imposing liability in the *Nally* case.

One year later, in *Employment Division, Department of Human Resources of Oregon v. Smith*, the Rehnquist Court undermined another key tenet of the church's defense in *Nally*. At virtually every step of the judicial process, from trial court to the California Supreme Court, Ericsson, Cooksey, and Lee had argued that only a compelling state interest would support the burdening of religious free exercise. The *Oregon v. Smith* ruling changed all of that. Now the state need only show that the regulation was facially neutral, meaning it placed no greater burden on religious organizations than secular ones. The test that appeared in *Sherbert v. Verner* and was so well illustrated in *Wisconsin v. Yoder* no longer existed. Under *Oregon v. Smith* a facially neutral law, otherwise constitutional, will pass muster under the free exercise clause no matter how great the burden, even to the extent of prohibiting a particular form of religious conduct altogether. As the mortar holding the wall of First Amendment protection together began to crumble, others stepped up where Walter and Maria Nally had been, and continued the assault on the cathedral.

Writing for the *Christian Century* four months after Lawton Posey's article appeared, Oliver Thomas, special counsel to the National Council of the Churches of Christ, outlined the growth of the expanding liability for clergy. For the most part liability centered around sexual misconduct in the counseling process. Although Ohio and Nebraska courts continued to reject these claims in the 1990s, courts in Texas, Colorado, and Oregon were among the jurisdictions providing access to the courts for victims of such conduct.

Thomas's article highlighted the 1996 New Jersey case of *F. G. v. MacDonell*, wherein that state's appellate court recognized the tort of clergy malpractice. Unlike the California appeals courts in *Nally* that offered relief through some traditional theory of tort liability, this case recognized a specific theory of recovery against the clergy. The New Jersey Supreme Court reversed that holding, but conceded that although clergy could not be sued under a malpractice theory, they were still liable for the same standards of conduct as ordinary citizens. The New Jersey Supreme Court declared "that a pastor, by accepting a parishioner for counseling, accepts the responsibility of a fiduciary." Thomas explained that "the court acknowledged that if the underlying dispute turns on a question of church doctrine, the claim may be barred by the First Amendment." Emphasis on "may."

MacDonell, like virtually every case that followed *Nally*, dealt with sexual misconduct by a clergyman in the counseling realm. What has not occurred since *Nally* is another case involving pure counseling, where belief is so closely connected to conduct that separating the two becomes difficult. Sex cases are easy to resolve. Sexual misconduct by a clergyman is so far outside the realm of what everyone, clergy and layman alike, consider proper conduct, that it does not pose the problem confronted in *Nally*. The U.S. Fifth Circuit Court as much as confirmed this notion on February 11, 1998, when it unanimously affirmed a jury verdict of $85,000 in *Sanders v. Casa View Baptist Church*.

In *Sanders*, two women sued a clergyman for using his counseling role to engage in sexual intercourse with them. The United States District Court for the Northern District of Texas had dismissed the plaintiffs' claims against the church, but allowed the claims for marriage counseling malpractice and breach of fiduciary duty to go to a jury. The jury found that the marriage counseling was essentially secular in nature, despite attempts by the defendant to cast his efforts as inherently ecclesiastical. The jury found no evidence of prayer, scripture, or discussion of other religious topics. This was malpractice of a secular nature under the guise of religious activity.

The legacy of *Nally* lives on despite the absence of a subsequent case with the complex interconnection between belief and conduct. In the years following the case there have been no fewer than twenty-seven law review articles nationwide that address the issue of clergy malpractice. Every one of them cite the case and most have titles such as, "Nally v. Grace Community Church of the Valley: Absolution for Clergy Malpractice?" "Nally v. Grace Community Church of the Valley: Clergy Malpractice—A Threat to Both Liberty and Life," and "Clergy Malpractice after Nally: 'Touch Not My Anointed, and to My Prophets Do No Harm.'" Most of the literature seeks a possible ground to reconcile suing the clergy with the First Amendment. One article, written in 1997, "The Sanctuary Crumbles: The Future of Clergy Malpractice in Michigan," concedes that clergy liability for sexual misconduct, negligent counseling, and breaches of duty is only a question of "when," not "if." The author identified four lawsuits in Michigan alone involving clergy misconduct.

If one peruses the Internet he or she can find attorneys that now include "clergy" among the laundry list of malpractice cases they handle. In 1993 *American Jurisprudence*, one of the oldest and most respected legal publications, published volume 47 of its "Trials" series titled "Clergy Malpractice for Negligent Counseling." The author is Juan Desrosies Barker, Ed Barker's wife.

It's not just the legal community that seems to see the inevitable course of liability in this area: the clergy itself is preparing for the continuing assault. At Woodmen Valley Chapel, a nondenominational congregation in Colorado Springs, Colorado, the church leadership developed a Ten Commandments they call "Ten Ministry Guidelines for Moral Integrity." Among the caveats are no visits to the opposite sex alone at home and no counseling for the opposite sex more than twice without a spouse present. Church spokesman Dave Wayman stated flatly, "it just makes sense." Although Woodmen Valley's rules focus on sexual misconduct, other churches recognize the potential for liability in the mental health area.

The trustees at the First Baptist Church in Maryville, Tennessee, plan to recommend what historian Martin Marty only suggested tongue-in-cheek years ago: for parishioners who seek counseling help to sign a disclaimer promising they will not litigate in the event of a dispute. Oliver Thomas drew up the contract for First Baptist and he now warns that pastors talking to people about their problems have to be "wise as serpents and harmless as doves." Among his suggestions:

1. Hold yourself out to the counselee as a pastoral counselor addressing spiritual truths and using spiritual tools.
2. Make sure the counselee understands that you are not licensed to provide medical or psychological counseling or therapy and that you would be happy to refer the counselee to a professional.
3. Stay within the boundaries of your areas of expertise.
4. Acknowledge that some surface problems of a counselee may be caused at least in part by physical, hormonal, or environmental influences, and that therefore a physician may be the better professional to minister to such needs.
5. Ask your insurance agent to look into obtaining professional liability insurance for your counseling ministry.
6. Remember that anyone, including clergy, is still answerable for intentional or outrageous misconduct.

———

Walter Nally has repeatedly told me that his goal was and is to "stop the killing," to prevent what happened to Ken from happening to other people. He insists John MacArthur's church continues just as it had before Ken's death. Admittedly, in the immediate aftermath both MacArthur and Sam Ericsson stated the church would continue to counsel as it always had. Over the course of researching and writing this book I spent a good portion of time playing devil's advocate in discussions with Walter Nally. Although I agree that Grace Church continues to counsel people in accordance with the biblical beliefs that it embraces, I do not believe the *Nally* suit and the years since the final appeal have been lost on the church or its pastors. Although I never met Reverend MacArthur face to face, I spoke at length with him on the phone, listened to his tapes, and read his trial testimony and some of his many books. He is a bright man with a firm grasp of the realities of the world in which he lives, worships, and ministers. During our telephone interview he admitted to being uncertain how *Nally* would have been decided if it were tried today. I find it hard to believe that the suit had no impact on how Grace Church counsels.

Even if John MacArthur's church continues to maintain the large staff and counseling program it had in the 1970s, not everyone has followed suit. Reverend Charles Darwin of Park City's Baptist Church in Dallas, Texas, ministers to an 8,500-member congregation. Today he refers twice as many people to professionals outside the church as he did four years ago—and "he doesn't like it one bit." In 1996 Darwin directed three part-time counselors, working upward of fifty hours a week, to see members of his congregation through the many changes in their lives. The legal exposure became too great for the church to bear. It cut its staff by two-thirds and today Darwin worries about where his referrals end up.

The secular community sees the same trend. David Kelly, director of Kenwood Psychological Services in New York City, says referrals from pastors and other clergy have surged by 20 percent since 1990. Kelly attributes the referrals less to fear than to ministers being more able to recognize their own limits. Marcia Grenell, a psychotherapist in Falls Church, Virginia has experienced a 50 percent increase in referrals from clergymen in the last three years.

––––––

As I finish this book I have no doubt that *Nally* was and is a landmark legal case. It was a hydraulic hose that blew for almost ten years and in its aftermath not only had the legal foundations we all knew prior to its filing been forever altered, but America had discovered something about itself. One nation, under God, no longer meant what it had to our ancestors, or even the generation that immediately preceded us. God may remain omnipotent and without blame, but we no longer believe his servants are or should be cloaked with the same immunity. Many Americans are actually afraid of organized religion; ironically, organized religion professes the same fear of the country America is or is becoming.

Landmark cases mean very little to the loser. As my interview at the Nally home began to wind down in July 1999, Maria Nally leaned over and asked me why I had such an interest in "Kenny's case." I tried to explain to her about the Landmark Law Cases series, the impact of the case on later law, and even my knowledge of the case dating back to law school. She understood but it did not move her. The more I thought about it, why should it? Ken is dead and the people she and her family felt were responsible essentially walked away. The suit took an incredible emotional toll over the course of a ten-year roller-coaster ride that ultimately left them empty. To the extent she has been unable to let go, the case continues, even if only as a bad memory.

Wally, Ken's brother, put it much more succinctly. Now a successful banker, husband, and father of two children, the bottom line was they lost. He conceded that he understood that for me this case fit into a somewhat larger picture, but for him and his parents it all boiled down to "Kenny got screwed," and the people responsible got away. His father was even more blunt. When I asked Walter Nally what he thought he had accomplished, he said, "nothing."

As I made the six-hour drive from Los Angeles to Phoenix that night I thought more about how they felt. Dred Scott had no idea of the long-term effect of his case. He just knew he was still a slave unless his owner decided otherwise. The bakers in *Lochner* only knew that work conditions would not be changing and that, legal rhetoric aside, work remained a dangerous place. Landmark means little to the vanquished, or at least those who feel vanquished.

I do not think Ed Barker would have felt that way. As I hope I have shown, the Nallys may have lost the case, but they seem to have represented the growing weight of opinion as to the issue of clergy liability. The first one to try to breach the wall was a strong bet to fail. But the law today is not where it was in 1980. The Nallys and Ed Barker can take a good portion of the credit. *Nally* redefined the debate, both in terms of the legal issues and the policy considerations. Ed Barker's legal skills forced that reevaluation.

During my interview with David Cooksey I asked him about Barker. The two did not really know one another very well before the case began and after the case ended their paths did not cross again. Within three years Barker had died. But Cooksey paid Barker a high compliment. He said, "Ed took a case that on its face had very little to offer in the beginning and rode it a long way, rode it all the way to the California Supreme Court." One of my big regrets in this project is never having been able to meet Ed Barker. I think I would have liked him.

In addition to the law and other interests, I am a historian of religion and community. I believe that to be an American historian one must study both because the two are crucial to America's birth and development. Aside from the law, it was these two elements that made this project so compelling for me. Although the importance of religion is obvious, the central role of community cannot be overlooked. As I interviewed people for this book, particularly those from the church, I got a feeling that life as a member of the Grace Church community offered a tremendous sense of security. That did not necessarily surprise me. Security and a sense of belonging are the most enduring aspects of community. What did surprise me, and maybe it should not have, was how alienated outsiders, or nonchurch members, felt when dealing with Grace.

All the legal issues aside, one of the components that drove this suit was the black-and-white attitude Ken took toward his own family once he became a Grace Church member. They either converted to Grace Church or they were all going to hell and there was no middle ground. Ken did not just find a new faith, he found new friends, new interests, and a new set of rules and mores. These are the very components of community. The Nallys came to identify Ken's beliefs as those of Grace Church. For Walter Nally it was as if this new community had torn his son from his old community, a community that the father was a part of and did not want to see his son leave, particularly in the manner he left. Those feelings grew more intense as Walter Nally came to know the aspects of Ken's life that neither he nor Grace Church ever shared with the Nallys. Maybe they should not have. Maybe Walter Nally just failed to come to grips with the conflict that confronts many fathers and sons. But in a very real sense when Walter Nally went to court with Grace Church, two communities went to war. The short answer to all of this is "too bad, get over it, that's what happens when children grow up and leave home." Maybe so. But it is not the only answer.

Jerry Scarpetti testified as a witness in the trial. Barker called him to rebut John MacArthur's statement that there were no other suicides among Grace Church members. There had been at least one and Scarpetti knew so. Then and now he struggles with the suicide of his friend, Glen Steffan, who was a Grace Church member. Steffan became a member through Scarpetti's efforts when he had been a member of Grace. Steffan committed suicide one year before Ken. Scarpetti left Grace and today embraces the Muslim faith. In the course of our interviews he placed into perspective the community dynamic of this case and the tragic events that gave rise to the suit. He said that in every religious community there are insiders and outsiders, believers and nonbelievers. The true test of how close a religion is to God is how it treats its outsiders. Maybe the courts were right. Grace Church did all it could and no one could have helped Ken. Had Walter Nally and his family not felt like outsiders perhaps it would have ended there. But they did feel alienated and the suicide was just the beginning.

Grace Church and other Christian religious institutions may scoff at Jerry Scarpetti's notion that treating people like outsiders may have actually made matters worse in the *Nally* case. But an article that appeared in the *Brigham Young University Journal of Public Law* three years after *Nally* ended not only recognized the inevitability of state regulation of the clergy, but suggested that the best remedy might be to treat nonbelievers with a little bit more compassion. The author, Thomas Taylor, an associate with the Salt Lake City firm of Christensen and Martin, held a Master's of Divinity from Yale. Before going to law school he served as an assistant minister at Saint Michael's Lutheran Church in New Canaan, Connecticut. The answer to avoiding liability for churches and ministers could be found in the same book Grace Church and so many others relied upon, the Bible. In *I Timothy* are the requirements for religious leadership:

> If anyone aspires to the office of bishop . . . [he] must be above reproach, the husband of one wife, temperate, sensible, dignified, hospitable, an apt teacher, no drunkard, not violent but gentle, not quarrelsome, and no lover of money. He must manage his own household well, keeping his children submissive . . . [,] [and] *he must be well thought of by outsiders.* (emphasis added)

Maybe the lesson of *Nally* is that beliefs should be protected, but the best way to do so is to treat everyone like an insider, irrespective of his or her belief.

Clergy liability and religion's struggle to find its place in American culture did not end with *Nally*. Ericsson was fond of referring to the case as the second Monkey Trial, or *Scopes II*. As this book headed to press *Scopes I* had come back to the forefront of debate almost seventy-five years after the case ended in Tennessee with John Scopes's conviction. It reappeared in Kansas, the heartland of America. On July 13, 2000, the People for the American Way Foundation sponsored a rendition of *Inherit the Wind*, with Ed Asner as William Jennings Bryan. The audience warmly applauded the cast, but the purpose of the play and panel discussion that followed was not lost on them. In 1999 the Kansas state school board voted to deemphasize evolution in science testing standards. In so doing it made the state the next battleground for social theory. A Gallup poll in 1999 found 68 percent of Americans in favor of teaching both creationism and evolution. By a margin of 55 to 40 percent they opposed replacing evolution with creationism. The same debate has heated up in at least thirteen other states. Linda Holloway, who chaired the Kansas board when it approved deemphasizing evolution, is seeking reelection. As she put it, the *Scopes* debate continues, "but creationists are the ones under attack now."

1952 Walter and Maria Nally marry.

1954 Kenneth Nally born.

1956 Grace Community Church of the Valley holds first service.

1965 Nallys move to Tujunga, California.

1969 John MacArthur becomes pastor at Grace Community Church of the Valley.

1974 Born and raised a Catholic, Kenneth Nally becomes a born-again Christian and joins Grace Community Church.

1978 Between January and April Kenneth Nally undergoes a series of formal counseling sessions with defendant Duane Rea after expressing suicidal thoughts. During the course of these sessions he reveals that he has attempted suicide on prior occasions while a student at UCLA. Thereafter, Kenneth continues to speak with church counselors, including Rea and Rich Thomson, on an informal basis.

1979 On March 12, Kenneth attempts suicide by taking an overdose of a prescription drug and is hospitalized at Verdugo Hills. While hospitalized he confides in several of Grace's ministers that he is sorry he failed and will try again if given the opportunity. After his release he spends six days with defendant John MacArthur and his family, and then returns home.

1979 Sometime between March 30 and April 1 Kenneth Nally shoots himself in the head with a shotgun at a friend's home.

1980 On March 31 Walter and Maria Nally file a $1 million negligence and clergy malpractice suit in Los Angeles Superior Court against Grace Church, John MacArthur, Lynn Cory, Duane Rea, and Richard Thomson.

1981 On October 2, after almost eighteen months of discovery, Judge Thomas Murphy grants the defendants' motion for summary judgment, dismissing the suit on the grounds that there is insufficient evidence to sustain the claims asserted by the Nallys.

1984 On June 28, the 2d circuit court of appeals overturns Murphy's dismissal by a 2–1 vote, saying that the issues of whether the church and its ministers were guilty of outrageous conduct in Ken's suicide should go to trial, thereby opening the door for the trial of all issues.

1985   On May 16, after almost four weeks of trial and upon the completion of the plaintiffs' case, Judge Joseph R. Kalin grants the defendants' motion for nonsuit, stating that based on the evidence produced at trial the First Amendment of the Constitution's separation of church and state protects Grace Church and its ministers.

1987   On September 16, the 2d circuit court of appeals once again reverses the trial judge's ruling and reinstates the suit, stating that the church counselors had a special relationship with Kenneth Nally sufficient to give rise to a legal duty to take affirmative steps to prevent his suicide.

1988   On January 21, the California Supreme Court agrees to hear the case.

1988   On November 23, the California Supreme Court dismisses the *Nally* case on the grounds that the church had no special relationship that gave rise to any duty on its part to the Nallys and thus the church cannot be held legally responsible for Kenneth's suicide.

1989   The U.S. Supreme Court denies certiorari, refusing to hear the appeal and thereby ending the *Nally* case.

Agarwal v. Johnson, 25 Cal. 3d 932 (1979)

Barron v. Baltimore, 32 U.S. 243 (1833)

Bellah v. Greenson, 81 Cal. App. 3d 614 (1978)

Brandenburg v. Ohio, 395 U.S. 444 (1969)

Braunfeld v. Brown, 366 U.S. 599 (1961)

Byrd v. Faber, 565 NE 2d 584 (Ohio 1991)

Cantwell v. Connecticut, 310 U.S. 296 (1940)

Carrierri v. Bush, 62 Wn.2d 536 (1966)

Christoffsen v. Church of Scientology, 644 P 2d 577 (Or. 1982)

Corp. of Presiding Bishops v. Amos, 483 U.S. 327 (1987)

Davidson v. City of Westminster, 32 Cal. 3d 197 (1982)

Destefano v. Grabrian, 763 P 2d 275 (Colo. 1988)

Everson v. Board of Education, 330 U.S. 1 (1947)

F. G. v. MacDonell, 677 A 2d 258 (N.J. 1996)

Goldman v. Weinberger, 475 U.S. 503 (1986)

Handley v. Richard, 518 So. 2d 682 (Ala. 1987)

Hester v. Barnett, 723 S.W. 2d 544 (Mo. 1987)

Hustler Magazine v. Falwell, 485 U.S. 46 (1988)

In re Edward C, 126 Cal. App. 3d 193 (1981)

Katona v. County of Los Angeles, 172 Cal. App. 3d 53 (1985)

Lemon v. Kurtzman, 403 U.S. 602 (1971)

Lewis v. the Holy Assn', F.Supp. (Mass. 1983)

Meier v. Ross General Hospital, 69 Cal. 2d 420 (1968)

Minersville School District vs. Gobitus, 310 U.S. 586 (1940)

Molko v. Holy Spirit Assn., 46 Cal. 3d 1092 (1988)

Nelson v. Dodge, 68 A.2d 51 (R.I. 1949)

O'Neil v. Schuckardt, 112 Idaho 472 (1986)

Oregon v. Smith, 110 S.Ct. 1595 (1990)

People v. Edwards, 194 Cal. App. 3d 430 (1987)

Reynolds v. U.S., 98 U.S. 145 (1878)

Sanders v. Casa View Baptist Church, 134 F. 3d 331 (1998)

Searcy v. Hemet Unified School District, 177 Cal. App. 792 (1986)

Sherbert v. Verner, 374 U.S. 398 (1963)

Simrin v. Simrin, 233 Cal. App.2d 90 (1965)

Stationers Corp. v. Dun and Bradstreet, 62 Cal. 2d 412 (1965)

Strock v. Pressnell, 527 NE 2d 1235 (Ohio 1988)

Tarasoff v. Regents of University of California, 17 Cal. 3d 425 (1976)

Tate v. Canonica, 180 Cal. App. 2d 898 (1960)

Texas Monthly v. Bullock, 489 U.S. 1 (1989)

Tresemer v. Barke, 86 Cal. App. 3d 656 (1978)

U.S. v. Ballard, 322 U.S. 78 (1944)

U.S.. v. Lee, 455 U.S. 252 (1982)

Vistica v. Presbyterian Hospital, (1967) 67 Cal. 2d 465

West Virginia State Board of Education v. Barnette, 319 U.S. 624 (1943)

Wisconsin v. Yoder, 406 U.S. 205 (1972)

Wollersheim v. Church of Scientology, 212 Cal. App. 3d 872 (1989)

Note from the Series Editors: The following bibliographical essay contains the major primary and secondary sources the author consulted for this volume. We have asked all authors in the series to omit formal citations in order to make our volumes more readable, inexpensive, and appealing for students and general readers. In adopting this format, Landmark Law Cases and American Society *follows the precedent of a number of highly regarded and widely consulted series.*

———

In February 1981, I entered Baylor Law School as a twenty-three-year-old, bright-eyed law student embarking on what I hoped would be a long and prosperous career. Hard work and a little luck left me with the enviable task nine months later of finding a suitable topic for an article for the *Baylor Law Review.* I had finished seventh in a class of sixty-seven, and as a member of the top 10 percent was invited to join the ranks of the legal elite, or so I thought. Never one to shy from the unusual or the bizarre, I took it upon myself to investigate what had been a mere aside during the course of a lecture in torts class. Discussing liability and duty, the professor mentioned that "even priests were being sued today." What he referred to was the *Nally* case. In March 1980, Walter and Maria Nally had introduced America to the unheard-of concept of clergy malpractice. The target was no fringe organization or fly-by-night cult group, but Grace Community Church of the Valley, the largest Protestant church in southern California, a church led by one of the most respected fundamentalists in the country, John MacArthur. To me this looked like a great topic.

As it turned out I would have been better served in my efforts to become a publishing member of the law review if I had chosen a topic of more interest to the practicing legal community, such as search and seizure or the new revisions to the Texas Deceptive Trade Practices Act. Despite some hard work and what I thought was a fine effort, the *Baylor Law Review* declined to publish my piece. Perhaps it was too esoteric, or more important, inappropriate for publication in a journal sponsored by a conservative southern Protestant institution of higher learning. My law review article, *Clergy Malpractice: Bringing*

Uniformity to the Law, marked the end of my first career as a legal writer. However, the case was far from over in 1981 and its eight-year sojourn through the California court system not only shook the foundations of the legal and religious community, but revealed significant aspects of American culture and society.

Because the theory of clergy malpractice was so novel and remains somewhat of a mystery today, there was very little in the way of specific secondary literature to rely on in writing this book. I owe a tremendous debt of gratitude to Walter and Maria Nally, not only for allowing me into their home and speaking with me but for allowing me access to the tremendous volume of material they had preserved about the case. Much of the book is based on the pleadings, trial transcripts, depositions, notes, and appellate decisions in the case. I also relied heavily on the large volume of newsprint media coverage and television coverage, all of which the Nallys preserved and provided me generous access to. Beyond merely allowing me to interview him, Walter Nally maintained an ongoing discourse with me, for the most part over long distance, as we discussed certain aspects of the case. After all these years everyone I interviewed had some level of emotional legacy from the case. As one might imagine, Walter's was by far the most intense. Over the course of researching and writing this book I spent hours talking to Walter. Many times I disagreed with his take on something, and it was in this debate over issues and events that I was able to flesh out unresolved questions of my own.

A good portion of the book is based on the personal interviews I conducted with the parties, lawyers, reporters, and witnesses in the trial. In addition to Walter and Naria Nally, I interviewed Kenneth's brother, Walter Jr., at the Nally home in Tujunga, California. Mike Casper, Kenneth's childhood friend, and Jerry Scarpetti, a witness at trial and a former member of Grace Church, also spoke with me at the Nally home.

As an attorney, I am grateful to David Cooksey and Sam Ericsson, the attorneys who tried the case for Grace Church, and Juan Barker, Ed's wife. I interviewed Cooksey at his office in Van Nuys and he provided me with his copy of the trial transcript, without which an important portion of this book could not have been written. Juan Barker graciously shared a morning and part of an afternoon with me at her Simi Valley law office, providing valuable insight not only into the case, which she witnessed as a young associate, but into Ed Barker himself, who died of cancer in 1991 and took so much of this story with him. Ericsson spent several engrossing sessions with me on the phone and provided facts and information that helped me tell the stories behind the story.

John MacArthur, Rich Thomson, and Pat Rotisky of Grace Church allowed me to interview them. While interviewing Rotisky at Grace's office, she generously allowed me to take copies of many of Pastor MacArthur's books and gave me an updated copy of his vitae. MacArthur granted me a phone interview while he was on business in Ft. Worth, Texas. I spoke with Thomson by phone from his church in Houston, Texas. Both men openly shared their thoughts on the case and the circumstances that led up to it.

Judy Gabriel, a freelance writer in California, also spoke to me about her perceptions of the case. As a reporter for the *Daily News*, she covered every day of the trial in 1985 from jury selection to dismissal. Although she did not have the benefit of her notes, she gave me important insight to the drama that unfolded in the courtroom.

I made generous use of a large collection of tapes made by MacArthur at Grace Church. The tapes provided background on MacArthur's life and the growth and development of Grace Church and gave insight into his religious beliefs and Grace Church. One tape, *The Day God's Word Went on Trial*, contained the post-trial press conference, a sermon at the church following the trial, and an interview with Ericsson.

I owe a debt to Michael Symanski, a news reporter who covered the appeal in 1987 and later coauthored an unpublished manuscript with Walter Nally, about the case, *The Father, the Son and the Preacherman*. In addition to allowing me to interview him, he gave me complete access and use of the material in the manuscript as well as documenting where the information came from. Likewise, Peter Birchwood of Great Britain, a friend of the Nallys and proprietor of Celtic Research, a genealogy research service, also coauthored an unpublished manuscript with Walter Nally, *Empty Salvation*. Like Mike Symanski's work, it provided good background information and research that helped me tell this story, and Birchwood also allowed me total access and use of the material within the manuscript.

I want to give special thanks to the present justices and staff at the

California Supreme Court, particularly Robert Wandruff in the court administrator's office. Through the court's good graces and his efforts, I received an audiotape of the *Nally* oral arguments in June 1988. Part of the challenge in writing history is to make events come alive for the reader. The ability to hear the litigants and judges debate the issues was invaluable.

Despite the absence of an extensive body of secondary literature on clergy malpractice I did benefit from a wide range of primary and secondary material that helped tell this story. The works listed below are far from an exhaustive compilation of the sources used, but they do reflect the sources that were most helpful.

There were only two monographs on pastoral counseling and clergy malpractice. Robert W. McMenamin, *Clergy Malpractice* (Buffalo, N.Y.: W. S. Hein, 1986), and H. Newton Maloney, Thomas L. Needham, and Samuel Southard, *Clergy Malpractice* (Philadelphia: Westminster Press, 1986) not only helped me understand the issues, but provided excellent insight into the fear and uncertainty that existed as *Nally* made its way to the California appeals court for the second time.

Jon Roberts, *Darwinism and the Divine in America: Protestant Intellectuals and Organic Evolution, 1859–1900* (Madison, Wisc.: University of Wisconsin Press, 1988), Gary Smith, *The Seeds of Secularization: Calvinism, Culture, and Pluralism in America, 1870–1915* (Grand Rapids, Mich.: Christian University Press, 1985), and George Marsden, *Fundamentalism and American Culture: The Shaping of Twentieth Century Evangelicalism, 1870–1925* (New York: Oxford University Press, 1980) proved helpful in explaining the beginnings of secularization and the rise of fundamentalism in America.

John Woodbridge, Mark Noll, and Nathan O. Hatch, *The Gospel in America: Themes in the Story of America's Evangelicals* (Grand Rapids, Mich.: Zondervan Publication House, 1979), Craig M. Gay, *The Way of the Modern World, or Why It Is Tempting to Live as if God Doesn't Exist* (Grand Rapids, Mich.: W. B. Erdmans, 1998), William McPherson, *Ideology and Change: Radicalism and Fundamentalism in America* (Palo Alto, Calif.: National Press Books, 1973), Martin E. Marty, *The Fire We Can Light: The Role of Religion in a Suddenly Different World* (Garden City, N.Y.: Doubleday, 1973), and Martin Marty and R. Scott Appleby, *The Glory and the Power: Fundamentalist Challenge to the Modern World*

(Boston: Beacon Press, 1992) provided good background into post–World War II secularization and the rebirth of fundamentalism.

Likewise, Flo Conway, *Holy Terror: Fundamentalist War on America's Freedoms in Religion, Politics and Our Private Lives* (Garden City, N.Y.: Doubleday, 1982), David Bollier, *Liberty and Justice for Some: Defending a Free Society from the Radical Right's Holy War on Democracy* (New York: F. Ungar Publishers, 1982), and Clyde Wilcox, "Evangelicals and the Moral Majority" in the *Journal for the Scientific Study of Religion* gave me a good feel for the backlash in America against fundamentalist Protestantism.

Edlon G. Ernst's *Pilgrim Progression: The Protestant Experience in California* (Santa Barbara, Calif.: Fithian Press, 1993), and Gregory H. Singleton, *Religion in the City of Angels: American Protestant Culture and Urbanization* (Ann Arbor, Mich.: UMI Research Press, 1979) provided essential background information for the rise of fundamentalism in southern California.

For background on Los Angeles I relied upon *The City*, edited by Allen J. Scott and Edward W. Soja (Berkeley: University of California Press, 1996), John M. Findlay, *Magic Lands* (Berkeley: University of California Press, 1992), John L. Chapman, *Incredible Los Angeles* (New York: Harper and Row, 1967), and Howard J. Nelson and William A. Clark, *The Los Angeles Metropolitan Experience* (Cambridge, Mass.: Ballinger Publishing, 1976).

To understand the conflict within the pastoral counseling profession I relied on numerous journals of the period. By far the most useful were *Counseling and Values* and the *Journal of Pastoral Care*. Within the pages of these and similar journals the debate among the clergy and other religious counselors over just how far a pastor could go in counseling severe mental problems played out. In addition, James Allen Peterson, *Counseling and Values: A Philosophical Examination* (Cranston, R.I.: Carroll Press, 1989), and Kenneth S. Pope and Melba J. T. Vasquez, *Ethics in Psychotherapy: A Practical Guide for Psychologists* (San Francisco: Jossey-Bass Publishers, 1991) allowed me insight into the legal and practical problems of religious counseling as well as the ethical problems confronting those counseling suicidal patients. These works combined with Herbert Hendin, *Suicide in America* (New York: W. W. Norton, 1995) gave me an understanding of the nature and extent of suicide at the time Ken Nally died.

To get a firm grasp of the development and explosion of nonprofessional counselors I also relied on a wide range of contemporary journals. The most useful were *American Journal of Orthopsychiatry, American Journal of Psychiatry, Professional Psychology, American Journal of Public Health, American Psychologist,* and *Personnel and Guidance Journal.* In addition to the journals, the paraprofessional counseling field was the topic of several full-length studies. Arlene Wood Weiner, *Mental Health for the Non-Professional* (Springfield, Ill.: Charles C. Thomas Publisher, 1980), Michael Gershon and Henry Biller, *The Other Helpers: Paraprofessionals and Nonprofessionals in the Mental Health Field* (Lexington, Mass.: D. C. Heath and Company, 1977), Alan Gartner, *The Paraprofessionals and Their Performance: A Survey of Education, Health and Social Service Programs* (New York: Praeger Publishers, 1971), and Sam Alley et al., *Paraprofessionals in Mental Health: Theory and Practice* (New York: Human Science Press, 1979) helped me understand the degree to which paraprofessionals, like those at Grace Church, had become an indispensable part of the mental health services offered to Americans after World War II.

I used some of Pastor John MacArthur's writings to understand the conflict between purely biblical counseling and secular psychiatry and psychology. *Anxiety Attacked* (Wheaton, Ill.: Victor Books, 1993), *Charismatic Chaos* (Grand Rapids, Mich.: Zondervan Publishing House, 1992), and *The Power of Suffering* (Wheaton, Ill.: Victor Books, 1995) gave me insight into this issue. *Reckless Faith* (Wheaton, Ill.: Crossway Books, 1994) helped me to understand John MacArthur's core beliefs, something I wanted to know even if it was not central to this book.

Thanks again to Walter Nally, I enjoyed the use of almost nine hours of videotape. From excerpts of the local nightly news I saw Barker, Cooksey, Ericsson, and Judge Joseph Kalin during trial. There were also brief shots of MacArthur, Rea, Thomson, and other witnesses testifying. These short pieces allowed me to get a feel for the intensity of the case and just how much it consumed the community and nation. Included within the video were home movies of the family, including the excerpt shown at trial, national and local news magazine shows covering the period the case was active, and the *Phil Donohue Show*, shot after the final appeal was denied.

The pure legal issues proved to be the area of the book I needed the least help with. However, I did rely on Laurence Tribe, *American Constitutional Law* (Mineola, N.Y.: Foundation Press, 1978), Kermit Hall, *The Magic Mirror: Law in America* (New York: Oxford University Press, 1989), and *The Oxford Companion to the Supreme Court of the United States* (New York: Oxford University Press, 1992) to concisely explain the status of the law as Walter and Maria Nally prepared to file their suit. For background into the California legal climate, particularly the unrest within the supreme court, I used Preble Stolze, *Judging Judges: The Investigation of Rose Bird and the California Supreme Court* (New York: Free Press, 1981), and Betty Medsger, *Framed: The New Right Attack on Chief Justice Rose Bird and the Courts* (New York: Pilgrim Press, 1983). Robert Egelko covered the supreme court for the *California Journal* and his work between 1986 and 1988 helped me to understand the changes and makeup of the court that ultimately decided *Nally*.

To assess the legal ramifications in the decade following *Nally* I relied heavily on legal journals and law reviews. Among the most important were *Journal of Church and State, Brigham Young University Journal of Public Law, Brigham Young University Law Review, University of Detroit Mercy Law Review, Trial Magazine, Whittier Law Review, Mississippi College Law Review, Journal of American Academy of Psychiatry Law, South Carolina Law Review, Denver University Law Review, Santa Clara Law Review, Utah Law Review, Pace Law Review, University of Dayton Law Review, North Carolina Central Law Review, Drake Law Review,* and *Villanova Law Review*. Within these publications I found virtually every perspective on clergy malpractice after *Nally*. They all shared one common message: *Nally* had forever altered the law.

INDEX

California, *continued*
  Constitution, 166, 173, 177
  County Counsels Association, 164
  County Supervisors Association, 165
  Penal Code, 149
  SB 1, 159–160
  State Senate Judiciary
    Committee, 159–160
  State University Northridge, 102, 143
  Supreme Court, 2, 87, 91, 96–97, 152, 156, 163–164, 166, 203, 209
  Trial Lawyers Association, 142
California, Court of Appeals
    Second Circuit, 137, 202
  division one, 86–93, 95, 143, 187, 189
  division seven, 143, 166–169, 183–184, 186–188, 193
Cantwell v. Connecticut, 56, 58, 88, 116, 133, 149, 193, 215
Carrierri v. Bush, 78–79, 215
Catholicism, 4–5, 8, 18–19, 35, 137, 141
Christian Century, 202–203
Christian Coalition, 52
Christian Legal Society, 62, 83, 132, 161, 163, 201
Christian Voice, 49–50
Christoffsen v. Church of Scientology, 90, 215
Church Mutual Insurance
  Company, 77, 79
Church-State Magazine, 160
Cleary, John, 77–79
Clergy, 100–101, 137
  as counselors, 4, 80–82, 101, 146, 204
Clergy malpractice
  insurance for, 77–80
  legal theory, 6, 58, 97, 133, 141–142, 146, 167–168, 183, 186, 190
  public debate over, 80–82, 202–206

standard to be applied, 73–75, 85
Cole, Justice John L., 143–144, 146, 148, 151–152, 183, 188
Colorado Supreme Court, 141
Congress for Religious Freedom, 160
Cooksey, David, 62, 64, 65
  discovery stage, 67–69
  first appellate decision, 95–96
  post-*Nally*, 201–203, 209
  pre-trial, 99
  second appellate decision, 153, 158
  summary judgment, 76, 78, 83, 86
  supreme court decision, 161, 164–165, 199
  trial, 104–105, 107, 109–111, 115–120, 124–129, 131–132, 134, 137–138
  voir dire, 101–103
Corporation of Presiding Bishops v. Amos, 168, 180, 215
Cory, Joanne, 17
Cory, Lynn, 8, 16, 23, 28, 31, 35
  discovery stage, 75
  first appellate decision, 88
  post-*Nally*, 201
  summary judgment, 84, 86
  trial, 107, 112, 116, 123, 126

Daily News, 106, 139, 141
Dallas–Ft. Worth Metroplex
  (DFW), 50
Dallas Times Herald, 48
Dalsimer, Dennis, 99
Dalsimer, Judge Vincent, 86–90, 93, 96–97, 99, 143
Dannemeyer, William, 49
Darrow, Clarence, 180
Darwin, Charles (Darwinism), 36, 48
Darwin, Reverend Charles, 207
Davidson v. City of Westminster, 183, 215
Deukmejian, Governor George, 154